3.71
4.95

D0422292

NEGOTIATION
FROM
STRENGTH

NEGOTIATION
FROM
STRENGTH

A Study in the Politics of Power

by C O R A L B E L L

LECTURER IN INTERNATIONAL POLITICS
IN THE UNIVERSITY OF SYDNEY

Alfred · A · Knopf :   NEW YORK

1963

L. C. catalog card number: 63-9119

THIS IS A BORZOI BOOK,
PUBLISHED BY ALFRED A. KNOPF, INC.

FIRST AMERICAN EDITION

As military inequality is reduced, negotiation becomes
possible.   DEAN ACHESON, 1950

Certainly we must seek to negotiate from strength
and not from weakness.
                          WINSTON CHURCHILL, 1950

Our policy must be to help make the West strong
enough to induce the Russians to want to compromise . . . if we continue to do this the point will
soon be reached when the Russians are ready to negotiate sensibly.   DR. ADENAUER, 1952

We are approaching this thing (negotiations) from
a greater position of strength than ever before.
                          PRESIDENT EISENHOWER, 1955

There is no one in Germany who has the slightest illusion about negotiation with the Soviet Union from
a position of strength.   DR. ADENAUER, 1955

If we do have to negotiate, we will be negotiating
from strength.   VICE-PRESIDENT NIXON, 1959

It is only when we have military force strong enough
to convince the Russians that they will never be able
to gain any advantage through military strength that
we can hope for fruitful negotiations.
                PRESIDENTIAL-CANDIDATE KENNEDY, 1960

We are not dealing in the world these days from a
position of weakness. . . . I have no doubt the Soviet
government knows a good deal about our strength and
has an accurate assessment of it.
                          DEAN RUSK, 1961

Unless we are prepared to place everything at risk,
we cannot hope to save anything from disaster.
                SECRETARY OF DEFENCE McNAMARA, 1962

Preface

Most of the research for this book was done in 1959, which the author spent in America on a Rockefeller Fellowship, chiefly at the School of Advanced International Studies in Washington and at the Institute of War and Peace Studies of Columbia University. The author would like to record her gratitude to the Rockefeller Foundation for making the work possible, to Professors W. T. R. Fox of Columbia University and R. W. Tucker of Johns Hopkins University for their many kindnesses, and to her own university, Manchester, and Professor W. J. M. Mackenzie for the grant of study-leave. The book was first conceived as a Ph.D. thesis for the University of London.

The author would like to acknowledge her debt also to a number of people, mostly in Washington, who made time in heavily burdened lives to answer questions about events and policies with which they had been concerned. Not all of them can be named here, but among those who can be are Mr. Dean Acheson, Mr. Paul Nitze, and Dr. J. R. Oppenheimer.

Finally, she owes a heavy debt to the Library and Press Library of Chatham House, on whose archives much of the study rests. Exercises in recent history must necessarily be tentative, and those who engage in them cannot fail to be aware of how lavish are their own opportunities for misinterpretation and plain error. For what remains of them in this study, despite the help of these most valuable institutions, the author acknowledges her sole responsibility.

Contents

NEGOTIATION
FROM
STRENGTH

[I]

An Aspiration Made
Explicit

A PHRASE has haunted Western diplomacy since 1950: the
phrase "negotiation from strength." This study is concerned
chiefly with the circumstances in which it became current
as a formulation of Western policy towards the U.S.S.R. and
with the degree to which the substance of policy has corresponded to the phrase. It will also examine the meanings that
have been attached to "strength" and to "negotiation," and the
reasons for the relative ineffectiveness both of the effort to build
situations of strength and of the pressures towards negotiation.
Since Western decisions in the period under review were made
primarily in Washington, this is a study in American foreign
policy, but of America in a situation of coalition, responding to,
resisting, and sometimes being frustrated by her NATO allies,
especially Britain. Indeed, the whole idea of negotiation from
strength has been debated in a sort of Anglo-American dialogue,
with occasional interventions from the other NATO powers.

The no-man's-land that lies between defense and diplomacy has tended until recently to escape the scrutiny both of writers on strategy, who assumed that the political framework for military decisions would be provided for them, and of those concerned with foreign policy, who assumed that military matters must be left to military men. Every government that has both a defence establishment and a foreign policy makes, it must be inferred, some conscious or unconscious assumptions about the relation between military power and diplomatic leverage. Yet the question of what particular kinds of military means are relevant as sanctions for particular kinds of foreign-policy ends is one which now contains so many ambiguities that it is not easily susceptible to any simple or convincing answer. In any case, when such a question is asked by policy-makers (as it is, by implication, whenever a defence budget is framed), it is complicated by the necessary presence in the policy-makers' minds of a number of other questions about such matters as the state of the economy and the political prospects of the party—questions which, since they are more familiar and more easily resolved, tend in fact to supply the answer to the quite different question about diplomatic ends and military means.

In so far as this study is a history of the West's effort to improve its military strength *vis-à-vis* the U.S.S.R., and the reasons why that effort was less than successful, it is a study in this sort of political double-think, and its effects. In so far as it is a study of the reasons for the postponement of negotiation, it may seem no more than a spelling-out of Kennan's observation that the search for an ideal military posture is the enemy of negotiation. But beneath the surface of events there are involved in this strand of history questions that have a wider relevance in the study of politics. What is "an effective decision"? How many people have to feel what degree of conviction to turn aspiration into intention and intention into an actual policy?

That there should be a gap between intention—or proclaimed intention—and what is actually done is even less a matter for surprise in foreign affairs than in other departments of politics.

But when the disparity between hopes and achievement is very striking—and it will be maintained that ten years under the sign of negotiation from strength had produced an actual Western negotiating position, by 1960, much inferior to that with which the process began in 1950—then it may be hoped that a history of the episode concerned will provide some insight into the relation between aspiration and reality in foreign policy.

The idea of negotiation from strength has had, at least in the period under review, the true mirage-like quality of some of the most effective political myths: shimmering promisingly, always a little farther off, across a stony waste of effort, keeping its distance at each apparent advance. It will be argued later that the difficulty of replacing it by any alternative aspiration for the Western alliance, even after its irrelevance to the probable power balance of the immediate future became apparent, was not a matter merely of failure of imagination by the policy-makers concerned, but of its integral relationship to a whole theory of international politics.

The phrase "negotiation from strength" first became widely used as a sort of shorthand for the aspirations of the Western alliance in its relationship with the U.S.S.R. early in 1950, in consequence of certain speeches by Dean Acheson (then Secretary of State) and Winston Churchill (then Leader of the Opposition). This is not, of course, to say that the idea was a new one: probably every diplomatist in history has been conscious of the advantages of negotiating from whatever kind of strength he can muster. Nor is it to say that the phrase had never been used before: it may well have been, though it was not common until the speeches of 1950 gave it popularity. The real justification for choosing the beginning of 1950 as the starting point of this case history is that Acheson's use of the phrase corresponded to an evolution of American policy, and that Churchill's response was the beginning of a continuing debate between America and Britain on this subject.

To establish the precise points at issue in this debate, and the way in which earlier positions were gradually modified, it is necessary to quote fairly substantially from the main speeches concerned. The most precise definition by Acheson of the original meaning of the policy (though he did not actually use the phrase) was in a small meeting of corporation and advertising executives in the White House on February 16, 1950.[1]

The only way to deal with the Soviet Union, we have found from hard experience, is to create situations of strength. Wherever the Soviet detects weakness or disunity—and it is quick to detect them— it exploits them to the full. When we have reached unity and determination on the part of the free nations—when we have eliminated all the areas of weakness that we can—we will be able to evolve working agreements with the Russians. . . . No good would come from our taking the initiative in calling for conversations at this point. . . . The Russians know that we are ready, always have been ready, always will be ready, to discuss with them any outstanding issue. We have discussed with them all important outstanding issues, not once but many times. It is clear that the Russians do not want to settle those issues as long as they feel there is any possibility they can exploit them for their own objectives of world domination. It is only when they come to the conclusion that they cannot so exploit them that they will make agreements, and they will let it be known when they have reached that decision.

This speech was a development of remarks he had made about a week earlier, in a press conference on February 8.

What we have also observed over the last few years is that the Soviet Government is highly realistic and we have seen time after time that it can adjust itself to facts when facts exist. We have also

---

[1] This speech was extempore, and was not released to the press until March 9, 1950, reportedly after some pressure by journalists on the State Department (The *New York Herald Tribune*, March 11, 1950). Text in *Department of State Bulletin*, March 20, 1950, Vol. XXII, No. 559, pp. 427–9. See also the volume of Acheson's speeches edited by W. McGeorge Bundy *The Pattern of Responsibility* (Boston: Houghton Mifflin Company; 1952), pp. 19–43.

seen that agreements reached with the Soviet Government are useful
when those agreements register facts or a situation which exists, and
that they are not useful when they are merely agreements which do
not register the existing facts. . . . So it has been our basic policy to
build situations which will extend the area of possible agreement;
that is to create strength instead of the weakness which exists in many
quarters. [He cited the rebuilding of Germany, E.R.P., the arms
programme, and Point 4 aid as ways in which this was being done.]
Those are ways in which in various parts of the world we are trying
to extend the area of possible agreement with the Soviet Union by
creating situations so strong they can be recognized, and out of
them can grow agreement. . . . I don't need to go over with you again
the fact that, growing out of the last war and other conditions before
the war and between the wars, there have been created all over the
world those situations of weakness. Every time one of those situations
exists, and they exist in Asia and they exist in Europe, it is not only
an invitation but an irresistible invitation to the Soviet Government
to fish in those troubled waters. To ask them not to fish, and to say
we will have an agreement that you won't fish is like trying to deal
with a force of nature. You can't argue with a river, it is going to
flow. You can dam it up, you can put it to useful purposes, you can
deflect it, but you can't argue with it. Therefore we go to work, as I
said, to change those situations of weakness so that they won't
create opportunities for fishing and opportunities for trouble. But so
far as agreement for agreement is concerned I think we have discovered that even the simplest thing growing out of the war, which
is to make peace, perhaps not with your enemies but at least with
your friends, has become impossible.[2]

There was an element of the fortuitous in Acheson's enunciation of this concept at this particular time. The doctrine itself was
connected, as has been said, with an actual evolution of military-
diplomatic policy which had begun in the previous September,
and which will be examined later. But the choice of this particular
time to give it expression was conditioned by two other factors.

[2] *Department of State Bulletin*, February 20, 1950, Vol. XXII, No. 555,
p. 273.

The first, but less important, was that Acheson, who had then been in office about a year, was conducting a general review, in a series of speeches at this period, of the commitments and intentions of American foreign policy. It was reported that President Truman had asked him to do so.[3] (The famous speech of January 12, 1950, to the National Press Club, defining the American defence perimeter in Asia, which was later alleged to have provided a "green light" for the attack in Korea, was one of this series.) But a much more important reason for his statement of position was that the Administration was at that particular moment under considerable pressure to make clear its position and its intended direction in the Cold War.

A week before the first of the two Acheson statements, on January 31, 1950, President Truman had announced his decision to proceed with the making of the H-bomb.[4] The public announcement of this decision (as against the decision itself) may be ascribed either to the success of Washington correspondents in ferreting out some information about its probability, or else to Truman's sense that there should be no more concealment of developments in this field from the American public than was strictly necessary. Whatever the reasons for it, the announcement brought into the open an anxiety that had been privately expressed before the decision was made, especially among influential scientists, about the general direction of American policy.[5] Professor Einstein denounced the militarization of American life and pleaded for a general renunciation of violence and the setting up of at least an embryo world government. Twelve eminent scientists asked for an undertaking that the United States should not be the first to use the new bomb.[6] Harold Stassen called for a bi-

---

[3] J. and S. Alsop: *The Reporter's Trade* (New York: Reynal & Hitchcock; 1958), p. 69.

[4] Harry S. Truman: *Memoirs. Vol. II. Years of Trial and Hope* (New York: Doubleday & Company; 1956), p. 309.

[5] The testimony in the Oppenheimer case, four years later, made clear the intensity of feeling that went into this secret debate, between September 1949 and January 1950. See below, pp. 39 ff.

[6] *The Economist*, February 1950.

partisan mid-century conference.[7] Senator Brien McMahon, Chairman of the Joint Congressional Atomic Energy Committee, proposed in the Senate that the United States should offer to finance a five-year world-wide Marshall Plan, involving the expenditure of $50 billion, in return for agreement on the control of atomic energy.[8] Senator Millard E. Tydings, Chairman of the Senate Armed Services Committee, suggested that the President should call a world disarmament conference.[9]

This predictable outburst of concern evoked by their own announcement was an embarrassment to the Administration, which was committed to the view that the balance of power had swung against America in the previous few months, that time was needed to redress it, and that the present was therefore not a good moment to hold or even suggest a new conference.[1] Against this background, Acheson's two statements may seem merely pieces of diplomatic temporizing, official tranquillizers for a case of nuclear anxiety. It is not altogether unreasonable, in view of his later position, to read into his earlier one an element of rationalization of an aversion to negotiations. Certainly in his use of the phrase the emphasis is very heavily on strength, and only lightly on negotiations. Nevertheless, as has been said, an evolution of policy underlay the phrase, so that it would not be accurate to dismiss its use at this point as simply an improvisation to fob off awkward demands. A more detailed examination of Acheson's concepts of strength and of negotiation and the relation between them will be made later. For the time being, the point to note is the development of the public debate.

Acheson's press conference of February 8 received a good deal of editorial notice, substantially favourable in America and Britain, rather cold in France.[2] But it might have passed without much

---

[7] Ibid.

[8] *Congressional Record*, February 2, 1950, pp. 1338–40.

[9] Ibid., February 6, 1950, pp. 1473–8.

[1] *The New York Times*, February 12, 1950.

[2] See *The New York Times*, February 9, 10, and 11, 1950; *Christian Science Monitor*, February 10, 1950; The *New York Herald Tribune*, February 9 and 12, 1950; *The* (London) *Times*, February 10, 1950; *Yorkshire Post*,

impact on the public mind, at least in Europe, had it not happened to coincide with a general election in Britain. (The election, which was held on February 24, 1950, returned the Labour
Party to office, but with so reduced a majority that the Government survived for only twenty months.) Foreign policy was
hardly raised as an election issue in the early part of the campaign,[3] but on February 15, in a clear reaction to the Acheson
press conference a week earlier, Churchill brought the question
up in a speech at Edinburgh.

It is my earnest hope that we may find our way to see a more exalted
and august foundation for our safety than this grim and sombre
balancing power of the bomb. . . . I have not, of course, access to the
secret information of the Government, nor am I fully informed about
the attitude of the United States; still I cannot help coming back to
this idea of another talk with Soviet Russia upon the highest level.
The idea appeals to me of a supreme effort to bridge the gulf between the two worlds, so that each can live their life, if not in friendship, at least without the hatreds and manœuvres of the cold war. . . .
It is not easy to see how things could be worsened by a parley at the
summit if such a thing were possible.

The Labour reply to this initiative was prompt but not particularly deft. Attlee, speaking at Lincoln, said the matter of negotiations with Russia was in the hands of the United Nations, and
that he could not make any further pronouncement on the subject until he had talked the matter over with the Foreign Secretary. Bevin, in a broadcast, recapitulated the story of previous
negotiations and said slightingly that the problem was not one
which could be solved by "stunt proposals." Morrison a few days
later committed the Labour Party even more definitely to regard
the proposal as an electioneering stunt.

February 9, 1950; *News Chronicle*, February 10, 1950; *Daily Telegraph*,
February 10, 1950; *Le Monde*, February 10, 1950; *Combat*, February 11 and
12, 1950; *Le Populaire*, February 10, 1950.
  [3] See H. G. Nicholas: *The British General Election of 1950* (London:
Macmillan & Co.; 1951), pp. 102 ff.

This is hardly a time for soap-box diplomacy. I do not rule out high-level talks between nations who are taking different views about the affairs of the world if and when it is clear that such talks would be advantageous. In the light of what our Foreign Secretary said on the wireless last night it is clearly his view, as it is certainly mine, that such an effort in the spirit of electoral stunting would be anything but useful. . . . It seems to me that the most unwise and injudicious way of launching such a proposal is by the Leader of the Opposition during the heat and excitement of a General Election. Moreover, these things would need careful preparation between us and the Soviet Union. The United States would be involved, and it could cause unnecessary friction if we suddenly took the issue out of the hands of the United Nations for delicate discussions are taking place.

And he advised his listeners, in any case, not to appoint anyone so "flamboyant" as Churchill, if talks should eventuate.[4]

To this, Churchill replied in his final election broadcast.

Why should it be wrong for the British nation to think about these supreme questions of life or death, perhaps for the whole world, at a time when there is a General Election? . . . The only time when the people have a chance to influence and, in fact, decide events is at a General Election. . . . Why should they be told it is a "stunt" or "soap-box" diplomacy to speak to them of the great world issues upon which our survival and salvation may depend?[5]

Politically and morally Churchill had the best of this exchange, though there is no evidence to show that his proposals either lost or won seats.[6] However one views the motives for his raising of the question of negotiations, the fact that it was done at this time secured it the maximum of notice. The original speech, the replies of the Labour spokesmen, and reactions to the idea abroad dominated the headlines of the British press for several days at the height of the election campaign. The Labour replies to the proposal had a weary, uninventive tone, and the imputation that

[4] Ibid., p. 105.
[5] Ibid.
[6] Ibid.

Churchill had raised the question purely as an election stunt was probably as much resented as believed. It is, after all, the business of the Leader of the Opposition to suggest alternative policies to those of the Government: if he can manage to do so just before the polls it may be electorally profitable, but his proposals should not therefore be dismissed as electoral stunting. There was a reasonable case to be made against negotiations at this time, but the Labour leaders hardly even tried to make it.

The point of interest is that it was partly the accident of timing of Acheson's speech (based in turn on the timing of the H-bomb announcement) that made a Conservative leader rather than a Labour one the champion in Britain of the idea of negotiations with Russia. This proved to be of some importance in later Anglo-American discussions, because of the grossly over-simplified stereotype in the American press and among the public, and even in Washington policy-making circles, of the difference in foreign-policy attitudes between Left and Right in Britain *vis-à-vis* Russia. The Labour Foreign Secretary, Ernest Bevin, had, one might say, been following a policy of "building situations of strength," without actually using the phrase, ever since the clashes of 1946 with Russia had shown that the 1945 election slogan "Left can get along with Left" was not necessarily a sound prediction. The Brussels Treaty and the North Atlantic Alliance were testimonies to his endeavours in this field. The Centre and Right of the Labour Party therefore were already solidly identified with the line of policy set forth by Acheson. Dissent or questioning could only be expected from the Labour Left (where it existed, but was too familiar to have much publicity value or influence) or from the Conservative Opposition. One cannot of course assume that each of the post-war Conservative leaders presented with that particular foreign-policy issue at that particular moment by Acheson's speeches would have reacted as Churchill did. It was a combination of the timing of the Acheson speech and Churchill's own temperament or his sensitivity to the movements of history that was decisive. Possibly the most unfortunate repercussion of the raising of the issue at an election period was not in Britain, where it was only very briefly a party question, but in America, where the belief that this issue was merely one that European politicians raised at intervals for reasons of electoral advantage lingered throughout the period under review, though Churchill's persistence—even obsession—with the idea at times when it had no conceivable electoral relevance ought to have dispelled any such illusion.

The first foreign-policy debate of the new Parliament, on March 28, 1950, was a continuation of the election exchanges. This debate was a curiously moving and dramatic occasion: the shadow of death was already visible upon the Foreign Secretary, Ernest Bevin, and Churchill's speech, luminous with the special magnanimity which is so notable in his last few great speeches in the Commons, received an ovation from both sides of the House. Referring to his pre-election Edinburgh speech, he said:

I cannot help coming back to this idea of another talk with Soviet Russia upon the highest level. The idea appeals to me of a supreme effort to bridge the gulf between the two worlds so that each can live their life, if not in friendship, at least without the hatreds of war . . . Certainly we must seek to negotiate from strength and not from weakness. We all agree on that. . . . We should do well to study the recent and most important pronouncements on foreign policy by the American Secretary of State, Mr. Acheson, whose gifts and services are so widely recognized. . . . But if there is a breathing-space, if there is more breathing-time, as I feel and do not hesitate to say, it would be a grave mistake of a different order to suppose that, even if we have this interlude, it will last for ever, or even last more than a few years. Time and patience, those powerful though not infallible solvents of human difficulties, are not necessarily on our side. . . .

He went on to say that as regards atomic weapons the position *vis-à-vis* Russia was already worse than four years ago.

Therefore, while I believe there is time for a further effort for a lasting and peaceful settlement, I cannot feel that it is necessarily a long time, or that its passage will progressively improve our own security. Above all things, we must not fritter it away. . . . Man at this moment of his history has emerged in greater supremacy over the forces of nature than has ever been dreamed of before. He has it in his power to solve quite easily the problems of material existence. He has conquered the wild beast, and he has even conquered the insects and microbes. There lies before him, if he wishes, a golden age of peace and progress. All is in his hand. He has only to conquer his last and worst enemy—himself.[7]

There was little effort in the debate to make specific the objectives of negotiation with Russia, except in the speech of Julian Amery, then a back-bencher, who said it must be the task of statesmanship, while American atomic supremacy persisted, to obtain from the Russians a settlement that would ensure their retreat behind the Curzon line, and the breaking of the monopoly of power by the Communist parties in the countries of Eastern Europe.[8] Eden, summing up for the Opposition, devoted his speech chiefly to Germany, showing much less interest than Churchill in the prospects of negotiation with Russia except for a concluding remark that when various measures for strengthening the Western coalition had been taken it should be possible to negotiate with Moscow on a basis of strength and "no method of negotiation ought to be excluded."[9]

Ernest Bevin, replying for the Government, linked the notion of "building situations of strength" closely with the progress of NATO. In a section of his speech dealing with a forthcoming meeting of the North Atlantic Council, he said:

I beg of the House and the country not to despair because of present circumstances. I think the day is not far distant when the growth of this power, which has been divided and separated so much in the past, the growth of this unity, not so much union, unity of spirit, unity of action and the comradeship between us, will create a situa-

---

[7] H. C. Deb. (House of Commons Debate), 5th Series, Vol. 473, col. 199 seq.
[8] Ibid., col. 221.
[9] Ibid., cols. 317–18.

tion that will leave no alternative but to negotiate and to settle once and for all this problem that has cursed the world for so long.[1]

It will be observed that in this debate in March the ideas set forth in Acheson's February speeches had already begun to undergo the process of "approximation" which is frequently the fate of political ideas. The most obvious change is the addition of the idea of "the summit" to the prospect of negotiations—that is to say that the negotiators should be heads of government rather than Foreign Secretaries or Ambassadors. Such a proposal was not only alien but entirely repugnant to Acheson's notion of efficient diplomacy and a considerable embarrassment to any American Government in view of the nature of the American political system and the diversity of the President's functions. The origin of this Churchillian idea is clear enough: the meeting is envisaged as a continuation of the war-time personal diplomacy of Roosevelt, Stalin, and himself. But the American image of the personal diplomacy of Yalta and Potsdam tended to be one of disaster and betrayal as far as the Republicans were concerned and of a rather dubious incursion into the bad old style of European power politics, excusable only in war-time emergency, as far as Liberals and Democrats were concerned. This distrust of Presidential personal diplomacy was a sort of overlay on a general American scepticism of American diplomacy as such, which may be unreasonable but is historically deep-seated, visible as early as Jay's Treaty.[2] The stereotype of the American innocent abroad, perpetually being "sold a bill of goods" by slick Europeans, is a commonplace in the bogus homespun philosophy of the Ameri-

---

[1] Ibid., col. 33.

[2] Of 1794, regulating relations between Britain and the U.S. See F. Monaghan: *John Jay* (Bobbs-Merrill Company; 1955), pp. 388–400, for a description of the reception of the treaty. One may still hear the note of traditionalist disapproval of Presidential personal diplomacy as late as 1961, for instance in this comment on the Vienna meeting: "Summit meetings constitute a dangerous departure from a Republic's policy, and seem to be more in conformity with customs and policies followed in the days of absolute monarchy." (The *New York Herald Tribune*, June 14, 1961.)

can cracker-barrel sage: "We never lost a war or won a conference."

However, there was also a more subtle change in the idea. Acheson had spoken of two processes: a building of strength in various ways (not all of them military) and the later emergence of prospects of agreement depending essentially on recognition of facts rather than on bargaining. The telescoping of these two ideas into the single phrase "negotiation from strength" deprives his picture of the future of its careful diplomatic haziness, gives it a much blunter, rather hectoring sound, changes the emphasis between the two elements, and makes the concept far more positive than it originally was. The original phrases were directed to the discouragement of immediate demands for negotiation by holding out the prospect that at some unspecified future time negotiations could be undertaken in rather more favourable circumstances for the West than at present: strength-building was to be the reality of policy for the moment and negotiation a fairly distant aspiration. What emerged from the March debate, on the other hand, was a kind of promise of negotiations, qualified by a rather ambiguous reservation as to the best time to hold them. The hope held out in Acheson's words is of agreements registering acceptance of a situation that has been changed by other means: the hope behind the British debate is of agreements that will themselves in some way change the situation. Negotiation is seen as actual bargaining about facts, rather than as merely registering recognition of facts.

In a sense one can therefore say that in this initial exchange the British position has already been established as in some respects more optimistic than the American. But in one respect it was less so. "Time and patience are not necessarily on the Western side," Churchill said, and time has proved his point. The implicit assumption behind Acheson's phrases, that after a period of competitive strength-building the net advantage would be with the Western powers, cannot but seem in retrospect to have been far too lightly made. Some of the reasons why it proved to be mistaken will be considered presently. But in fairness to Acheson's understanding of the situation in 1950, it must be pointed out that he had clearly, even at this stage, a more accurate notion than most members of the Administration of what the rigours of competition in strength-building with the U.S.S.R. were likely to be. This was demonstrated in his concept, also enunciated about this time, of "total diplomacy," that is to say the primacy of foreign policy,[3] the need to relate the decisions of domestic policy to the stringencies of external policy. But neither Acheson nor his successor, nor either of their respective Presidents, was in a position to modify the scale of national priorities in America as drastically as this concept would have required. Acheson was conscious of this: he once remarked that he sometimes felt like a man standing on a dock with an oar, trying to get the dock to move.[4] It was not until 1955 that there began to be a general understanding of the degree of advantage possessed by an autocratic government in deciding what proportion of national resources should go into the means of military strength and diplomatic leverage, and not until 1957 that the almost unconscious assumption of an inherent Western technological advantage was dispelled.

In a consideration of Acheson's position on both strength and negotiation it is important to distinguish between successive periods of time. The tone of his analysis of Soviet policy in these statements of February 1950 was notably mild, with a sort of philosophic acceptance of Soviet pressure on the West as one of the facts of international life. "You can't argue with a river, it is going to flow." And there is no great insistence on military forces as the basis of strength. After the Korean attack of June 1950, there is a much greater emphasis on rearmament as the basis of diplomatic strength. For instance, in a television interview of September 10, 1950, he said: "The goal for which we are struggling is to settle, so far as we can, the great issues between East and West. To settle these differences we have got to talk on equal

---

[3] See McGeorge Bundy: op. cit., pp. 23 ff.
[4] *The New York Times*, April 8, 1950.

terms. We cannot have one party very strong in terms of armament, and the other party very weak."[5] On October 8, he said:
"Building the strength of the free nations is not by itself a method
of settling differences with the Soviet leaders. It is a way—and
the only way—to prevent those differences from being settled
by default."[6]

This hardening of position was natural and no doubt inevitable:
the pressures of Acheson's last two years of office, both external
and domestic, were of a kind to keep his mind on power-building
rather than negotiation. But since, despite his efforts, no substantial margin of negotiable strength was built either during his
term of office or still less (in his own view) during the Republican
Administration, the pre-conditions of successful negotiation, as
he saw them, have never been achieved. Since 1955, therefore,
he has been even less enthusiastic about negotiations and about
any change of stance in Europe than the spokesmen of the Republican Party. In 1957 he wrote: "The only agreements which
are possible now would be disadvantageous to us and would not
diminish the dangers of nuclear war."[7] A view he stated in 1959:
"Power can be limited only by countervailing power,"[8] expresses
the essence of his diplomatic theory, and his positions on negotiation are deductible from it. In the early part of the period under
review his reading of the power situation was more hopeful than
in the later part. Since the actual change in power relations since
1950 has been unfavourable to the West, and since his best expectation of negotiations is that they should register power relationships accurately, it is logical that he should have been less
sanguine about negotiations in 1960 than he was in 1950.[9] Never-

---

[5] *The New York Times*, September 10, 1950.
[6] *The* (London) *Times*, October 9, 1950.
[7] *Power and Diplomacy* (Cambridge, Mass.: Harvard University Press;
1958), p. 39.
[8] "Prelude to Independence," *Yale Review*, Summer 1959, p. 490.
[9] See, for instance, *The New York Times* of October 2, 1959 (seq.), for a
running argument between Acheson and Herter over whether negotiations
should take place concerning Berlin.

theless, it is not unfair to Acheson to see in his attitude in 1950 a hint of the free-thinking clergyman, with his own reservations about the pearly gates, feeling it psychologically proper nevertheless to inspire the Sunday-school class to virtue with the prospect of ultimate bliss crowning a period of meritorious endeavour.

The idea of negotiation from strength shares with that of the balance of power (to which it is closely related)[1] an element of built-in ambiguity in that *strength* may imply *parity* or *superiority*, just as *balance* may mean *equilibrium* (as of scales) or *surplus* (as of accounts). In Acheson's use of the phrase, it may be asked, did *strength* mean *parity of strength* or *superiority of strength?* The evidence of the military plans made at this period[2] suggests that even parity would be something of an exaggeration for Western ambitions when they had to be translated into hard figures for armed forces. On the other hand, the emotional overtones of the phrase, certainly as used by commentators and by other policy-makers, and perhaps sometimes as used by Acheson himself, conveyed the hope or expectation of an advantage in strength. And since the precise exchange rate, as it were, between the atomic strength in which America was superior (and expected to remain so) and the conventional forces in which Russia was superior (and was expected to remain so) was obscure, one cannot write down an acceptance of something below parity in conventional forces as necessarily ruling out a hope for an over-all advantage.[3]

---

[1] Acheson might have said, for instance, that his policy was to redress the balance of power before entering negotiations. But this would have been a tactless expression for a Secretary of State to use, since the concept of the balance of power is regarded as sinister by many Americans.

[2] See below, pp. 40 ff.

[3] Acheson ought not to be held responsible for journalistic glosses on his policy, but the following example provides something of the emotional tone in which the idea of negotiation from strength was widely presented:

The idea of "peace through strength"—through overwhelming strength—is the basis of present Western policy, and it holds out the most realistic hope of peace we have had for the last six years. America is alone potentially stronger than all the rest of the world put together. But as long as

We come now to a consideration of the relationship between "negotiation from strength" and other currents of opinion in the American attitude to Russia. How new was the line of thought suggested by Acheson in these speeches? Certainly not as new as some of the press comment implied: *The New York Times,* for instance, called it "a turning-point, a sort of watershed,"[4] but it would have been more accurate to call it intensification of a pre-existing policy, or the making explicit of an old aspiration. The belief that the Western powers were at a disadvantage in negotiations *vis-à-vis* the Soviet Union because of their political and military weakness may be seen to be affecting the Western attitude to negotiations as early as the breaking-off of the Foreign Ministers' Conference in Moscow in 1947 by the then Secretary of State, Marshall. According to one American source, the State Department regarded it as a matter of high strategy that major negotiations with the Russians should be averted from that time until the outbreak of the Korean war.[5] This interpretation may be

> America's strength remains potential, while Russia's is actual, and as long as Russia can hope to add further parts of Europe and Asia to her power-sphere by political manœuvre, there is no unchallengeable overbalance of strength on the Western side. . . . We embarked on the process of establishing this overbalance of power a year ago, and we have made astonishing progress towards security in this one year.

This version of Western policy was provided not by a Right-wing American journal, but by a Left-Liberal British one (*The Observer,* November 11, 1951—leading article by Sebastian Haffner). A tendency to count Western chickens before they were hatched was particularly notable about this period—cf.

> With American re-armament advancing into mass-production stage, British and French re-armament gathering speed, and Japan and Germany about to be added to the Western Grand Alliance, Russia faces the certainty that her expansionist career will be at an end by 1953 or 1954 at the latest. . . . She can recognize that she has overplayed her hand and seek accommodation and a settlement by renouncing her post-war conquests in Europe and accepting her true status as a Great Power of the second class. (Ibid., September 23, 1951.)

[4] February 11, 1950.

[5] *Christian Science Monitor,* July 26, 1950. W. W. Rostow, in *The United States in the World Arena* (New York: Harper & Brothers; 1961), confirms this interpretation. See p. 209.

exaggerated, but it is at least clear that the State Department was profoundly sceptical of the value of high-level talks: Stalin's hints at a peace conference in May 1948 and again in 1949 were coldly received, and such lower-level negotiations as did take place were not conducted with any eagerness for serious bargaining.[6] It would be exaggerating the coherence of Western policy to represent the period from late 1947 to early 1950 as one of deliberate building of strength, certainly as far as military strength was concerned (in 1950 there were still negligible Western combat forces on the Continent), but there was a very substantial recruitment of economic and diplomatic strength during the period, and the desire to improve the West's negotiating position *vis-à-vis* Russia was clear in many of the major diplomatic moves that this entailed.

At first sight, the enunciation of the Truman Doctrine (that first improvised measure of strength-building for a threatened area) at a time when Marshall was actually in Moscow for a Foreign Ministers' Conference may seem an obvious instance, but coincidence rather than policy provided this appearance. The actual timing of the Truman Doctrine was not based on calculation of its effect on the conference, but on the exigencies of the British economic situation, Bevin having told the Department of State that Britain could not maintain its aid to Greece and Turkey beyond February.[7] However, Marshall himself, according to Paul Hoffman, said that he conceived the idea that later became the Marshall Plan during the tedious and fruitless negotiations of the conference.[8] That the plan as first proposed took the form of a scheme for the general rebuilding of Europe, rather than for the strengthening of Western Europe to balance against Russia, was due to the astute persuasions of George Kennan, who was

---

[6] See *The United States in World Affairs* for 1948 and 1949 (New York: Harper & Brothers for Council on Foreign Relations; 1950 and 1951).

[7] See Joseph M. Jones: *The Fifteen Weeks* (New York: Viking Press; 1955). This is an account by an ex-member of the Department of State of the processes of policy-formation in the period from the Truman Doctrine to the Marshall Plan. See especially pp. 129–239.

[8] *Life*, July 18, 1955.

able to assure the State Department that if it was offered in this form there would be no prospect of the Russians actually participating[9]—a development that would have roused elements in the Senate to vigorous resistance to the whole project. Kennan's prediction of course proved accurate, and the Marshall Plan must be accounted not only the most successful single strength-building measure of American policy, on the economic and political plane, but also, in the Russian refusal of association and refusal to permit the satellites to join, one of the most notable of America's psychological warfare successes.

Curiously enough, the business of putting together and ratifying the North Atlantic Treaty, in 1948 and 1949, despite the crucial role it was to play later in Acheson's concept of positions of strength, was accompanied by very little in the way of optimistic forecasts of negotiation from strength,[1] probably because it was done in the atmosphere engendered by the Czech coup and the Berlin blockade, when the Western powers felt themselves hard pressed to maintain a *status quo* policy, and a revisionist one appeared far beyond their diplomatic and military means.

The most reasonable summation is that negotiation from strength was not a new doctrine, but that it made explicit an aspiration that had been implicit in Western policy since 1947, or even since the first intimations in 1944–5 of how intransigently determined Russia was to maintain her power sphere in Europe at the farthest reaches to which the war had brought it. However, this statement must be qualified by considering the relationship between the idea of negotiation from strength and the idea of containment, which from the time of the publication of George Kennan's famous article in the July 1947 issue of *Foreign Affairs*[2]

---

[9] Jones: op. cit., p. 253.

[1] See *North Atlantic Treaty*: Hearings before the Senate Foreign Relations Committee, 81st Congress, 1st session (Washington: U.S. Gov't Printing Office; 1949).

[2] *The Sources of Soviet Conduct* by "X." The article was a development of a cable sent to the State Department in February 1946. See *The Forrestal Diaries* (New York: Viking Press; 1951), p. 46.

had been assumed by informed observers to represent the basic motivation of American policy towards Russia.[3]

In one sense there was no necessary inconsistency between the two ideas. Policy in foreign affairs has to operate on a number of different planes simultaneously, and containment was a concept for the day-to-day level of operations, whereas negotiation from strength operated at the aspiration level, and provided a sort of happy ending for the containment story. On the other hand, containment is clearly a *status quo* concept: it aims to keep the situation from deteriorating. Negotiation from strength is *prima facie* a revisionist one: it aims to improve things—for instance, to negotiate the Russian troops in Europe back behind the Russian frontier, thus (it was assumed in this early period at least) making a profound change in the world balance of power.

This distinction between the nature of the two policies is rather more important from the point of view of academic analysis than it was in actual practical policy, since the implicit revisionism of negotiation from strength was in the degree of velleity rather than will, and the acceptance of the *status quo* in containment was of a bare and reluctant sort. But it ought not to be altogether discounted, especially as it was connected with a change of personalities in the Policy Planning Division of the State Department. George Kennan (General Marshall's appointee) was succeeded at the end of 1949 by Paul Nitze (Acheson's appointee). There had been considerable divergencies between Acheson and Kennan on various matters, including the Truman Doctrine.[4] These divergencies between the two men grew much sharper in later years, especially after Kennan's Reith Lectures of 1957. Acheson's views on the relationship between military power and diplomatic leverage are robust, straightforward, and hard-headed, with no great inclination for ambiguities and some impatience with dissentient views. He once dismissed Kennan's analysis as "mystical."[5]

----

[3] See Walter Lippmann: *The Cold War* (London: Hamish Hamilton; 1947).

[4] See Jones: op. cit., pp. 155-6.

[5] See his article in Foreign Affairs, April 1958, for his general attitude towards Kennan's later proposals.

The most important and substantial difference between the idea of containment and the idea of negotiation from strength is that they implicitly offer two alternate notions about a possible end to the power struggle with Russia, which may be called respectively the "domestic change" thesis and the "diplomatic adjustment" thesis. The first holds broadly that abatement of the power struggle is to be looked for only through a process of change within Russia: the nature of the change expected may be put crudely as in a remark by Dulles in 1955 about the Soviet system being on the verge of collapse[6] or delicately as in Kennan's phrase about "an erosion from despotism."[7] And of course when this idea is used as a policy concept there are great variations as to how far the West can or should attempt to promote such changes. But essentially the hope is domestic change in Russia, and there is an underlying premise (which might be regarded as historically dubious) that a non-despotic Russian state would be less likely to be in conflict with the West.

The difference between these two implicit assumptions about possible ends to the power struggle is interesting because of its relation to theories, conscious or unconscious, about the causation of war. Broadly speaking, one may see the causation of war as lying in the nature of the state, or in the nature of the relation between states, or in the nature of man. From the first assumption of war as inherent in the nature of the state—whether of despotic states in general, or of Communist despotisms in particular, or (from the other camp) of capitalist states as such—it would logically follow that domestic change in the enemy is the only substantial hope of peace. From the second theory, of war as inherent in the nature not of individual states but of the relation between them, it would logically follow that diplomatic adjustment was a possible hope of peace, or at least of the avoidance of any particular war. On the third theory, seeing war as inherent in the nature of man, one would presumably have to pin one's hopes

---

[6] See below, p. 126.

[7] *American Diplomacy*, 1900–1950 (London: Martin Secker & Warburg; 1952), p. 144.

for long-range peace to psychoanalysis, or Christianity, or the transforming effects of socialism on humanity.

It would of course be expecting an unnatural degree of consistency to assume that the statesmen and commentators obliged to contemplate Russian-American relations should entirely cleave to one or another of these concepts, but distinguishable preferences are visible among them. Acheson uses both the "domestic change" and the "diplomatic adjustment" thesis, but with a fairly clear preference for the latter.[8] Dulles's preference was almost entirely for the "domestic change" thesis: when he was occasionally forced into speaking of diplomatic adjustment, his words had an unconvinced ring. Kennan, though the original popularizer of the "domestic change" thesis in 1947, changed his position fairly radically, and had become an adherent of diplomatic adjustment by 1957.[9] Walter Lippmann, on the other hand, was a strong adherent of the "diplomatic adjustment" thesis from his first cogent criticism of Kennan in his 1947 pamphlet, *The Cold War*.

On the whole, European statesmen and commentators were more optimistic than their American counterparts about diplomatic adjustment, and Americans have been much more optimistic than Europeans over the hope of domestic change, in the special sense of disintegration in Russia.

There are, of course, other possible positions than either of these which may be taken about the outcome of the power struggle between America and Russia. For instance, one might hold that it will merely die away like that between Catholics and Protestants or between Moslems and Christians, without either domestic change or formal diplomatic adjustment, or that it will inevitably end in war, or inevitably end in the defeat of the West without war. No doubt these possibilities have been present in the minds of people concerned, but they cannot be said to have

---

[8] For an example of his use of the "domestic change" thesis, see his speech at Detroit, July 24, 1951. *Department of State Bulletin*, August 6, 1951, XXV.

[9] See his Reith Lectures of 1957, published as *Russia, the Atom and the West* (O.U.P.; 1958).

played much part in the policy debate, since the bulk of both the Democratic Party and the Republican Party (and in Britain the Labour Party and the Conservative Party) shared what may be called a central "government" position, preoccupied with the "containment/negotiation from strength" complex of ideas. The variations as to the degree of hope or scepticism with which the idea of negotiation is regarded are important, but there is not much essential difference of views regarding the nature of the power struggle with Russia, or the limits within which it may be conducted.

More radical voices may be heard from outside this central government position, from both a Left and a Right opposition, independent of the formal parties. The Left opposition in America is rather a vestigial remnant in the period after 1950. It may be characterized as holding the theory that the whole conflict was mistaken or unnecessary, a misunderstanding that could be cleared up if the right people were in power in America. This was the mood of the "Wallace or War" slogan in the 1948 Presidential election. However, Henry Wallace's candidature was the last political gesture of the radical Left in America. It withered away like a frost-sensitive plant as the full rigours of the Cold War set in. It is interesting to speculate as to the direction in which the Wallace vote of 1948 went in the 1952 election. In so far as it was a "Left" vote it presumably should have gone to the Democrats, but in so far as it was a "peace" vote it may well have gone to Eisenhower, who after all campaigned largely on the promise of a settlement in Korea.

After about 1948, few Americans (apart from Communist party members and a handful of neo-Marxist academic analysts[1]) were prepared to persist with the Left thesis that the causes of friction with Russia were to be found in the nature of *American* society. This is an interesting position, when one considers the spectrum

---

[1] The most important and interesting of the latter group was C. Wright Mills. See his *The Causes of World War III* (London: Martin Secker & Warburg; 1959).

of opinion, since it is the symmetrical opposite of the "domestic
change in Russia" thesis, seeing domestic change in America as
the prerequisite of a settlement.

The Right opposition or preventive-war school of thought de-
serves more extended attention, both for its intrinsic interest and
because a fascinated exaggeration of its importance has been a
damaging element in the European image of America. As Bernard
Brodie has said, the project of preventive war has been pressed
sotto voce by various voices throughout the period since 1945,[2]
and it has had some influential adherents, though it cannot be
called a genuinely influential school of thought. Its adherents
have been mostly in, or closely connected with, the armed forces,
especially the Air Force and the Navy. Truman's Secretary of
Defence, Louis Johnson, was reported to have "privately talked
preventive war" and his Secretary of the Navy, Francis Matthews,
went so far as to urge publicly that the United States become "the
first aggressors for peace" and "pay any price—even the price of
instituting war—to compel co-operation for peace."[3] (Truman
remarks that Matthews had heard so many "Admirals and other
high Navy people" talk preventive war that he had "repeated the
phrase without realizing just how far it took him away from my
policy."[4] For the whole period until 1955 the idea tended to recur
in crises when the balance of power seemed likely to swing against
the United States, for instance in the Indo-China crisis of 1954
and the Formosa crisis of early 1955. In these two crises the idea
was associated chiefly with the names of Admiral Radford and
Admiral Carney, then Chairman of the Joint Chiefs of Staff and
Navy Chief of Staff respectively. A more or less off-the-record
speech by Admiral Carney in 1955 particularly alarmed that sector of American opinion which dissented vigorously from the preventive-war idea. Senator Estes Kefauver, for instance, said on

[2] "Unlimited Weapons and Limited War," *The Reporter*, November 18,
1954.
[3] *The New York Times*, August 26, 1950.
[4] *Memoirs*, Vol. II, p. 383.

NEGOTIATION FROM STRENGTH

March 30, 1955, that there were forces in the Eisenhower Administration "so powerful and apparently so eager for a war with China that they are becoming almost impossible to resist."[5]

But it must be emphasized that, highly placed though these spokesmen may have been, there is no indication that either Truman or Eisenhower took them seriously. Truman publicly reprimanded Matthews and dropped Johnson from his Administration. Eisenhower, when asked about preventive war at a press conference in August 1954, said that "it was impossible now" and he "would not listen seriously to anyone who came and talked to him about such a thing."[6] Dulles also was careful to repudiate any suggestion of State Department interest in the notion of preventive war. The question was put to him directly in connection with the John Paton Davies case. Davies, a former member of the Policy Planning Staff who was dismissed by Dulles in 1954 on the grounds of lack of discretion, asked for permission to publish the papers in his own case, including one he had written in 1950, advocating a "preventive showdown" with Russia.[7] Dulles refused to publish the papers on the ground that they would include many top-secret papers of the Policy Planning Staff. He added that "any idea of preventive war was wholly out of the question as far as the United States were concerned: it was not in any sense part or parcel even remotely of U.S. foreign policy," and he "did not want to create the impression that the way to favor in this or any other administration was to be an advocate of preventive war against the Soviet Union."[8]

The proposals, such as they were, for preventive war never in fact had any real prospect of proving adequately persuasive, for

---

[5] *The New York Times*, March 31, 1955.

[6] Ibid., August 17, 1954.

[7] Apparently in order to exempt himself from any imputation of "softness towards Communism."

[8] *The New York Times*, November 10, 1954. The publication of a book by General Thomas Powers was forbidden by the Secretary of Defence in 1959 (*The New York Times*, August 21, 1959), apparently on account of its advocacy of preventive war.

two reasons: a natural moral revulsion against the idea, and the fact that the power relations between America and Russia have never been such as to make it really feasible. Before the Russian acquisition of air atomic power, Western conventional forces were so weak that Europe had to be regarded as a hostage to the Red Army. Since that date, it has been clear that such a war could only be launched at unacceptable cost and ruin, first in Europe and later in America itself. As Bernard Brodie says: "Actually, there probably never was a time when preventive war would have been technically—not to say politically—feasible. When we had the atomic monopoly we did not have enough power; and when we developed the necessary power we no longer had the monopoly."[9] Something called the "policy of restraint" is occasionally adduced as the reason for the failure of America to put its atomic monopoly to diplomatic advantage *vis-à-vis* Russia in the period 1946–9. The phrase suggests that America felt itself strong, in this period, but was restrained from using its strength by some definable set of moral or political considerations. This is a misleading picture: the margin of American advantage, as seen by the policy-makers, was never so clear that any specific body of considerations was needed to justify refusal to attempt to exploit it. In any case, the normal inertia of a democracy in foreign policy, the normal dislike of democratic leaders for taking any decisions other than those forced upon them by the other side, operated as an effectively restraining factor on any nice calculation of advantage this year against probable disadvantage ten years hence.

Since 1955, with the growth of Soviet long-range striking power, the doctrine of preventive war has had no serious following, but there has been much growth of the doctrine of pre-emptive war. There is a clear theoretical distinction between the two, even though the difference in practical results might be difficult to discern. Preventive-war doctrine was the outcome of a period when victory (in the sense of a power-political position more

[9] Op. cit.

favourable at the end of the process than at the beginning) seemed possible: pre-emptive war (which has been flippantly defined as the "We won't strike first unless you do" doctrine) aims rather to minimize the damage to the homeland when war has become inevitable, by striking first at, and reducing as far as possible, the effective striking forces of the other side. This is an evolution that belongs to the final stage of the relative growths of strength, and will be discussed later.[1]

---

[1] One may discern, in a number of articles on pre-emptive war, an effort to overcome the moral revulsion against striking the first blow, by stressing the point that the blow would be directed at armed forces rather than civilian populations. See "No Need to Bomb Cities to Win War" by Col. Richard S. Leghorn (U.S.A.F. Reserve), in *U.S. News and World Report*, January 28, 1955, and "Must the U.S. Take the First Blow?" (Ibid., December 13, 1957).

The Constituents
of Strength

When Acheson made his statements about negotiation
from strength in February 1950, there had already been in progress for about four months, within the counsels of the American
Government, a great, impassioned, confused debate about the
nature of the military strength to be built by America in the next
strategic period. This underwater explosion of conflicting opinion
had been set off by an actual literal bomb, the first Soviet atomic
bomb, whose firing was detected in September 1949. The notion
of negotiation from strength may be regarded as the fleck of
foam which showed on the surface of policy above the hidden
convulsion: the two main pressure waves down below affected
respectively hydrogen weapons and conventional forces.

A detailed account of some of the secret arguments of September 1949–January 1950 was made available to the world in
1954 through the Oppenheimer inquiry,[1] and those portions of

---

[1] *In the Matter of J. Robert Oppenheimer*: Hearing before the Personnel
Security Board, Washington, April–May 1954 (Washington: U.S. Gov't
Printing Office; 1954).

policy not covered by the inquiry have since been touched on in other sources. Some areas of the history of this period are still only dimly visible through the shadow of "classification," but enough is available to make out the outlines of the story.

As soon as the Soviet atomic explosion was detected in September 1949, the consciousness that one strategic period—the period of American atomic monopoly—had ended, and that the decisions for the next must be taken swiftly, brought many divergent interests into play. That a thermo-nuclear weapon could probably be made, but that there were substantial and unresolved technical difficulties in the way of making it, had been known since the late war years. Some of the scientists who in the original effort at Los Alamos had been concerned with fusion rather than fission reactions (especially Dr. Edward Teller) were strong advocates of a "crash programme" for the development of thermo-nuclear weapons, as were General Vandenberg, the Air Force Chief of Staff, and General Bradley, the Chairman of the Joint Chiefs of Staff. The Atomic Energy Commission, which had already in hand a programme for expanding the production of atomic weapons, was doubtful, and ultimately divided three to two against the crash programme: technically it was a question of whether the prospect of success with the H-bomb was sufficient to justify the diversion of effort and material from the A-weapons programme. The General Advisory Committee on Atomic Energy, whose chairman was Dr. Oppenheimer, was asked for an opinion, and reported against. It was Oppenheimer's role in the formulation and presentation of this opinion, in the main, that made him vulnerable to the delayed but effective revenge of the inquiry four years later.

In these circumstances Truman handed the problem to a special committee consisting of Acheson, Secretary of Defence Louis Johnson, and the Chairman of the Atomic Energy Commission, David Lilienthal. They made two recommendations: that all efforts should be made to determine whether an H-bomb could be constructed, and that there should be "a re-examination of our foreign policy and our strategic plans, both diplomatic and military."[2] The second of these recommendations was to result after a further three months' work in a National Security Council paper which might be described as the original appreciation and recommendations for the second period of the atomic age. For the moment, however, we will be concerned with the more dramatic of the two recommendations, that regarding the hydrogen bomb.

As was previously said, it was the announcement of this decision, and the uneasiness it produced, that first evoked Acheson's use of the concept of negotiation from strength. But the main point of interest in the decision itself is how far, if at all, those who were charged with advising the President on this question concerned themselves with the problem of relating this particular form of military strength to American diplomatic leverage, and whether they believed it would provide effective backing for negotiation.

On the whole, the answer to the second question is clearly "no." Reading the transcript of the evidence in the Oppenheimer inquiry, one is struck by the absence of optimism, even on the part of those who were strongly "for" the bomb, that its possession could readily be transmuted into diplomatic advantage. The efforts to produce it were justified rather on the ground that it was necessary to prevent any further deterioration of the American position *vis-à-vis* Russia. This was particularly the case with the President. He is said to have asked only two questions: "Can they make it? And if so, how can we not?"[3]

Equally striking is the degree to which, before the Soviet explosion, the United States Government had avoided letting its right hand know what its left hand was doing. This applied

---

[2] Truman: *Memoirs*, Vol. II, p. 309.
[3] The arrest of Klaus Fuchs about this time was one of the chief factors in the American belief that Russia might be well advanced towards a thermonuclear bomb. Fuchs had been present at some of the discussions of the bomb in the war years.

even to the advisers with whose aid the President reached his decision. Lilienthal said in his evidence at the Oppenheimer inquiry that the A.E.C. "had before it no diplomatic or political evaluation for the effect of such a weapon pro or con on such matters as the Cold War, or the effect on our alliances and other diplomatic and international relations."[4] Nor did they seem to have much more specific advice on the military usefulness or otherwise of the new weapon: when General Bradley was asked to give an opinion on the military value of a bomb a thousand times the size of the Hiroshima bomb, he apparently replied that it would be principally psychological.[5]

One is left with the impression that even though the whole debate after the Soviet atomic explosion turned around the question of which kinds of military power were politically useful, very few of the participants in the debate were sufficiently at home in the three fields of knowledge—that of the scientists, concerned with relative technical possibilities; that of the military, concerned with the likely demand for particular kinds of weapons; and that of the diplomatists, concerned with the relative likelihood of the sorts of situations in which weapons might be used—to have worked out any firm views on this point. Only Oppenheimer, with his brilliant fertility of mind, seems to have been confident of his ability to make judgments in all three fields, and his ventures into strategy and politics created a dangerous resentment among those who felt that he was poaching on their preserves, or that his technical judgments were moral judgments in disguise.

It was not really surprising that most of the people concerned were provided with no coherent view of the requirements of American policy, since security barriers cut them off from some of the necessary information. Kennan, for instance, though still at this time in charge of the Policy Planning Division of the State Department, and therefore more concerned than anyone else with the long-term relationship between America's power and its commitments, was apparently expected to formulate

---

[4] Oppenheimer transcript, p. 400.
[5] Ibid., p. 407.

his views in ignorance of America's actual military strength; "I
have never known the number of our bombs or the real facts of
their destructiveness or any of those things."[6] Lilienthal, though
chairman of the body concerned with supplying to the military
their most formidable weapons, was in ignorance of the full
measure of the country's reliance on them: "General Bradley
stated rather flatly that they had no reserve except the A-bomb in
the event of any aggression in any part of the world. . . . This
seemed to me really quite harassing . . . our earlier discussions of
what kind of programme we should have did not have the
advantage of knowing the limitations of the military establishment at that time."[7] He was perturbed at the direction of policy:
he spoke of "an illusion of security which a number of G.A.C.
members attributed to our possession of the A-bomb, an over-
valuation of the security that could be secured from large bombs
alone, as distinguished from a balanced military establishment."[8]
He also remarked that the Atomic Energy Commission had not
received from the armed forces any request for a weapon of
greater destructive power than a stepped-up fission bomb which
they were planning at the time.[9]

The question of whether the possession of nuclear weapons
would enable the *Russians* to negotiate from strength (assuming
that America was not also in possession of them) was obviously
under consideration at the State Department: Kennan said in his
evidence that it was a matter he "had occasion to argue many
times here in Washington." He was doubtful that the Russians
would attempt to use weapons of this sort as a means of pressure.[1]
Acheson's view on this point was not made specific at the inquiry,

---

[6] Ibid., p. 366.
[7] Ibid., pp. 404–5.
[8] Ibid.
[9] Ibid., p. 403. See also *The New York Times*, October 4, 1954, for an
article by Lilienthal.
[1] Oppenheimer transcript, p. 363. Since the development of Khrushchev's
technique (from 1956) of attempting to use Soviet missile strength as a form
of diplomatic leverage, it is clear that Kennan's assumption was far too
optimistic.

but it is clear from Truman's final decision that it was to the contrary.

All in all, the American decision on the H-bomb must be held to have proceeded less from any conviction that its possession would strengthen America's hand diplomatically (or perhaps even militarily) than from the fear that a failure to build it would provide the Russians with a margin of potential advantage.

If there had in fact been any expectation in 1950 that the addition of nuclear weapons to the American armoury would lead to a period of decisive Western superiority (a perceptible moment for negotiating from strength), the expectation would have been disappointed, because, though America produced a thermonuclear explosion some nine months before the Russians, it did not test "a droppable bomb" until March 1954, as against August 1953 for the Russians, and it seems probable that these weapons began to reach sizeable numbers in the armouries of the two sides about the same period—the second half of 1954. There was, however, a time, from November 1952 to August 1953, when a belief in the American nuclear advantage was held in some policymaking circles, and had a serious—indeed, disastrous—effect on decisions. But that episode belongs to the history of the Republican Administration.

The second of the two recommendations of the Acheson-Johnson-Lilienthal committee, that for a general review of American strategy and foreign policy, was also accepted by Truman. There had been earlier urgings within the Department of State that such an effort should be made, but most of the actual work on it, which was shared by the Departments of State and Defence, was done between January and April 1950. The review was embodied in a National Security Council document known as N.S.C. 68, and reached the President on April 7, 1950. N.S.C. 68 is one of the major milestones in the evolution of American policy in the post-war period, and though it is still classified, a good deal may be learned of its substance.

Truman's account is confined to generalities: he says that it contained an analysis of the world situation—"close attention was given to the effect of Russian atomic strength as it was likely to develop over the next few years"—and that the recommendations "aimed at building up rapidly the combined political, economic and military strength of the free world."[2] From other sources it may be learned that a substantial and expensive programme of rebuilding American strength was called for: the level proposed approximated to partial mobilization. The concept of "a year of maximum danger," which was used in the early period of NATO, apparently first appeared in this document, the year named being 1954, the estimated date by which Russia was expected to have a reasonable stockpile of atomic weapons.

There was some discussion of the possibilities of negotiation with Russia in the final section of the paper, but only in generalized terms and with a fundamental assumption that any successful negotiation must reflect an improved power relationship.

Though N.S.C. 68 was a joint product of the Departments of State and Defence (the official chiefly responsible at the Department of State being Paul Nitze, Kennan's successor as chief of the Policy Planning Division and later Assistant Secretary of Defence for International Security Affairs in President Kennedy's Administration), Acheson and the Secretary of Defence, Louis Johnson, did not by any means see eye to eye on policy. Johnson was as dedicated to economy and the balanced budget as any of Eisenhower's advisers later, and differed sharply from Acheson on the desirable rate for the rebuilding of American armed strength. According to a senior State Department official of the time, N.S.C. 68 was only "got past" Johnson by presenting it to him already signed by all the other persons concerned, including the Joint Chiefs of Staff.[3]

---

[2] Truman: *Memoirs*, Vol. II, pp. 311–12.

[3] The differences between Acheson and Johnson were well known in Washington at the time, and the subject of some press comment. The inspired "leak" to a sympathetic journalist is one of the established techniques of internecine warfare in the U.S. public service, and seems to have been used by the State Department in this case. At any rate, Johnson thought so;

Given the preconceptions of Congressmen, the economic and political climate of Washington in the spring of 1950 was calculated to favour Johnson's view of the situation rather than Acheson's. America had been in a state of mild recession for most of the previous year, and Congress was in the mood for retrenchment rather than expansion of government spending. The budget presented in January 1950, which took no account of the programme that was to be foreshadowed in N.S.C. 68, already required some increase in taxation. Approval for a further large increase in defence costs would certainly have been difficult to obtain. Therefore, though work was continued from April to June on translating the recommendation of N.S.C. 68 into military budgets and forces levels, it remained uncertain whether the programme would actually go into operation.

What put effective political impetus behind it was the attack in Korea, which not only caused Johnson to revise his position entirely but also transformed Truman's situation *vis-à-vis* Congress as far as defence costs were concerned. To a degree that now seems a trifle surprising, the attack in Korea was accepted as the beginning of a new phase in Soviet policy, a phase in which the U.S.S.R. was showing itself willing to take the risks of open hostilities, possibly in Europe as well as elsewhere. And it must be remembered that Korea was "read with" the Russian atomic explosion as evidence that the increasing adventurousness of Russian policy was related to a growth in military strength. Though this view was most prevalent in Washington it had some European adherents, especially in Germany, which was naturally inclined to see a possible parallel to the Korean situation in its own case. Therefore, if Korea constituted a first mortgage on

there is an entertaining account of his reactions in Alsop: *The Reporter's Trade*, p. 148. On N.S.C. 68 generally, there is some material in Walter Millis's *Arms and the State* (New York: Twentieth Century Fund; 1958). The author's information was derived from interviews in Washington. A detailed analysis of N.S.C. 68 by Paul Hammond is to be published in *Strategies, Budgets and Defense Policies: Three Studies in the Making of National Security Policy* (Columbia University Press, forthcoming).

American strength, it also provided the major incentive for the
dispatch of more troops to Europe. The reasoning behind the
comparative subordination of Asia to Europe, even at the crisis
point of the Korean war, was expressed by Admiral Forrest P.
Sherman at the MacArthur hearing: "If we lose Western Europe
we will have great difficulty in preventing a subsequent build-up
in Soviet power; with the shipyards and airplane factories, all of
the productive capacity of Western Europe lost, we would have
an increasingly difficult time in holding our own; whereas if we
lose all of the Asiatic mainland we could still survive and build
up and possibly get it back again."[4]

The Atlantic Treaty had of course been in existence for about
a year at the time when serious attention began to be given to
force levels in Western Europe, after the approval of N.S.C. 68.
But in its original formulation the treaty was seen as a political
rather than a military obligation. The most ambitious common
purpose that can be ascribed to its members at the time of signature in April 1949 was the inhibiting of any further extension
of the Soviet *Machtgebiet* in Europe, by a political and psychological solidarity, rather than by an Atlantic army. The first
theory of NATO was engagingly called "the dumb-bell concept":
it envisaged the treaty as a link between two separate centres of
power, one in America, the other in Europe. This notion did not
survive the dispatch of a military and State Department team
(including Paul Nitze) to Europe in the spring of 1949, to
investigate the situation, since it became abundantly clear that
the idea of an independent power centre in Europe was unrealistic for the time being.

In the Senate hearings on the treaty in July 1949, even its
opponents do not appear to have expected it to entail the degree
of peace-time commitment of American troops to Europe that
developed later. The Secretary of State denied categorically that

[4] *Military Situation in the Far East*: Hearings before the Senate Armed
Services and Foreign Relations Committees, 82nd Congress, 1st session,
May–August 1951 (Washington: G.P.O.; 1951), pp. 1585–6.

the peace-time stationing of U.S. troops abroad in large numbers was contemplated, and the Army Chief of Staff described the alliance as essentially political.[5] Opposition to the treaty was confined to the remnants of the radical Left (Henry Wallace called it the product of an alliance between "certain elements in the Catholic Church," "British imperial interests," and "our own big-business interests"[6]) and Conservative groups suspicious of its constitutional effects. None of these adequately forecast the treaty's future as the basis of the major American deployment of forces overseas, though such an argument might well have been damaging to the Administration's case. The Senators' questioning turned largely about the cost of arms aid to Europe. This issue could have been kept separate from that of ratification of the treaty, and Conolly and Vandenberg believed it should have been,[7] but Acheson candidly insisted that the treaty implied military help, and this straightforwardness proved an effective strategy.[8]

The origin of NATO's coalition army may be seen in the Senate's insistence on an integrated strategy for Europe. The funds allocated for NATO were divided into three parts: $100 million to be available immediately, $400 million to be available as soon as the North Atlantic Council had produced defence plans, and $500 million to be expended after June 30, 1950. The Senate's rider concerning defence plans was intended to ensure that the projected aid would not be devoted to purely national ends. A ready source of such plans as it demanded existed in

---

[5] *North Atlantic Treaty*: Hearings before the Senate Committee on Foreign Relations, 81st Congress, 1st session, April 27–May 3, 1949 (Washington: G.P.O.; 1949), pp. 47, 292 ff.

[6] Ibid., p. 463 ff.

[7] *The Private Papers of Senator Vandenberg* (New York: Houghton Mifflin Company; 1951), pp. 502–18.

[8] Approval of ratification was given in the Senate by 82 to 13 votes on July 21, 1949. The grant of $1,000 million for military aid to Europe was approved by voice vote on September 28, 1949. (*The U.S. in World Affairs*, 1949 [New York: Harper & Brothers; 1950], pp. 82 ff).

the Military Liaison Committees attached to the Brussels Pact, and the associated Joint American Military Advisory Group.

From these sources emerged the plans which were to be later taken over by the NATO command. Since the Western effort to rebuild conventional forces in Europe through the mechanism of NATO became an important part of the concept of "situations of strength" as it developed, it is necessary to examine in some detail the successive strategies and forces goals of NATO, and the degree to which they could be held to assist in, or inhibit, the realization of particular diplomatic objectives. In the discussion of military matters there is always difficulty in separating the wheat of actuality from the chaff of official claims and journalistic speculation. But a reasonable amount has been disclosed about NATO's military affairs by official spokesmen like Lord Ismay[9] and General Norstad,[1] and by well-informed military analysts, especially Roger Hilsman, Alastair Buchan, and Hanson Baldwin.[2]

Three sets of military plans were devised in the period before the NATO command became active: the first in case of war in the immediate future, the second assuming a year or two of defence build-up, and the third geared to a longer period of danger. The short-term plan was in effect a plan for the evacuation of troops from the Continent in case of emergency, assignment of

---

[9] *NATO: the First Five Years* (Utrecht; 1955).

[1] Various interviews and speeches, especially those reprinted in *NATO Letter* IV, No. 12 (December 1956) and *NATO Letter* V., No. 12 (December 1957).

[2] Dr. Hilsman has written accounts of NATO's strategy in *Alliance Policy in the Cold War* (ed. Wolfers. Baltimore: Johns Hopkins Press; 1959) and in *NATO and American Security* (ed. Knorr. Princeton: Princeton University Press; 1959). Mr. Buchan's account is in *NATO in the 1960's,* especially Chapters 1–3 (London: Institute of Strategic Studies; 1960). Hanson Baldwin reviews military affairs for *The New York Times;* see also his *The Great Arms Race* (London: Stevens & Sons; 1958). The author has leaned particularly on the writings of Dr. Hilsman, who is at present a director of intelligence and research at the State Department, and whose position in Washington, even before this appointment, kept him in close touch with policy-makers.

troops to withdrawal routes, and authority to commandeer ships in British and allied ports. "This was the plan for the immediate future, the period of the oft-repeated and undoubtedly apocryphal remark of the NATO staff officer whose reply as to what the Soviet troops needed to reach the Pyrenees was simply 'shoes.' The cry among those who were fond of the sardonic was 'On to Lamballe,' an obscure village in Brittany on one of the withdrawal routes."[3] A plan of this sort was of course the only realistic one in view of the fact that the Western powers had only twelve divisions in Europe,[4] as against a probable 175 Soviet divisions, and, moreover, that the Western forces were not deployed to meet an attack but were scattered through Germany and Austria on occupation duties, with little armour or artillery or tactical air support.

The medium-term plan was aimed at remedying some of these deficiencies. It called for the shifting of supply lines (which had previously run parallel to the front from Hamburg and Bremerhaven, and in many places were within a few miles of Soviet armour), the building of new airfields in proper tactical positions, the establishment of supply dumps and hospitals, the "fleshing-out" of corps and army supporting troops, and the re-deploying of combat forces in position to meet an attack. This medium-term plan contemplated that, in the event of an actual attack, the Western forces would retreat to positions behind the Rhine and attempt to hold there, but it was conceded that the chances of holding would not be good.[5]

---

[3] Roger Hilsman: Unpublished paper in files of Library of Congress Reference Service.

[4] Ismay: op. cit.

[5] Hilsman: op cit. This realization produced a certain jockeying for position, when the build-up was actually on, as to which allied nation was to get which sector of the front. The southern position, in Bavaria, was considered the worst, since the chances were that a force there would be pinned against the Alps. The centre position offered the best chance of retreat into France and another stand, perhaps, at the Pyrenees. (Ibid.)

The long-term plan was an assessment of the forces needed to defend Western Europe in the event of a major war. The two lines envisaged as being defended were the old Western Front from Basle to the mouth of the Rhine, and the Brenner-Trieste area. This military problem was a familiar one for Western staff officers: it meant covering the major approaches adequately, using apparently the figures for division fronts derived from the experience of the Second World War; the intervening areas were to be lightly screened and a reserve kept of about one third the total force. The general consensus was that a force of about a hundred divisions would be needed, assuming that the attacker would need about a three to one majority to dislodge them.

This target figure of about a hundred divisions (ninety-six was the number finally settled on) was of some later importance in the counsels of NATO, so there are certain points to be noted about it. First, the general assumption when it was set was apparently that the Third World War would not be markedly different from the last stages of the Second World War. It would hardly be exaggerating to say that the influence of atomic weapons on the course of the war appears to have been discounted: this may be interpreted as meaning either that atomic weapons were not at this time (late 1949–early 1950) available in sufficiently large quantities to be judged likely to put much of a crimp in Russia's ability to wage war (there are other indications to this effect) or that, even though they were available, their impact on warfare was rather played down by the officers concerned. They would be Army officers, in the main, and many of them remained resolutely sceptical about the transforming effects of the new weapons even much later. Stemming from this assumption about the nature of the possible war, there was a further assumption that the full total of divisions need not be available until sometime after D-day. The screen force, required on the line before D-day, was to be thirty-five to forty divisions, of which seven or nine were to be in Italy, to cover the Brenner-

Trieste area, two to three in Scandinavia, and only twenty-five on the Central Front.

There are, to a layman, two surprising things about the military history of NATO. The first is that its strategic concepts have borne so little relation to the ostensible political or diplomatic ambitions of its members. The second is that though the states to whom was allotted the task of raising the forces proposed for the Central Front have included some of the most notable and successful military powers of modern history—the United States, Britain, France, and later Germany, with assistance from Canada, Belgium, Holland, Norway, and Denmark—they have never succeeded in reaching actual forces figures commensurate with even their minimal strategic objectives. According to taste, one may interpret this as a morally gratifying demonstration of the peace-loving nature of democracies or as a politically dismaying demonstration of their inability to match intention with performance unless the knife is visibly at their collective throat.

The point being made is that the objective set down in this initial period for the joint efforts of the United States, Britain, France, Canada, Holland, Belgium, and Denmark, twenty-four to twenty-five divisions in readiness and a further forty to forty-one mobilizable at short notice,[6] was a comparatively modest one by the standards of the past: France alone, for instance, raised a hundred divisions at the onset of the Second World War. The usual explanation in terms of shortage of military manpower or disadvantage in relative population figures, *either* of the 1950 decision that the necessary divisions could not be raised without German participation *or* of the later decision that a conventional defence of Europe was not feasible, simply does not stand up to an examination of the relevant figures.

---

[6] These figures are given by a number of authorities, including Hilsman (op. cit.), and F. O. Miksche: *The Failure of Atomic Strategy* (London: Faber & Faber; 1959). According to Miksche, the divisions not actually on a war footing were to be maintained at 75 per cent of strength. See p. 48.

The twelve member nations of NATO in 1950, when these plans were being made, represented about 350 million people. By the later accession of Greece, Turkey, and Western Germany, their numbers rose to about 430 million. As against this, the Russians commanded a population of about 260 million, if one includes the satellites, though their captive position in the Soviet sphere might be judged to make them as much a military liability as an asset in the event of conventional hostilities. It is only if the Chinese are added that manpower totals are, *per se*, unfavourable to the West, and for various reasons, if only of transport, it is clear that what China could add to the manpower total available for attack *in Europe* can be disregarded. This is particularly the case when one is considering the earlier period, about 1950. And a larger proportion of total manpower is mobilizable in economies of the highly developed Western European type than in those of less-developed character: there is, as it were, more fat to cut.[7]

It would therefore be more accurate to describe the failure of the original Central Front powers to contemplate the raising of the required divisions as an illustration of the difference, for democracies, between political decision-making in peace-time and such decision-making in war-time. However, one factor that should be borne in mind is that these decisions had to be taken at great speed, with little leisure for reflection on the limits they might later impose on the negotiating position of the West. The crowded and crisis-ridden months of July and August 1950, between the attack in Korea at the end of June and the North

---

[7] It might be argued, in contravention of this general point, that the refusal of the Western powers to tie up any large percentage of their manpower resources in the unproductive function of soldiering represented an unavowed but realistic assumption that the real battle would prove to be the economic and political contest between two systems of society and that the mobilization of large armed forces would actually damage Western prospects in this second battle. But this argument fails to take adequate account of the diplomatic meaning of military strength.

Atlantic Council meeting early in September, were the crucial period of choice for the future of NATO. As late as the May 1950 meeting of the North Atlantic Council, though the proposals of N.S.C. 68 had by then been adopted in Washington, and strategic guidance had gone to regional planning groups instructing them to make plans on the hypothesis of possible war in 1954,[8] no urgency was apparent. Both Truman and Acheson were still at this time reluctant to consider the rearmament of Germany, and apprehensive that any such proposal would severely damage America's relationship with the European members of NATO.[9] But by August, after the Korean attack, the State Department had committed itself to a "package plan" including an American Supreme Commander, five to eight American divisions in Europe, and a defence line east of the Rhine. The Joint Chiefs of Staff insisted that a rearmed Western Germany must be included in this project, as otherwise the American troops would be committed to potential disaster.[1] Thus, one may say that these early plans for the military future of NATO obviated the possibility of a negotiated neutralization of Germany, since almost as soon as the actual effort to rebuild Western military strength began, the project of a conventional defence for Europe which would contemplate any future for Germany other than its military integration with the West was discarded. Some political considerations would in any case have indicated the same course of action as the demands of the military. Dr. Adenauer had already asked, under the impact of Korea, for a reinforcement of allied troops and permission to raise a force of the same strength and character as the People's Police in Eastern Germany,[2] and Acheson had to bear in mind also not only the deficit in the

---

[8] Ismay: op. cit., p. 102.
[9] Truman: *Memoirs*, Vol. II, pp. 252–3.
[1] Millis: op. cit., p. 33.
[2] Sir Ivone Kirkpatrick: *The Inner Circle* (London: Macmillan & Co.; 1959), p. 240.

Western division count and the possible political effects in
Western Germany of its exclusion from Western military planning, but the political and military disincentive effects in the
rest of Europe of creating a defensive system which would seem
geared to the protection of Western Germany without requiring
any contribution in German manpower.

Truman has printed portions of Acheson's private reports to
him of the September 1950 meeting of the North Atlantic Council.

Bevin, who really agreed with me, had been put under wraps by his
Government and was not permitted to say anything. This grows out
of the current debate in the House of Commons on this very subject.
. . . On the part of Schuman the difficulty was deeper. His attitude
was that he was not able or willing, as the spokesman of his Government, to take any decision, even in principle, in regard to German
participation until the forces of the Government could face the
psychological reaction to the creation of German armed force. . . . I
think we showed that it was quite possible to deal with the German
Government on the issue, not as supplicants, but merely as agreeing
to proposals already made by Adenauer to contribute units of European forces, and to force him to accept conditions to our acceptance
of his proposal."[3]

During the course of this conference, according to Truman, the
British Government changed their instructions to Bevin, permitting him to join Acheson in working for a united defence
force with German participation. By the end of the conference,
all the members of NATO except France had accepted the idea
in principle, though some of the smaller powers were unenthusiastic. After further discussions, joined by Moch and Shinwell, and further assurances by America as to their contribution
to the financing of the programme of rearmament, the French
agreed on the principle of the inclusion of German manpower

---

[3] Truman: *Memoirs*, Vol. II, pp. 255–6. The report is dated September
15, 1950.

in the defence of Europe, but not as to the means by which it should be done. This was to prove the most damaging of all possible compromises for the future of Western policy, since it resulted in four years of wrangling even more fatal to the prospects of negotiation than to the building of strength.

The period from September 1950 until the end of 1952 is the only segment of NATO's history that can be said to be marked by any convinced or wholehearted effort to build a defence for Europe based primarily on conventional forces. Early in 1953 the results of this effort were judged discouraging enough to inspire a search for alternatives. "By 1953," General Norstad has said, "we were permitted to plan on a fairly full integration of atomic weapons into our forces.[4] The change was not sudden: 1953 and 1954 must be classed as transitional years, and the formal public avowal of the new strategy did not take place until December 1954.

In assessing the degree to which NATO can be said to have failed in the effort to raise conventional forces, one must distinguish with some care between three sets of military statistics: the NATO armed forces, the armed forces of NATO countries (a much larger figure), and the armed forces available on the Central Front. It is this last figure which is the most significant, in view of the actual area of friction and potential incident between East and West in Europe, and in view of the suppositions of the NATO strategists as to the logical objectives of any possible Russian attack. That is, the figure one must be chiefly concerned with is that providing troop-cover for the line from Basle to the mouth of the Rhine, and its northern extension in the Scandinavian area. But if it is misleading in one direction to quote the total armed forces of the NATO powers against the same figure for the Communist *bloc* in Europe,[5] it is almost as mis-

---

[4] NATO *Letter* IV, No. 12 (December 1956), pp. 34–7.

[5] This figure can be held to show a substantial Western margin of superiority, if an appropriate date is chosen, as for instance this table. (Statistics taken from F. O. Miksche: op. cit., p. 63).

leading in the other direction, to quote the NATO figures for the Central Front against the entire division strength of the Communist *bloc:* the official figure for this, a somewhat conventional one, has been usually given as 175 Soviet and eighty satellite divisions.[6] A more appropriate figure, probably, is that for the Russian forces in Central Europe, usually estimated at forty-one to forty-two divisions, of which twenty are in Eastern Germany or nearby.[7] As against this, Western forces on the Central Front, non-existent (as far as combat troops were concerned) until late 1950, had grown, according to Liddell Hart, to eighteen divisions by the end of 1952, but seem to have remained static near this point for some five years.[8]

According to Ismay, 1953 was "a year of consolidation"[9]— which appears to be a euphemism for no numerical increase and to apply also to 1954. In 1955 there was probably a net decline because of withdrawals of French troops. Only from 1956 did the Central Front forces again begin to increase slowly, through

Men Under Arms, January 1958			
West		*Communist* bloc *in Europe*	
Belgium	145,500	Soviet Union	4,150,000
Canada	119,000	Satellites	1,070,000
Denmark	45,700		
France	879,000		
German Federal Republic	180,000		
Britain	870,000		
Greece	131,000		
Italy	358,000		
Netherlands	143,000		
Norway	33,000		
Portugal	55,000		
Turkey	421,000		
U.S.A.	2,857,500		

The total for the West is thus 6,237,700 and for the Communist *bloc* in Europe 5,220,000, showing a Western superiority of 1,017,700.

[6] See Ismay: op. cit., p. 112.
[7] *The* (London) *Times*, December 15, 1958.
[8] *Manchester Guardian*, March 9, 1953.
[9] Op. cit., p. 104–9.

the addition of German forces, to reach twenty-one and a third divisions by 1960.[1]

It is true that if one looks at other statistics of NATO than those for the Central Front, the numbers look rather more impressive. In 1952 the admission of Greece and Turkey to the organization produced a substantial increment, at least on paper, in the form of fourteen Turkish and eight Greek divisions. To call these forces a paper addition to NATO strength is not intended to disparage them but merely to point out that they represented an alteration in the statistics of the Western coalition rather than increase in its strength. They were not newly created or even newly disposable forces, but existing ones fully committed to the defence of their respective countries, and as far as NATO itself was concerned, militarily the additional forces were more than offset by the additional military commitment involved. The Italian forces for the Brenner-Trieste area rose to seven divisions in 1951 and nine in 1952, and have since declined to only seven. In fact, on a division count there has been rather more NATO strength in the Southern Command than in the Central Command. And there are, of course, other indices of NATO strength than simple divisional numbers: for instance, numbers of tactical aircraft available to the NATO command, which increased from 400 in December 1949 to 1,000 in April 1951, when Shape was activated, to 6,000 in December 1954.[2] One can say that the effort to increase tactical air strength began earlier and was longer sustained than the effort to create land forces, though it was not wholly successful. Again, on the ques-

---

[1] Institute of Strategic Studies, The Military Balance 1960 (London, 1960), p. 8. Under the impetus of the Berlin crisis, the figure of twenty-five divisions was reached at the end of 1961. See a speech by General Norstad, Guardian, November 14, 1961.

[2] This figure is derived from Ismay, though not directly given by him. He claims (p. 107) that numbers of aircraft almost doubled between 1951 and 1954, and gives (p. 102) 3,000 as the number available in 1951. On the other hand, Miksche gives the number of aircraft available on the Central Front as late as 1958 as 3,685 (op. cit., p. 62).

tion of the infra-structure, fixed equipment necessary for the efficient use of NATO forces, one may say that effort was more sustained than in the building of actual forces, with improvements being made fairly steadily through the NATO period.

But it seems doubtful that these qualitative improvements, and the growth of air strength, did much to improve the relative balance *vis-à-vis* the U.S.S.R., since commensurate improvements were being made at the same time in the Soviet forces. Their original piston-engined planes were replaced by jets, the proportion of armour and artillery was increased, transportation greatly improved. Therefore, though the initial stage of quantitative strength building represented a considerable redressment of Western as against Soviet strength, the second stage of qualitative improvement was probably not much more than a balance to a similar process of Soviet improvement. This continued to hold good in the post-1954 stage of the introduction of atomic weapons, as in the stage of improvement of conventional weapons.

It would not be accurate to say that the failure to raise adequate conventional forces was the only reason for NATO's abandonment of its original strategy. The remorseless progress of military technology, that sorcerer's apprentice, bringing accretions of destructive power with the insistence of the sleepwalker, would in itself have tended towards change even if the conventional forces had been adequate. But the shortfall in conventional forces was the major influence on strategic decisions and the reasons for that shortfall are in themselves worthy of analysis as an example of the inherent difficulties of coalition policy.

There is one governing background factor which applies to all the countries concerned, the fact that the psychological impact of the Korean war diminished rather quickly, and almost disappeared once the truce negotiations there were under way in 1951. Apart from this, the blend of political and economic considerations which affected the contributions of each to the joint forces was different in every country.

Let us start with the United States, which made the greatest armament effort absolutely (as no one looking at the figures could deny) and perhaps also relatively, though this is rather more debatable.[3] American armed forces at the outbreak of the Korean war numbered about 1.5 million men (as against the 12 million men that America had had under arms on VE-day). The first post-Korea goal for the armed forces was about 3 million men, scheduled for mid-1951, but after the entry of China into the war the target figure was raised to 3.5 million, and in October 1951 raised again to 4 million, though in fact this figure was never reached.

Expenditure on defence rose even more steeply, from less than $12 billion in 1949–50 to $21 billion in 1950–1, and $41.4 billion in 1951–2. Along with these measures went a substantial degree of economic mobilization: a state of emergency was declared in December 1950, a National Defence Production Act was passed to give the President power over much of the nation's economic life, a vast stockpiling programme was begun, and the Mutual Defence Assistance appropriations, especially those for the NATO area, were vastly increased. Louis Johnson was replaced as De-

---

[3] The defence expenditures of the European powers, while much smaller absolutely than those of the U.S.A., and smaller also as proportions of national income, did not represent smaller burdens on the national communities concerned, since national incomes in Europe at the time proportionally to the United States ranged from less than half even for the richest, to only a fifth for the poorest.

G.N.P. per capita *in* 1950 *at European price weights*

U.S.A.	100	Belgium	47
U.K.	48	France	40
Denmark	49	Netherlands	39
Norway	47	Germany	32
		Italy	21

Milton Gilbert and Associates: *Comparative National Products and Price Levels* (Paris: O.E.E.C.; 1958.)

fence Secretary by General George C. Marshall in September 1950.[4]

Considering the size of the U.S. armed forces at their peak, the number of divisions disposable overseas was rather low, and Korea at the crisis period absorbed seven divisions. But it was less other commitments and technical questions of military organization that governed the size of the American forces available for the NATO area, than the political repercussions in America of assigning troops to Europe. On the eve of the crucial NATO meeting of September 1950 Truman announced his intention of substantially increasing U.S. forces in Western Europe. He had in fact at the time no additional forces to send (testimony at the MacArthur inquiry later revealed that at the end of 1950 there was just one division left in the country), but he (or Acheson) considered it a necessary earnest of intentions to Europe. This was one of the most courageous and radical of all Truman's decisions; radical in its break with the past, courageous in that it was bound to evoke a great wave of political feeling.

Congress was in recess when the announcement was made on September 9, but, even before it resumed, the first speeches in what was to be called "the Great Debate" were to be heard. There was already friction between America and her European allies at this time over their comparatively laggard efforts in Korea and in particular over the differences of policy on China and on the possibility of extending the war. The distrust of and disappointment with Europe which are never far below the surface in American popular feeling came to a head in this debate.

The ex-Ambassador to London, Joseph Kennedy, on December

---

[4] This was not because Johnson continued his earlier opposition to increased arms expenditure nor, as was rumoured at the time, because he was an advocate of preventive war, but because of a dispute between him and Truman over the appointment as Secretary of the Air Force of Thomas Finletter. For a detailed account of the American rearmament effort, see the succesive annual volumes of *The U.S. in World Affairs* (New York: Council on Foreign Relations) for the period since 1949.

12 comprehensively denounced current U.S. policy, the United Nations, and Europe, and called for withdrawal from such "unwise commitments" as Korea, Berlin, and the whole idea of defending Western Europe.[5] Ex-President Hoover, in a speech on December 20 which received an overwhelmingly favourable response from the country, spoke up for an armed two-ocean isolationism, with America holding the Atlantic and Pacific Oceans in combination with Japan, Formosa, the Philippines, and possibly Great Britain and the Commonwealth, but not "another man or another dollar" for Western Europe until the Europeans had themselves raised and equipped combat divisions "of such huge numbers as would erect a sure dam against the red flood."[6] As was said in Europe, he was against aid until it became unnecessary.

When Congress resumed in January, almost the first fifteen weeks were taken up with debating troops for Europe. Senator Robert A. Taft, a leading contender at the time for the Republican Presidential nomination in 1952, made it clear in a speech on January 5 that his position was not far removed from ex-President Hoover's, and that he had grave doubts (which he was to develop later in his book A Foreign Policy for Americans)[7] about the stationing of American forces in Europe.

The Administration was able to produce, during the Committee hearings,[8] an impressive weight of evidence for the strategic and economic importance of Western Europe to American defence, especially in the matter of the bases essential for an American atomic strike at Russia. Much time in the hearings was devoted to the relative effort and sacrifice of America and her European allies in providing forces for the common defence. The Administration gallantly made out the best possible case

[5] Vital Speeches of the Day XVII, January 1, 1951, pp. 170–3.
[6] The New York Times, December 21, 1950.
[7] New York: Doubleday & Company; 1951.
[8] Assignment of Ground Forces of the United States to Duty in the European Area: Hearings before the Senate Foreign Relations and Armed Services Committees, 82nd Congress, 1st session (Washington; 1951).

for its European allies. Its evidence included a report to Congress by General Eisenhower, at the beginning of February, on his return from his first visit to Europe as NATO Commander, in which he maintained that the Europeans would themselves produce most of the forces necessary to defend the area.[9] General Marshall reassured the Congress that it was proposed to send only four new divisions to Europe, to add to the two already there. But the suspicion of European "free-loading" on the U.S. effort persisted: Senator Knowland's proposal to limit the U.S. divisions sent to one for every six provided by the Europeans was evidence of it. The Senate finally approved the sending of the four additional divisions on April 4, 1951, by a vote of sixty-nine to twenty-one. But it included a rider that "it is the sense of the Senate that no ground troops in addition to such few divisions should be sent to Europe in implementation of Article 3 of the North Atlantic Treaty without further Congressional approval." President Truman maintained his view that the Constitution endowed the President with power to deploy American troops as he saw fit, without Congressional authority,[1] but this resolution, in conjunction with the considerable vote against sending the four divisions, and the opinions expressed in Congress and the country generally, acted as an inhibition on the strengthening of American troops in Europe short of a major crisis. With the succession of the Republican Administration this inhibition was reinforced, since Eisenhower took a much less robust view of his powers *vis-à-vis* Congress than Truman.

So that in general one can say that the reasons why it was never feasible to include more than six (actually it has not been more than five for most of the period) divisions from America in the NATO line were much more political than military or economic.

---

[9] *Department of State Bulletin*, February 12, 1951.
[1] See *Powers of the President to Send the Armed Forces Outside the United States* (Washington: Senate Foreign Relations and Armed Services Committees; 1951).

It is true that the American effort meant new taxes: the general tax rate rose sharply between 1950 and 1952. But these taxes hardly put a dent in the general prosperity. The two-chickens-in-most-pots and two-cars-in-many-garages standard of living was maintained largely undiminished. The choice between guns and butter hardly begins to be necessary in America until much higher levels of expenditure are reached than were approached during the Korean war. An authoritative study of this question made by a committee including some distinguished economists found that expenditure on national security could rise to about $75 billion a year (at the 1956 level of national production) before America began to feel real economic strain. In the peak year of expenditure on the Korean war and general rearmament, 1953, the highest point reached was $51 billion. Throughout the period of intensive conventional rearmament, 1950–3, it was also possible to increase spending on all other items of national expenditure, including consumption. Security expenditure rose 168 per cent and other governmental expenditure 15 per cent, but consumption was able to rise 9 per cent and investment 15 per cent. This was, of course, because of the rapid increase in gross national product. The increase in total annual production ($56 billion) was almost twice the increase in the defence programme ($32 billion) in the years concerned.[2]

The European members of NATO seem *prima facie* to offer a better case for the view that the impediments to the growth of NATO's conventional forces were primarily economic. But this appearance is rather misleading, or at least one can say that if the initial check was of economic origin, the reasons for failure to take up the running again after this check had been overcome were primarily political. That is, the economic difficulties, while real, did not last for much more than the first year of the rearmament effort. The ten years of unexampled arms budgets,

[2] Gerhard Colm and Marilyn Young: *Can We Afford Additional Programs for National Security?* (Washington: National Planning Association; 1953).

1950–1960, have also been, after all, years of unexampled prosperity on both sides of the Atlantic. This remains true if consideration is limited to the "conventional forces" period of NATO, 1950–3. During these years the production of goods and services in the European members of NATO rose by 21 per cent and *per capita* consumption by 7 per cent. Only when attention is concentrated on the calendar year 1951, or the fiscal year 1951–2, does the defence burden look genuinely onerous. In that year expenditure on rearmament rose very rapidly. For NATO as a whole it reached a level of $55 billion as against a pre-Korea level of $20 billion, and the average proportion of gross national product spent on defence rose from 5 to 8 per cent, with Britain and France experiencing a sharper rise than most of the NATO powers, to 9.6 and 9.3 per cent respectively.[3] The economic strains and disequilibrium of 1951 in fact more or less settled the political and strategic course that NATO was to follow. But these economic strains were brought about less by NATO than by the Korean war, so that it may be said that while Korea, in the phrase of the time, "put teeth into NATO" it also established the limits of growth of those teeth. The higher taxes, sharp inflation, balance of payments troubles, and (in some areas) lowered real incomes of 1951 generated a political resistance to further rearmament that both the Left and the Right had to take electoral account of. The cost of living rose 9–10 per cent in the U.S.A., Britain, Canada, Germany, and Italy; 16–17 per cent in Sweden and Norway; and 20 per cent in France.[4] (It will be noted that the inflation hit non-rearming countries as hard as rearming ones.) Some of the immediate results of the rise in raw-material prices were favourable to Europe. The gold and dollar position of the sterling area improved so much through dollar purchases of raw materials (especially Australian wool

---

[3] See R. S. Ritchie: *NATO: The Economics of Alliance* (Toronto: Ryerson Press for Canadian Institute of International Affairs; 1956), pp. 56 ff.

[4] See *Annual Register* for 1950 and 1951 (London: Longmans, Green & Co.; 1951 and 1952).

and Malayan tin and rubber) that it was found possible to suspend further Marshall aid to Britain from the end of 1950. Initially, the world shortage of dollars was eased and European hard-currency reserves grew. In the second phase, however, the much faster rise in the price of raw materials than of manufactured goods worsened the terms of trade of the European members of NATO and brought about a return of severe balance of payments problems, together with a general scarcity of raw materials, and European difficulties in obtaining and paying for essential imports. Thus political forces were engendered which provided effective resistance to the original military aspirations of NATO.

The experience of Britain offers a particularly clear illustration of the political limitations on the ability of a government in a democracy to pursue an unpopular course of action in a period of less than immediate crisis. The Labour Government which was in office when the Korean war broke out undertook an expenditure of defence over the next three years of £4,700 million,[5] as well as increasing the period of conscription to two years. The Chancellor of the Exchequer proposed, in the words of his economic survey, "to meet most of the cost of rearmament by sacrificing for the time being the improvements we had hoped to enjoy in the standard of living, and indeed cutting it back somewhat below its present level."[6] But this heroic exercise in political virtue conceded rather too little to the human weaknesses of the electorate. Consumption standards in Britain were still, in 1951, close to their post-war nadir, and there was some psychological truth in the *cri du cœur* of a Labour member during the defence debate that people couldn't make that sort of a rearmament effort on a meat ration of eightpence worth a week.[7] The rearmament programme exacerbated and brought into the

---

[5] See P. Calvocoressi: *Survey of International Affairs for 1950 and 1951* (London: Oxford University Press; 1953 and 1954).

[6] Cmd. 8195.

[7] H. C. Deb., 5th Series, Vol. 484, cols. 408–740.

open a split between the Right and Centre of the party, and its Left wing, led by Aneurin Bevan. Whatever one judges to be the actual reasons for Bevan's conflict with the official leadership of the party (and some of his colleagues believed that he resigned first and thought of reasons afterwards), his choice of the rearmament programme and the consequential charges that were imposed on the Health Service as the ground on which to fight represented an astute judgment of feeling in the party and the country. The Bevanite argument, developed in the pamphlet *One Way Only,* that the rearmament drive was on an excessive scale, "based on a gross overestimate of Soviet strength, and a cringing inferiority complex about Soviet political warfare,"[8] could not but seem agreeable by contrast with the demands of official policy.

Hampered by an unworkably small majority, a split in his own party, and a world situation that made it impossible to put the party's programme of social betterment into operation, Attlee decided to go to the country again, and saw his government defeated in October, though by a comparatively small margin. Ironically enough, Churchill, as incoming Prime Minister, proved a Bevanite with respect to the scale of the rearmament programme. As early as December 1951, he said it would have to be relaxed,[9] and in July 1952 announced that the whole programme was under review. There could be no strength without firm economic foundations and the defence programme must be kept within the nation's strength.[1] The balance of payments crisis was the biggest single factor in this change of policy. Rearmament

---

[8] Bevan's position was misunderstood in the U.S.A., where it was believed to proceed from excessive ideological sympathy with the U.S.S.R., whereas it actually rested on a belief that the Soviet industrial base was too narrow to support an attack on the West, which was probably true at the time but failed to take account of the rate of industrial growth in the U.S.S.R. See his speech during the defence debate, H. C. Deb, 5th Series, Vol. 484, cols. 733-4.
[9] H. C. Deb., December 6, 1951. Vol. 494, cols. 2611–13.
[1] Ibid., Vol. 504, cols. 1272–1403 and 1491–1612.

imposed a severe strain on the metal-using industries, which produced a major share of British exports. In a choice between the risks of an inadequate defence establishment, and the risks of inadequate external balances, in a situation of considerably relaxed world tension, the Conservative Party perhaps found it easier to deviate from the line of policy that its American ally hoped for than the Labour Party would have done in the same situation.

As to France, the main factor limiting her troop contributions to NATO throughout the decade was, of course, her colonial wars, first in Indo–China and later in North Africa. But, until the end of 1954, French policy was complicated also by the disastrous project of the European Defence Community and the European Army. When the plan for the European Army was first adumbrated, late in 1950, under the pressure of American insistence on German rearmament, the supposition was that French contributions would dominate its composition. In November 1950 Moch envisaged thirty European divisions by the end of 1951, and forty by the end of 1952, with France contributing half at each stage.[2]

In a sense the history of the failure of the E.D.C. project is a miniature of that of negotiation from strength. Both are histories of "hoping for a better moment," and both illustrate that delay is not enough. The four years of indecision over the E.D.C. were as much a matter of domestic as of international politics. Probably the best chance of its receiving Parliamentary approval would have been shortly after its formulations. As 1951 wore on, and the war in Indo–China began to take a heavy toll of French junior officers and N.C.O.'s, the question of maintaining equivalence in Europe with a new German Army began to look awkward enough to make postponement desirable. It was not politically possible to use conscripts in Indo-China, but the loss of officer *cadres* there impeded the training of conscripts for Europe. At the height of the war, the equivalent of the entire

[2] *The* (London) *Times,* November 3, 1950.

annual output of St. Cyr was consumed each year in Indo-China.[3]
Moreover, as Jacques Fauvet put it: "Time accentuated the conflicts inherent in the policy of European integration, and in
France's domestic politics."[4] Delay allowed the opponents of
the scheme time to develop their arguments, and deprived its
advocates of the sense of urgency. The nationalists could enlarge
on their theme of France as a mere cog in the wheel of Europe
and on the fear that the use of the French Army as a specific
for colonial trouble would be impeded: "Europe would be built
on the corpse of France." The neutralists had time to develop
the hope that France could opt out of the power struggle, though
some were for the E.D.C., seeing in a United Europe a prospect
of a more effective independence of America. Even the internationalists became divided: some were for it, but some wanted
either a less constricted Europe than that of the Six, or at least
Britain inside the E.D.C. to offset Germany (though the fear
of a *tete-à-tete* with Germany of which much was made at the
time by French spokesmen has been conspicuously absent from
the Common Market negotiations).

The degeneration of the situation in Indo-China in 1953 and
1954 produced a new argument against the E.D.C.: the belief
that if the treaty were ratified, the Russians might retaliate with
extra help through China to the Viet Minh. The upshot of all
the delays contrived by the friends of the treaty in the hope of
improving its chances was that it fell finally to a Prime Minister
who was dubious about the whole scheme to put it forward, and
at the least propitious moment, in the aftermath of defeat in
Indo-China and in a period of much French resentment against
America.

Dulles's threat of an "agonizing reappraisal" of American

---

[3] See the author's *Survey of International Affairs* for 1954 (London: Oxford University Press; 1957), pp. 12 ff., for an account of the connection
between the fighting in Indio–China and other aspects of French policy.
[4] *France Defeats E.D.C.* (ed. D. Lerner and R. Aron. London: Thames
& Hudson; 1957), p. 138.

policy in Europe if the treaty were not ratified is usually classed as one of his major diplomatic miscalculations, in that it helped produce the rejection he feared. Certainly the phrase irritated the French, and may well have affected the votes of one or two deputies. But it must be remembered that, from the point of view of France's allies, the next best thing to acceptance was rejection. Once the E.D.C. had been rejected, a new scheme for the military integration of Germany into the Western camp was devised, signed, and even ratified by France within four months.[5] The demise of the E.D.C. was a good deal less damaging to the "positions of strength" policy than the unconscionable four years it spent dying.

In fact, it was not on the side of strength but on the side of negotiations that the E.D.C. was most damaging to the Western powers. It did not reduce the strength contributed by the intending members so much as change its form and timing. The twelve German divisions projected were ultimately to be forthcoming: the French lack of divisions would no doubt have been as pronounced whatever the form in which they were to be contributed; the situation with regard to Italy and Benelux might not have been much different. But the four years spent pursuing this *ignis fatuus*, years during which negotiations with the Russians had to be abjured because of their possible effect on the E.D.C., were precisely the years in which the negotiating strength of the parties involved changed most radically. The delay postponed the arming of Germany beyond the point at which the prospective German Army was a negotiable asset to the West, and beyond the point at which the Western powers could make effective decisions about Germany. It is ironic to reflect that the quality in the E.D.C. scheme which in 1950 was seen—but not proclaimed— by many Frenchmen to be its major merit, that it afforded indefinite possibilities for wrangling over details and thus delaying a decision, ultimately redounded to the advantage of Germany and Russia, not France. If France had *rejected* the E.D.C. in

---

[5] See *Survey* (R.I.I.A.) for 1954, pp. 129 ff.

1951, she could perhaps have made her veto stick and forced the Western powers into a strategic concept not dependent on German forces. If she had *ratified* it in 1951, there might have existed in 1952 or 1953 some basis for a bargain over Germany. But by indecision, leaving the West with no settled position to negotiate from at the period when negotiation came nearest to being possible, she ingeniously combined the disadvantages of both courses.

The minor NATO powers could not of course be expected to contribute very substantially in actual forces to the strength of NATO. What is of most interest perhaps in their policies is the illustrations they provide of the complexities of coalition diplomacy. Small powers have not much choice in foreign policy: essentially they must choose between placing their reliance on the forbearance of their stronger neighbours (and opt for neutrality) or placing their reliance on helping maintain the balance of power between the great powers, and opt to ally themselves appropriately. Either choice carries an element of risk. In 1949, the remembrance of precisely how little declarations of neutrality had availed the would-be neutrals of World War II,[6] and the demonstration in the Czech coup of 1948 of how short-lived liberal governments were in the Soviet sphere of power, operated to convince the minor European powers of the advantages of alliance over neutrality. But the more vulnerable the small power, the less clear is the margin of advantage, and the less reasonable it must therefore appear to buy this marginal increment of security at any exorbitant price. One can see the calculation of relative loss or gain in the respective attitudes of a number of minor NATO powers. Denmark was perhaps the most vulnerable of all: Copenhagen was within half an hour's strike time of

[6] Twenty European powers declared their neutrality in September 1939, but only five—Ireland, Spain, Portugal, Switzerland, and Sweden—were able to maintain it. And even in the cases of these five, success in maintaining neutrality was less a matter of choice or virtue on the part of the small power than of good fortune in geographical situation or the usefulness of its neutrality to the great powers.

forward Russian airbases even in the conventional-forces epoch of NATO and within almost equally easy reach of Russian tanks based in Eastern Germany. Without West German forces there was clearly no prospect at all of any defence of the country, especially in view of the ruling strategic concept, before 1954, of a defence along the line of the Rhine. In the circumstances it would have been surprising if the Danes had been enthusiastic military-force builders within NATO. In fact, Denmark has only spent, on the average, about 3 per cent of its gross national product on defence (a far lower figure than much poorer countries like Greece and Turkey): it keeps only about 40,000 men under arms, and permits no foreign troops or missile bases on its soil.

Norwegian policy illustrates the operation of a different kind of political limitation on enthusiasm for the alliance. The decision of the Norwegian Government in 1949 to take part in the talks that led to the signing of the North Atlantic Treaty was influenced by several factors: an uneasy recollection of an effort made by Russia in 1946 to obtain a share of control of the Spitsbergen (Svalbard) area, awareness of the Soviet limitation on Finland's independence, shock at the Czech coup, and an uneasy consciousness of how useful the Norwegian coastline would be to Russia in the event of her being engaged in submarine warfare against the Western powers. However, this mood of alarm and revulsion at Russian tactics overlay a residual attachment to the idea of neutrality, a wistful belief that socialist solidarity ought to be possible between Norway and the U.S.S.R. (Norwegian politics tend to be dominated by the Labour Party, which has a radical-Left past as an ex-member of the Comintern), and a desire to avoid any measure that could be construed as showing an aggressive tendency against the U.S.S.R. With these reservations in mind, Norway, when it signed the pact, made a proviso that it would not grant bases for foreign military forces on Norwegian territory, except in the case of attack or threat of attack on Norway itself. The term of conscription has been kept to one year, though the percentage of G.N.P. devoted to defence has been reasonably high, 5.6 per cent to 7.4 per cent.

One may contrast the ambivalence of NATO, in terms of enhanced security measured against its political and economic costs in Norway and Denmark, with its relatively advantageous aspect for its three southern members, Italy, Greece, and Turkey. In the case of Italy in particular, association with NATO has helped solve more problems than it has created, especially on the economic side. This is despite the fact that Italian adherence to the North Atlantic Treaty, at the time it was signed in 1949, was anathema not only to the Left Socialists and the powerful Communist party (who of course still dislike it) but also to the nationalist Right, who have since become partly reconciled. But Italy at the time of the signature of NATO was still only two years removed from a fairly severe peace treaty, and from the status of a co-belligerent rather than an ally, and was still excluded (as it was to be till 1955) from the United Nations. So that membership in NATO was important as a mark of diplomatic re-acceptance into the comity of the European powers, and its only substantial security guarantee until admission into the U.N. in the package deal of 1955. Economically, Italy has made an even more notable though less publicized industrial recovery than Germany, its growth rate over the period 1950–9 averaging 3.8 per cent per annum, as against 3.6 per cent per annum for Western Germany. While the reasons for rapid economic growth are of course complex, the influence of Italy's choice of political alignment is apparent not only in the economic effects of direct American aid and military procurement but in the psychological conditions that affect domestic investment.[7]

Greece and Turkey occupy, even more clearly than Italy, the position of considerable net consumers of security. It is true that their armies are substantial, if one is considering purely numbers, but if one balances the question of the vulnerability of the area

---

[7] See survey of growth rates in Europe, prepared by the National Institute of Economic and Social Research: *The* (London) *Times*, August 1, 1961.

to be defended against the accretion of troops, one can see that the area has represented a net debit to NATO. Politically, one can say that the reason for these powers being recruited to NATO in 1952 was that membership in that organization and the extension to their own highly vulnerable position of the guarantees given by America were more reassuring to them than any alternative security arrangement. However, there are, of course, military assets in the air and naval bases covering the Eastern Mediterranean and Middle East, and the powerful radar probes and other instruments based in Turkey have been vital elements in the Western scrutiny of military installations in Russia.

These southern members of NATO, with comparatively underemployed economies, especially at the beginning of the period,[8] were less embarrassed than the northern members by the loss of manpower through conscription. Official NATO doctrine has been to advocate a standard period of twenty-four months. In contemporary conditions a conscript is reckoned to become a useful soldier only after a year's training, so that if the total period of service is much less than two years the training process is barely economic, in military terms. It absorbs the army's resources of experienced N.C.O.'s and officers to produce just-trained soldiers who cannot be used for a tour of duty of reasonable length, since they are practically due for discharge. Conscription is also expensive in national terms, in that it subtracts useful manpower from the economy and thus exacerbates economic frictions in a period of boom such as all but a few of the NATO powers have enjoyed fairly continuously since 1950. NATO has never, therefore, been able to induce member countries to adopt its views, and the members of the alliance have shown no consistency or agreement in their practice.[9] As a former

[8] Italy, for instance, had 1,615,000 unemployed in 1950. O.E.E.C. *Annual Economic Review* 1961, p. 163.

[9] *The* (London) *Times* summarized the position thus in 1955: "There are, of course, good reasons why Canada has no national service at all, while the United States has a two years' draft under its Selective Service law; why Italy's conscripts actually serve for 16 months, though the legal term is

Canadian Chief of Staff has put it, the game of "you find the military manpower" has dogged the counsels of NATO since its inception.

That the United States and Canada should regard with aversion the stationing of large conventional forces in Europe was inevitable, given their political histories and traditions. That the European members should prefer the remote dangers of military inadequacy to the immediate prospect of depleted external balances was logical enough. That political leaders should hesitate to impose on their people heavy taxation and long periods of conscription is hardly a matter for surprise. Yet these reasonable enough attitudes added up to the unreasonable fact that the Western powers between them were not able to raise even the twenty-five divisions required in readiness for the Central Front. And so the first NATO strategy fell to the ground, and a lethal new one had to be devised to replace it. It would not be too harsh to say that the military history of NATO appears to illustrate the fact that an immediate shilling on or off the income tax and an immediate six months on or off the conscription period are more politically efficient (in the sense of affecting decisions) than a distant prospect of nuclear Armageddon.

---

18 months, while in Portugal the rank and file serve for only seven months though the legal term is twenty-four. In Greece and Turkey, as in the United Kingdom, the call-up is for a straightforward two years, without any qualification. There are practical reasons too why a Danish signaller or lorry-driver serves for only 12 months while the infantryman or gunner serves for six months more; why the Frenchman has to serve a full eighteen months, but may not be sent to Indo–China, though the British conscript is sent to Korea or Malaya; why Norway's and Luxembourg's term is one year only."

[3]

A Change of Command

I T WAS SAID of Dulles during his first months of office in 1953 that he had to spend most of his time proving to Congress that he was not Acheson in disguise. But in fact the period at which he worked hardest at proving how much he differed from Acheson was the election campaign of 1952: the memory of his efforts to this end before the election overshadowed the whole period of his tenure as Secretary of State. Once he was in office, many of his policies—especially the more successful ones—were mere extensions of Acheson's. Yet there is a sense in which the change of Administration at the beginning of 1953 marked a real and crucial turning-point, and for the succeeding six years Dulles's personality so coloured and dominated not only American foreign policy but the whole Western strategy in international politics that it seems justifiable to consider it the period of his command.

On the question of negotiation from strength, one may say that his most important difference from Acheson in terms of impact on Western decisions was probably in his concept of the nature of the strength that should be sought as a backing for American diplomacy. This was a field in which not all the responsibility—or formally even the major part—can be assigned to him: it belonged to Eisenhower and his Cabinet generally, especially the Secretaries of Defence and the Treasury. But Dulles played an important part in the process by which Eisenhower in consultation with his Cabinet made these particular policies. Their nature and results will be considered later. This chapter will be concerned with the framework of circumstances and assumptions that governed his approach to the question of negotiation, and his diplomatic technique generally, since the history of his six years of office is difficult to understand without this background.

Dulles seems to have been sceptical of negotiation, by temperament and conviction, long before he came to the office of Secretary of State. In the earlier of his two books, *War, Peace and Change*[1] (which he wrote when he was much further from political power, and therefore more inclined to speak his mind frankly than in the later *War or Peace*[2]), it is apparent how much of his view of the normal state of diplomacy and international relations was derived from the experience of the thirties, and how much he was inclined to discount the element of compromise or negotiation or accommodation, as against that of power, in the relations between states. In fact, he hardly mentions negotiation, or diplomacy in its narrower sense, in what is intended as a general study of the processes of international politics. His solutions to the problems of conflict and change in international politics are what he calls "ethical" (including changes in human psychology) or what he calls "political" (involving supra-national institutions of a legalistic sort). The idea that the traditional diplomatic process involving bargaining, accommo-

---

[1] London: Macmillan & Co.; 1939.
[2] New York: The Macmillan Company; 1950.

dation, balancing, and compromise might have any role to play seems simply not to have interested him.

The circumstances in which he and the Republican Party sought power in 1952 would in any case have discouraged emphasis on compromise. A clever, brave, obstinate, egotistic man who enjoyed using his own very formidable capacities to the full, and whose chances of doing so in the office which he had almost a family commitment to seek[3] depended on the fortunes of his party—this was Dulles as the election campaign got under way in 1952. He was a tremendous "politician," not in the sense of being deeply involved with the machinery of his party but in the sense of one who loves decision, authority, the making of policy, and who believes himself better fitted than most men for the business of state—as indeed he was. According to his biographer, J. R. Beal,[4] he hesitated on the brink of taking office, but not much need be read into this hesitation, if it existed. He had, after all, put himself forward as a potential Secretary of State on pre-

---

[3] Two of Dulles's relatives had held the office of Secretary of State: his grandfather John W. Foster, and his uncle, Robert Lansing. He also had other family connections with the State Department, which he was fond of recalling. He dwelt on them rather heavily in his first talk to the State Department officials on taking office, to the irritation of some of his listeners, who felt that he was regarding the Department too much as a family fief. The chief influence of Dulles's formative years seems to have been his grandfather, with whom he lived as an undergraduate, and who arranged his first taste of diplomacy at The Hague Conference of 1907, got him his first job as a lawyer, and provided financial help in the early years of his marriage. The alternation in Dulles's early years between the comfortable but commonplace world of his father (a Presbyterian minister) and the world of the rich and powerful at his grandfather's house perhaps provides a clue to the assiduous moralizing of his later years—asserting, at least verbally, his father's values in his grandfather's world.

[4] *John Foster Dulles: 1888–1959* (New York: Harper & Brothers; 1959), p. 134. This is an expanded and revised version of an earlier campaign biography and not in any sense a detached or critical study. A later biography of sorts, *Duel at the Brink*, by R. Drummond and G. Coblentz (New York: Doubleday & Company; 1960), is a little more critical but still marked by obituary piety. A third view, Richard Goold–Adams's *The Time of Power* (London: George Weidenfeld & Nicolson; 1962), was published while this volume was in press.

vious occasions—in 1944 and 1948 with Dewey—before success
came in 1952, and he was to show himself sufficiently convinced
of the value of his own role to stay in office well into the terminal
stage of an agonizing illness. If he had any doubts about the job,
they were on the score of the administrative burden, not because
of hesitation as to whether he knew the right direction of policy.
Indeed, his conviction that he did know the right direction—
could keep, as was said, America's foreign policy in his hatband
—was strong enough to reduce to insignificance the policy-making function of the State Department.

The 1952 election campaign was one of the few in recent
American history in which foreign-policy questions played a
substantial part. And the issues were as much between sectors of
the Republican Party as between Republicans and Democrats.
Dulles's task was to devise a foreign-policy platform that would
not only help win the election but would prove broad enough
to accommodate all the elements of his party, from the Eisenhower internationalists through the Taft isolationists to the Mc-
Carthy malignants. He set about this task, it must be said, with
more zeal than scruple. Dulles was often called legalistic, but his
was the legalism not of a judge but of an advocate, an astute
attorney making out as telling a case as possible for his client,
committed to the side that had retained his services, rather than
to impartiality. This aspect of his personality is very apparent in
the electoral statement: he solved the problem of making it
palatable to all sections of the Republican Party by concentrating
on denunciation of the Democrats. The result cannot be regarded
as his actual estimate of the policies of Acheson. It accuses the
Democratic Administration of having "lost the peace so dearly
earned in World War II," and "squandered the unprecedented
power and prestige which were ours," of having "required the
National Government of China to surrender Manchuria," and
thus "substituted on our Pacific flank a murderous enemy for an
ally and friend," of having allowed "more than 500,000,000 non-
Russian people of fifteen different countries to be absorbed into

the power-sphere of Communist Russia," and of having brought on the Korean war through lack of foresight.[5] When Richard H. Rovere asked Dulles at Chicago how he reconciled some of the statements in the platform with positions he had previously taken, Dulles replied blandly that as an individual he could not subscribe to some of the statements he had drafted, but as a platform writer he was merely stating the Republican case against the Democrats.[6]

The main matter of substance on which Dulles offered an ostensibly radical change of policy from Acheson was the question of "liberation." The central feature of Acheson's policy *vis-à-vis* the Communist powers, as has been pointed out, was "containment" on the operating level and "negotiation from strength" on the aspiration level. The only feasible alternatives to the idea of "holding a line" in Europe and Asia, given the general political temper of America at the time, were those of setting up a different line somewhere else (Taft's continental isolationism) or pushing the line farther forward (i.e., "liberation"). The first of these alternatives ceased to be a possibility when Taft lost the nomination. The choice of "liberation" as an election slogan therefore became almost inevitable. James Burnham and others of the extreme Right had already spelled out this concept in some detail, but it need not therefore be concluded that Dulles was influenced by such writings. The idea is too obvious to need ascribing to any particular source.[7]

The most careful elaboration by Dulles of the idea of liberation is in an article in *Life* for May 19, 1952. "Courage," he says, "will not be maintained in the satellites *unless the United States makes*

---

[5] *The New York Times*, July 11, 1952.

[6] Richard H. Rovere: *The Eisenhower Years* (New York: Farrar, Straus & Cudahy; 1956), p. 61.

[7] Burnham's *Containment or Liberation* (New York: John Day Co.) was published in 1952. See also W. H. Chamberlain's *Beyond Containment* (Chicago: Henry Regnery Co.; 1953). Dulles, when he wrote *War or Peace*, was already interested in the idea that the Soviet structure of power could be shaken by forces latent within it.

it publicly known that it wants and expects liberation to occur"
(italics in the original). "The mere statement of that wish and
expectation would put heavy new burdens on the jailers and
create new opportunities for liberation." He proposed a seven-
point programme:

1. It should be made clear that U.S. policy seeks "as a peaceful
goal" the eventual restoration of independence in the "Moscow-
dominated nations of Europe and Asia" and will not be a party
to any "deal" confirming Soviet despotism.

2. The U.S. should welcome the creation in the free world of
"political task-forces to develop a freedom program for each of
the captive nations."

3. Escapes should be stimulated from behind the Iron Curtain
of those who could help develop these programmes.

4. The Voice of America and private committees for Free
Europe and Free Asia should be co-ordinated with such programmes.

5. American economic, cultural, and commercial relations
should be co-ordinated with freedom programmes, "calling off
or licensing intercourse as seemed most effective from time to
time."

6. Diplomatic relations with the present puppet governments
should be ended "if and when that would promote the freedom
program."

7. The United States should seek to bring other free nations to
unite with it "in proclaiming a great new Declaration of Independence, and policies towards the captive nations."

However, he was careful to add a disclaimer of intent to induce
armed revolt in the satellites: "We do not want a series of bloody
uprisings and reprisals. There can be peaceful separation from
Moscow, as Tito showed, and enslavement can be made so un-
profitable that the master will let go his grip."[8]

It may be noted in passing that this article in *Life* also contains

---

[8] *A Policy of Boldness*, pp. 146 ff.

an indication of the position on "massive retaliation" which was to startle the world when elaborated at full length in 1954. Dulles expatiated on the impossibility of defending the whole of the free-world frontier, and said the only solution was for the free world to develop the will and organize the means to retaliate instantly against any aggression by Red armies, so that "if it occurred anywhere we could and would strike back where it hurts, by means of our choosing."[9] Aside from this article, Dulles pursued the theme of liberation in a number of speeches from April 1952,[1] with Eisenhower echoing the idea a few times, notably in a speech at Denver on August 13, in which he said that containment was not enough, and that the United States should aim at restoration of the liberties of oppressed peoples.[2]

Dulles tended to cast his condemnation of containment in moral terms: he called it "an example of non-moral diplomacy," indicating a willingness "to violate principle in order to gain immediate practical advantages," and accused the Democrats of being "careful to keep in a position where they could use the captive peoples as chips in some further poker game which they may play with Stalin."[3] One may perhaps reasonably construe as an example of the mechanism that psychologists call projection the attribution to the Democrats of a cynical political use of the plight of Eastern Europe.

If liberation was to be substituted for containment as the policy concept, what was to be substituted for "negotiation from strength" as the aspiration concept? The short answer is that, at this stage, the hope of a disintegration in the Soviet state and/or the Soviet sphere of power is postulated, and American policy at or beyond this stage is not spelled out. This "disintegration" thesis was not, it may be repeated, confined to Dulles or to

---

[9] Ibid., p. 151.

[1] See *The New York Times*, April 12; May 13, 17, 18, 23; June 11, 20, 22; August 28, 1952.

[2] *The New York Times*, August 14, 1952.

[3] *The New York Times*, October 11, 1952.

members of the Republican Administration, but he adhered to it
more consistently than most spokesmen for American foreign
policy, though he varied the terms in which he used the concept
from prediction of collapse to an almost Kennanesque hope for
an ultimate mellowing in Russia.

Like all-in wrestling, an election campaign may be held to
comprehend in its nature a deviation from rules observed on
other occasions, but even when something has been conceded
to normal electoral licence the "liberation" proposals must be
criticized on several grounds. One may say that they seem calculated to induce East Europeans to take action that would provoke Russian reprisals without necessarily loosening the Russian
grip of the area: that they constituted an effort to hoodwink
American voters of East European origin into a belief that there
existed some comparatively painless line of action, wilfully ig-
nored by Acheson, for restoring the freedom of their relatives, and
that they caused a good deal of alarm among America's allies in
Western Europe. Certainly, if the seed sown in this campaign
came to any harvest, it was in the Dead Sea fruit of the Hungarian revolution and counter-revolution. As far as "negotiation
from strength" is concerned, the point to note is that the "liberation" proposals ostensibly put it out of court by holding out to
the American electorate the prospect of other, better, less painful, and far more moral ways of obtaining the objectives of
American foreign policy than contemplating any form of diplomatic settlement with Russia, even one negotiated from a position of strength.

Ought one to put down the "liberation" campaign simply as
an irresponsibly cynical piece of electioneering on Dulles's part?
The chief consideration that militates against doing so is that he
had, long before this date, in *War, Peace and Change* set down
his conviction that the dynamic always tended to prevail over
the static in international politics.[4] This generalization was obviously derived from what he imagined to be the essential na-

---

[4] Pages 266–7.

ture of the relationship between the Axis powers and the Western democracies in the thirties, but it had a clear moral when applied to Western containment and the Russian pressure against it, and would necessarily entail the conclusion that the prospects for "containment" were poor, and that some alternative must be sought. Testifying to the Senate Foreign Relations Committee before his inauguration, he repeated that containment "was bound to fail because a purely defensive policy never wins against an aggressive policy. If our only policy is to stay where we are, we will be driven back."[5] One might most justly, therefore, ascribe the liberation speeches to a combination of genuine belief that containment must necessarily fail with a too facile assumption that an alternative was easy to come by. Alternatives to a ruling policy always look a good deal easier from the seats of opposition than from those of government. The sourest little epitaph for the "liberation" policy may be found in Dulles's own words four years later, when he told a North Atlantic Council meeting at the time of the Hungarian rising that America "could not accept the concept that each nation subject to injustice should attempt to remedy it by force, as this would set loose forces that would yield almost inevitably to World War III, particularly in view of the present predicament and power of the Soviet rulers."[6]

The partisan bitterness over foreign policy before and during the 1952 election, for which Dulles was certainly in part to blame, ruled out both 1952 and 1953 as possible periods of negotiation as far as the West was concerned. (It will be argued later that these were the years of nearest approach to an actual Western position of strength.) In 1952 Acheson was under such heavy attack that he had to spend most of his time demonstrating his anti-Communism, and he had no room for any kind of flexibility in negotiation, even in the long-drawn-out truce talks in Korea. In 1953 the Republicans had a little more leeway, at least on

---

[5] *The New York Times*, January 16, 1953.
[6] *Daily Telegraph*, January 12, 1957.

Korea (it was said later that Truman would have been impeached if he had agreed to the truce terms that Eisenhower obtained), but their general policy direction was predetermined by the manœuvres of the election campaign. It would have been almost impossible for a party which had built its claim to office on the equation of the Yalta agreement with treason to embark on any kind of negotiations in the period immediately after its return to power.

Furthermore, even if Dulles had been personally an enthusiastic negotiator, he would have found his room for manœuvre very much restricted by his relations with the leading personalities of his party, especially Senators McCarthy, Taft, Knowland, and Bricker, all of whom in their separate ways represented threats to his personal control of policy. The *sine qua non* of his attaining full power in his own field was ability on the one hand to engage the trust and confidence of the President and on the other to reconcile Right-wing members of the Republican Party to getting rather less change in the actualities of American foreign policy than they wanted. It is true that since the Republicans had very narrow majorities in Congress—two in the Senate, seven in the House—he might have built his majority instead on Democrats and liberal Republicans. But Eisenhower, though not greatly "a party man," was tremendously "a team man": one might say that his *métier* had been "keeping the team together," both in the Second World War and in NATO. He was hurt and puzzled when the divergencies of view among his political supporters turned out to be less easily reconcilable than those among his military subordinates.[7] One of the essentials for getting on with Eisenhower, as far as Dulles was concerned, at least at first, was getting on with the Republican Party and with Congress. The position of ascendancy within Eisenhower's Cabinet, and *vis-à-vis* the President himself, which was so striking towards the end of Dulles's life was a late and cultivated growth. During his

---

[7] See Robert J. Donovan: *Eisenhower: The Inside Story* (New York: Harper & Brothers; 1956), pp. 151 ff.

first months of office there were constant and confident predictions that he would be dropped from the Administration.⁸ Eisenhower's chief mentors during this period were the "old hands" of the party, especially those within Congress. Senator Taft was still the majority leader in the Senate and a great power within the party. After his illness and death in the summer of 1953, the Senate leadership fell to almost as formidable and intransigent a person, Senator Knowland. Senator McCarthy was rising to the peak of his malodorous power. Senator Bricker was working on a project that might have severely damaged the power of the executive in foreign affairs.

One may divide Dulles's period of office into three two-year terms, demarcated by elections. In the first two years, 1953 and 1954, with Congress dominated by McCarthy and the Rightwing Republicans, he was engaged chiefly in preserving various Acheson policies and preserving the power of the executive in foreign policy. In the second period, 1955–6, with a Democratic Congress, he had greater flexibility of action, but perversely these were the years of his severest unpopularity, and on the whole of his least diplomatic success, culminating in the great disastrous crisis of his relations with both allies and enemies in November 1956. The final two years, 1957 and 1958, showed him in some ways at his best, patching up the NATO alliance, milder with neutrals, bringing off his policy adroitly enough (whatever one thinks of its content) on Quemoy and Matsu, even beginning to show a little flexibility on the question of negotiation. Then there was the sad little epilogue of the first few months of 1959, a dogged struggle to retain his hold on life and on his job.

One may see both Dulles's achievements and his limitations in the degree to which he preserved Acheson's policies in spite of the pledge of change with which he came to office. In view of the dominant influences in the Congress that reassembled in 1953, this was no minor task. It is not usually realized how little repre-

⁸ Beal: op. cit., p. 149.

sentative of Republican tradition, or of feeling among the
stalwarts of the party, President Eisenhower's mild international-
ism was. He was not the man closest to their hearts when they
ran him for President: he was the man who could win the election. Senator Taft was "Mr. Republican," and one may see the
protest of party feeling at his being baulked of the Presidency
in the memorial now erected to him on Capitol Hill—a memorial
which astounds the visiting foreigner by commemorating a man
almost unknown outside his own country on very nearly the scale
and importance accorded to Washington, Lincoln, and Jefferson
—and to no one else.

But it was not Taft who was the dominant figure of the 1953
Senate but Senator McCarthy, and Dulles's relations with him
in 1953 offer a striking illustration not only of the forces which
inhibited the freedom of the Executive in foreign policy at this
period in America (especially as regards any proposals for
negotiations with Russia), but also of Dulles's streak of moral
callousness where the retention of power was concerned.

This may be called a period, in America, of reaction, but reaction in the simple literal sense rather than in the more usual
sense of counter-revolution: reaction chiefly to the events of
1950. Within a few weeks of each other, in January and February
of that year, there had come the conviction of Alger Hiss, the
arrest of Klaus Fuchs, the announcement of the making of the
H-bomb (itself a response to a Russian bomb produced, so it
was popularly assumed, by means of stolen American secrets),
and a few months later the early disasters of the Korean war.
And at this time it was beginning to be slowly understood, even
outside policy-making circles, just how large a swing against
America in the balance of power had occurred in 1949, with the
Communist victory in China and the Russian atomic explosion.

In taking account of the kid-glove deference with which Dulles
handled McCarthy, it is necessary to bear in mind the impact of
these events on the American public. The discovery of traitors, or
assumed traitors, in fairly high places was a far more traumatic

experience for Americans than a similar development would be for Europeans. Any country with a radical political party (radical in the sense of rejecting root and branch the social, economic, or political organization of the country and desiring to remake it according to the prescriptions of either the Right or the Left) is used to the idea that some of its citizens totally dissent from the national way of life. No doubt the idea of carrying such dissent to the point of handling over government secrets to a foreign power will still excite reprobation, but in America, with no recent political radicalism, no acceptance as legitimate of a political position that rejected "the American way of life," and a fervent general attachment to the institutions and habits that phrase connotes, the national indignation at treason was complicated by a shocked incomprehension of the dissent that occasioned it, a feeling that since some kind of mysterious political dry-rot had attacked various outwardly fair-seeming pillars of the establishment, there was no knowing how far into the foundations it might have spread. One ambitious young Congressman who was to do well out of this mood, Richard M. Nixon, put the popular view, as it affected the Department of State, in a nutshell: "Traitors in high councils of our own Government have made sure that the deck is stacked on the Soviet side of the diplomatic tables."[9]

However, Mr. Nixon rode this wave of feeling less spectacularly (if more profitably in the long term) than Senator McCarthy. A self-styled "Mick from the backwoods," looking in 1950 for a means of ensuring a new term in the Senate, McCarthy was perfectly suited politically to the adoption of the stance of a tribune of the people, crying out against the State Department and its upper-class, allegedly Anglophile Secretary. For McCarthyism was much more a popular phenomenon (in the literal sense) than it was understood to be in Europe. It was the expression of a mid-Western, new-immigrant, Irish-and-German-Catholic sus-

---

[9] Eric F. Goldman: *The Crucial Decade: America 1945–55* (New York: Alfred A. Knopf; 1956).

picion of Easterners, intellectuals, radicals, the British, and striped-pants fellows in the State Department whose sturdy Americanism had been sapped by Harvard and fancy foreign universities. The deliberately *louche* quality of McCarthy's manner and speeches and even appearance was well calculated to enhance his self-identification with the resentment of a simple, shirt-sleeves frontier democracy against a genteel and decadent Establishment, of ambiguous political views.[1]

McCarthy had, of course, been devoting himself to harassment of the State Department ever since the speech in February 1950 in which he claimed to have discovered "205—or 81—or 57" card-carrying Communists in its ranks.[2] But from the beginning of 1953 he was in a position to continue this flagellation even more disruptively, if he chose, since the Republican capture of a majority in the Senate had given him the chairmanships of the powerful Committee on Government Operations and its Permanent Subcommittee on Investigations. These chairmanships gave him a freer hand in choosing the subjects of his investigations and interpreting the rules of procedure as he thought fit.

He represented therefore a formidable political force for Dulles to reckon with, especially as Dulles had no political popularity of his own to set against McCarthy's, and no skill in popular persuasion at the electoral level; he had not even been able to secure his own election to the Senate when he tried in 1949.[3] And McCarthy's influence in the Senate was at its peak as Dulles began his insecure first months of office in 1953. Eight other Senators were thought to owe their seats largely to his campaign-

---

[1] See Goldman: op. cit., p. 138; and Richard H. Rovere: *Senator Joe McCarthy* (New York: Harcourt, Brace and Company; 1959), pp. 119–40.

[2] Rovere: op. cit., p. 100.

[3] The Truman Administration had actively backed his opponent, Senator Lehman, but Dulles's defeat cannot be ascribed chiefly to this. Of the three Secretaries of State whose terms of office fall within the scope of this study, only the last, Christian Herter, had electoral experience or success, or political prestige independent of his President. Herter was a popular and successful governor of Massachusetts, and exerted some influence within the Republican Party, at least at state level.

ing.[4] Nor was the fact that McCarthy was a titular Republican likely to save a Republican Administration from his attentions. He was clearly addicted, by 1953, to headlines and popular applause, and after the Republican assumption of power he seemed, if anything, to be in the mood for madder music and for stronger wine in the way of publicity.

It is necessary, in fairness to Dulles (since this episode was the shabbiest in his tenure of office), to emphasize that McCarthy was a genuinely formidable force at this time, too strong politically for Dulles to try conclusions with independently of Eisenhower, and that Eisenhower himself had no wish for such an encounter. Even he, like Nixon and like leading Senators of the party, was to some extent identified with the "twenty years of treason" thesis about the Democratic Administration. And he did not scruple to use the fanciful picture of a Democratic machinery of government riddled with subversives in his 1954 state-of-the-union message, when he announced with apparent pride that his Administration had dismissed 2,200 persons under the employee security system.[5]

According to Beal, the question of relations with Congress came up at the first two meetings of the Eisenhower Cabinet, and Eisenhower directed that there should be "one hundred per cent co-operation" with Congress, including McCarthy, an edict that Dulles passed along to the State Department.[6] Eisenhower had, of course, an assiduous determination to be "a constitutional President," in contra-distinction, by implication, to Roosevelt and Truman, who had been inclined to put the largest possible interpretation on their own powers. This determination to adhere to what his American critics called a "high-school civics course"

---

[4] Rovere: op. cit., p. 35.
[5] Though this figure was misleading. For an account of the method used to inflate the numbers, see Alsop: op. cit., p. 223.
[6] Beal: op. cit., p. 139. See also Donovan: op. cit., pp. 85–95. This is an adulatory Republican account of the Einsenhower Administration, and not likely to err on the side of harshness to the President.

notion of the President's relations to Congress put its mark on several aspects of American foreign policy.

As far as this attitude affected McCarthy, it meant that Eisenhower would not quarrel with him and that Dulles therefore would not or could not make any effort to stand between the Congressional wolves and endangered State Department members. Indeed, one might say that he helped ensure their being thrown out of the sleigh with all possible efficiency and dispatch by appointing as Security Chief of the State Department Scott McLeod, one of McCarthy's henchmen. Beal represents this appointment as a mere coincidence,[7] but even if one accepts his story that McLeod's connections were unknown to Dulles at the time of the appointment, it would be difficult to interpret Dulles's retention and backing of McLeod in office long after these connections became public knowledge, otherwise than as a deliberate sop to McCarthy.[8]

Possibly there was an element of what might be called "Hiss trauma" in Dulles's attitude to the State Department on the security question. He had, after all, himself been partly responsible for Hiss's appointment to the post of president of the Carnegie Endowment, and had presumably seen a good deal of Hiss in the days when they were respectively president and chairman of directors of that body, without feeling any particular suspicion that his loyalties were ambiguous. If the technique of "guilt by association" was to be pushed by McCarthy to its logical limits, Dulles would be quite as well qualified as Acheson to become one of its victims.[9] He once remarked grimly that he "was not going to be caught with another Alger Hiss on his hands."[1] At any rate,

[7] Page 140.

[8] On McLeod's tenure of office at the State Department, see also *The Reporter*, August 17, 1954; *Big Brother in Foggy Bottom*; and Alsop: op. cit., pp. 194 and 223.

[9] For an account of the Hiss case generally, and a summary of Dulles's evidence as a prosecution witness, see Alistair Cooke: *A Generation on Trial* (London: Rupert Hart–Davis; 1950), especially pp. 61 and 238 ff.

[1] Beal: op. cit., p. 141.

whether one ascribes his attitude to real shock at the evidence against a man who had been as familiar to him as Hiss, or merely to a cold-blooded resolution that he would not attract the sort of harassment that Acheson suffered through any squeamish notions of loyalty to subordinates, there is no denying that he carried his prudent washing of hands of "controversial characters" to the point of callousness. The case of John Carter Vincent was particularly notable. No charge of disloyalty was ever sustained against him, but he was nevertheless dismissed, Dulles himself blandly telling the victim that he suffered from one fatal weakness: his critics in the Senate talked louder than his supporters.[2]

It is possible to justify Dulles's prudent appeasement of the Senate in this manner by maintaining that, from the point of view of the national interest, he had to weight the preservation of morale in the State Department against the greater importance of preserving the substance of American policy and the American alliance structure, since the Right wing of his party was determined to mark in some way its divergence from the Democratic policies, and that the sacrifice of a few State Department officials was of little moment if it diverted attention from the continuance of essential policies. However, even when Senator McCarthy's ambitions extended beyond the purging of the State Department and he began organizing his own anti-Communist blockade, Dulles remained implacably determined not to quarrel with him. In March 1953 McCarthy announced that he had negotiated an agreement with Greek ship-owners to stop trading at Soviet and satellite ports. Harold Stassen, the Director of Mutual Security, had the courage to point out that in terms of the American Constitution this was a flagrant invasion of the prerogatives of the Executive Branch, but Dulles merely arranged a genial private luncheon with McCarthy.[3] His affabilities may well have been effective, because not much more in fact was heard of McCarthy's

---

[2] See Joseph C. Harsch: *"John Foster Dulles: a very complicated man,"* *Harper's*, September 1956.

[3] See *The New York Times*, March 28–April 10, 1953.

project, but the episode is another illustration of his determination
to buy off McCarthy by coaxing and appeasement rather than to
risk a quarrel with him. He did nothing to prevent McCarthy's
emissaries, Cohn and Schine, from disrupting the U.S. Information libraries in Europe in 1953, and when Eisenhower, com-
menting on this episode, indicated a mild disapprobation of book
burning, Dulles implied that perhaps it was not such a serious
vice after all.[4] Apologists for the Administration, such as Donovan, tend to present the final discrediting of McCarthy (through
his entanglement with the Army, and the Senate disapproval that
he thus incurred, and through the stands taken by a few private
persons) as an ultimate justification of the refusal of Eisenhower
and Dulles to challenge him in his days of triumph, but this
rationalization fails to take account of the fact that the serious
and still visible damage done by McCarthy to the American
image abroad (which was the aspect of his activities that most
obviously concerned Dulles) could have been reduced by a less
acquiescent stance on the part of the Administration.[5] The best
one can say of Dulles's "more anti-Communist than thou" technique with Senator McCarthy is that he was ultimately successful
in establishing a relation of confidence with the Senate, and this
of course was a first essential to the State Department's being able
to put its policy into effect. The episode in 1955, when the Senate
voted down McCarthy's resolution attacking the summit negotiations with Russia, is sufficient evidence of this, and though
many factors went into the Senate's rejection of McCarthy,
Dulles's having established himself as an even more dedicated
hammer of the Communists was not without importance.

Senator Bricker in his quite different fashion represented, like
McCarthy, an inhibition on the potential flexibility of manœuvre
of the Republican Administration, and like McCarthy he derived

---

[4] Ibid., June 14–July 10, 1953.

[5] In the review of his Administration which President Eisenhower made
for television in 1961, he advanced the claim that his own decision to ignore
McCarthy was an effective weapon against him.

his strength in part from the Republican resentment of twenty years of Democratic power. Again like McCarthy, he acquired an enhancement of power through Eisenhower's obsessive deference to the Senate, but Dulles coped with the threat involved to the Executive's control of foreign policy much more firmly, adequately, and honorably than in the case of McCarthy—perhaps because the threat in this case was of a legal and constitutional nature, and Dulles was therefore on more familiar ground.

The strong Executive control exercised over foreign policy by Roosevelt and Truman had produced a resentful suspicion in the Senate that it had been, or might be, squeezed out of its proper functions in the foreign-policy field, and more specifically a belief that some future President could take advantage of the opportunity offered by a treaty or multilateral convention to in effect change the legal position inside America in some important field. Since under the American Constitution the U.S. courts are empowered to interpret treaty obligations as law, the rights and duties enjoined in the U.N. Convention on Human Rights could theoretically be enforced through American courts if the U.S. Government were a party to the Convention. Senator Bricker proposed to obviate this possibility by the enactment of a constitutional amendment asserting the supremacy of U.S. law over the provisions of any treaty. He first introduced this amendment in 1952, when it failed of the necessary majority, but he reintroduced it in 1953, as soon as Congress convened. With the new composition of Congress, there was a serious possibility of his success. Moreover, Eisenhower was inclined to sympathize, according to Donovan, with Senator Bricker's urge to protect the constitution[6] and to feel that the amendment was justified on the basis that a President might impose on the country through a treaty legal obligations which would deprive the people of constitutional rights or invade the powers reserved to the states. However, Dulles stood by the view that the amendment would seriously curtail Executive control and make it impossible to

[6] Op. cit., pp. 232 ff.

conduct foreign policy effectively, and the defeat of the project must be ascribed largely to him. He convinced Eisenhower of its undesirability and, though it had originally been introduced into the Senate by sixty-four sponsors (who represented the necessary two-thirds majority), intensive Administration activity succeeded in whittling down this number so as to secure a rejection by forty-two to fifty on February 25, 1953. The amendment was brought back in 1954, with support drummed up meanwhile from such groups as the American Medical Association, the Daughters of the American Revolution, the Chicago Tribune, and the "Vigilant Women for the Bricker Amendment, a volunteer organization of housewives and mothers of boys overseas,"[7] but Dulles was again able to ensure that it was first watered down into milder forms, and then again defeated on February 24, 1954.[8] The prospect of the amendment re-emerging in some form did not altogether vanish until the death of Senator Bricker and the return of a Democratic majority in Congress.

Dulles's determination, in this episode, to resist any further legal impediments to the already rather constricted powers of the Secretary of State to negotiate with other governments represents one of the more constructive instances of his basic quality— his tenacious grip on power, and determination to conserve it. This was the dominant motif of his diplomacy. In some aspects it was a strength, as here; in others it was a weakness, as in his unwillingness to delegate authority, or to risk the negotiating away of any apparent position of advantage. Later in his career he showed considerable adroitness in manipulating, on the one hand, Eisenhower's wish to be a strictly constitutional President and, on the other, the Senate's wish to feel itself adequately consulted, by means of the use of Senate resolutions (the Formosa resolution, and the Eisenhower Doctrine, which was also in form a Senate resolution), to make a foreign-policy point.

---

[7] Donovan: op. cit., p. 239.
[8] See *The New York Times*, January 30, 1954; February 5, 1954; February 26, 1954; and *Christian Science Monitor*, February 3 and 4, 1954.

Between a President anxious to demonstrate his constitutional circumspection and a Senate jealous of its allegedly infringed prerogatives (and seeing its moment for restoring them), any Secretary of State appointed in 1953 would have found his room for manœuvre circumscribed. Within the limits so set, Dulles's mode of manœuvre was governed by the preconceptions he brought to the business of diplomacy. And oddly enough, though he had been franker in advance about these preconceptions than almost any other major politician of recent times, the basis of his theory of diplomacy was still widely misunderstood. There is a European stereotype of Dulles that sees him as another Woodrow Wilson or Cordell Hull, raised to the nth degree of moralistic and legalistic rigidity. Thus his aversion to negotiation with Russia or China has often been explained as a Calvinistic determination to have no commerce with the devil in the form of "atheistic Communism" (a phrase he was admittedly fond of), and the intransigence of Western policy during his term of office is seen as a mere transfer of his personal views to government policy.

This is a greatly over-simplified view of Dulles, and one that underrates his level of political sophistication. It is true that he was a churchman, the son of a minister, and given to uttering moral platitudes. But this was not because he was a simple man who saw the clash of interest and will in world politics only in moral terms: it was because he was a complex man who understood very well that the espousal of moral principles could be a useful weapon—even an essential weapon—in a struggle that took place on a number of levels, including the moral one, simultaneously.

Dulles was immensely conscious of the political utility of moral appeals. As late as 1948, he reflected, for publication, on their usefulness to the other side.

What has given Soviet Communism its tremendous influence over men everywhere in the world? It is the moral slogans which they have adopted and expressed. . . . What are those slogans of which they have seized hold? They are nothing but the same slogans—the same beliefs, I say here—for which America has stood as a Christian nation and for which the Church of Christ stands . . . the leaders of the Soviet Communist Party have been smart enough to see that the way to get influence in the world is to sponsor great moral principles.[9]

Comparing this passage with his own later technique, it is impossible not to feel that he decided to take a leaf out of the enemy's book. Not that he was always successful: he was a man of limited imagination who seemed unaware of how different an Indian assessment, for instance, of the relative moral stature of the Communist and the Western camps might reasonably be from an American one.

However, the point being made here is that though Dulles frequently spoke as if he were unable to distinguish between the American national interest and the laws of God, in the actual conduct of policy he had a clear though rather narrow concept of the American national interest and a technique for advancing it which was consistent (even over-consistent) and based on a coherent theory of power and diplomacy. Though he did use, as an aspiration or declaratory standard, the kind of legal and moral prescriptions which are loosely associated with the name of Woodrow Wilson, and which Europeans tend to imagine are the sole mode of American thought about world politics,[1] the reflections in his earlier writings, when he was not inhibited by office or the approach of office, are closer to the tradition of the Federalist

---

[9] "Moral Force in World Affairs," in *Presbyterian Life*, April 10, 1948, quoted in E. Raymond Platig: *John Foster Dulles, a Study of his Political and Moral Thought Prior to 1953* (Unpublished thesis, University of Chicago, 1957).

[1] One of the reasons for this European illusion is that so many well-regarded American analysts of foreign policy have mourned in print over the alleged American tendency to view world politics too simply in legal or moral terms. But if one concentrates on what has been *done* in American diplomatic history as against what has been *said*, it is by no means clear that the neglect of their country's power interests has been the besetting vice of Secretaries of State. And even in the theory, as against the practice, of international politics, America has other traditions than those of Wilson and Hull.

Papers (or even Hobbes and Machiavelli) than to that of Cordell Hull.

The presentation to the electorate in moralizing terms of a position adopted essentially on a power-political basis seems to have been with Dulles a deliberate, conscious, and frequently used technique. It should not be called a rationalization, since that word properly implies that the transposition takes place at the unconscious level, and in view of Dulles's own analysis of this technique when practised by the other side, it is difficult to believe it was unconscious in his own case.

Possibly it was his training as a lawyer that had habituated him to maintaining separately but simultaneously in his mind the arguments that may be made for one side of a case, the arguments that may be used for the other side, and the arguments that may be used in rebuttal of either side. The author observed an instance of his use of this rather schizophrenic technique in connection with the question of American non-recognition of the Communist government in China. In a television interview in Britain in 1958, Dulles produced a fluent justification of this policy, couched purely in power-political terms, with hardly a word of moralizing. In a similar interview in America a few weeks later, he produced an equally fluent justification couched purely in moral terms, with hardly a word about relative power positions. And he had himself written, in 1939, a cogent argument against what was to be later his own policy.

The policy of non-recognition derives its principal appeal from the fact that it affords a degree of moral self-satisfaction. . . . But non-recognition by governments, if we look upon it as a gesture of moral condemnation, is of dubious value. This is particularly so if the condemnation may appear to be tainted by hypocrisy, as for example . . . is the case if the state which condemns is a nation whose interests seem, at the time, to be preponderantly served by a maintenance of the *status quo*. . . . Under these circumstances a policy of non-recognition of the fruits of aggression serves as an irritant, rather than a pacificator. . . . International practice over the centuries has made it clear that recognition merely constitutes taking congnizance of certain admitted facts. No moral judgement is involved.[2]

This tendency of Dulles to shift his ground and his arguments to suit the case he was making for the moment was particularly prominent during the Suez crisis. Eden obviously felt its impact: he remarks tartly that he could not understand what the Secretary of State was intending.[3]

In the same way, Dulles's penchant for concluding military alliances, which was often attributed by his critics to mere legalism, or a tendency to regard treaties as an end in themselves or a substitute for power, was in fact compatible in his mind with as cool a scepticism regarding such arrangements as any proclaimed adherent of *realpolitik* could show. As late as 1952 he could write: "Treaties of alliance and of mutual aid mean little except as they spell out what the people concerned would do anyway."[4] Earlier, in *War, Peace and Change*, he had written even more bluntly: "In the absence of any central authority to pass judgement one cannot consider treaties, as such, to be sacred, nor can we identify treaty observance in the abstract with law and order. If we do not realize that treaties as such are neither 'law' nor 'sacred' we will fall into the common error of thinking that treaties provide a mechanism whereby international peace can be assured."[5]

The apparent inconsistency between this view and Dulles's assiduity in treaty-making while in office vanishes when one examines the actual function of these treaties in relation to Dulles's concepts of the motivation of Soviet foreign policy. This is an issue which brings into prominence what was perhaps the most interesting technical element in his diplomacy, his use of definition and ambiguity. The phrases for which he is least favourably

---

[2] *War, Peace and Change*, p. 88.
[3] *Full Circle: The Memoirs of Sir Anthony Eden* (London: Cassell & Company; 1960), p. 476. See also pp. 458, 461, 469.
[4] "Security in the Pacific," in *Foreign Affairs*, January 1952, p. 183.
[5] Page 47.

remembered, "massive retaliation" and "brinksmanship," are related to the same technique.

It has often been said that in reaction against Acheson's speech of January 12, 1950, which it became a point of Republican faith to maintain had encouraged the Russians to decide on the attack in Korea, Dulles made the central tenet of his post-Korean policy the necessity to avoid any kind of ambiguity that could encourage misapprehension, and therefore a tendency to take risks, on the part of Russian policy-makers. This is only partly true: Dulles also used the element of built-in uncertainty which Korea had given to American foreign policy, as seen from the Russian point of view (that is, the experience of the United States behaving contrarily to the way that the then Secretary of State had indicated), as a form of diplomatic leverage.

After all, though ambiguity is a source of danger in foreign policy, it is also an essential element in allowing for flexibility, permitting adaptability to circumstances and changes in power relationships. As a rule of thumb for *status quo* powers, one might say that it is always dangerous to lead the other side to believe that you intend *less* than is, in fact, the case, but it may be useful to lead it to believe that you intend rather more (though not so much more as to amount to provocation). What is required is, as it were, a zone of uncertainty with a clearly defined inner edge, that is, an unmistakable indication of the power area whose infringement will obviously lead to war, plus a certain protective shadow of ambiguity for those areas as to which it is necessary to preserve a free hand and take account of the circumstances of the time. This, in fact, is what Dulles seems to have striven for. The area in which it can be seen most clearly is in Asia, where Thailand, for instance, is within the perimeter of certainty, but Laos and Cambodia and Quemoy and Matsu are or were[6] in the zone of ambiguity, in that the nature of American reaction to the

---

[6] As the conflict over Laos sharpened in 1962 the development of American policy might be held to have resolved the earlier ambiguity there.

prospect of a change in their status shows some haziness of definition.

Dulles of course did not leave many such areas of ambiguity. SEATO and CENTO (the latter of which grew out of the Dulles notion of the "Northern Tier") and the mutual-defence treaties with countries like Iran and Pakistan were not, except in a minor and subsidiary way, attempts to create military organizations or military strength on the ground in the manner of NATO: they were so many devices for defining a perimeter, "Thin Ice" signs erected for the benefit of observers in Moscow.

Where the conditions in the area were unpropitious for doing this with treaties, as in the Middle East, Dulles would still mark out his perimeters with the help of a Senate resolution, such as the Eisenhower Doctrine. Unilateral declarations of this sort may obviously have advantages over treaties in certain circumstances. But a treaty organization, endowed with the paraphernalia of committees and secretariat and annual conference, carries a more convincing air, both to those it is intended to protect and to those on the other side, than a declaration. One has only to reflect how differently a treaty binding Britain, France, and America to preserve, as against change by force, the frontiers of Israel would have been regarded, in place of the Tripartite Declaration to the same effect, to realize how much the form of commitment to a particular *status quo* may affect the degree of conviction that it carries.

Dulles was tremendously insistent that the Western intention of preserving its own sphere of power *vis-à-vis* the U.S.S.R. should carry conviction. His proliferation of treaties was one aspect of this: the others were his enunciation of the principles of brink-manship and massive retaliation and his discouragement of sum-mit negotiations.

There is an element of deliberate bellicosity in the *Life* article in which the famous remark about willingness to go to the verge of war occurs. "Some say we were brought to the verge of war. Of course we were brought to the verge of war. The ability to get to the verge without getting into the war is the necessary art. If you cannot master it, you inevitably get into war. If you try to run away from it, if you are scared to go to the brink, you are lost."[7] The apparent relish for danger conveyed in these phrases, the hint that Dulles rather enjoyed sailing close to the wind[8] as Secretary of State, were received with so much dismay and resentment in Western Europe that Dulles issued a semi-recantation.[9] But it is clear that the original impression created by the article was the one intended, though intended rather for Russia and America than for Western Europe. In so far as the "brinkmanship" interview was making any point beyond the obvious one of reiterating the fact that America was prepared to accept the risks inherent in the preservation of its sphere of power, its point must principally be found in its timing, at the beginning of 1956, when the afterglow of the summit meeting was still diffusing a rosy warmth over the international political prospects. Dulles was clearly anxious that not too much reliance should be placed on the pacific nature of American foreign policy, which had been so much emphasized and publicized by Eisenhower's speeches at the summit, and anxious to convey that the determination to seek peace should not be construed as the whole of American policy. This insistence on not providing too peace-loving an impression may be seen earlier in Dulles's tenure of office, in the famous episodes of the "unleashing" of Chiang Kai-shek and the effort to convey through Nehru a message to the Chinese Government concerning the possibilities of American reaction in Korea. In the first case, it will be recalled that the Eisenhower Administra-

---

[7] James Shepley: "How Dulles Averted War," *Life*, January 16, 1956.

[8] He was in fact a skillful and rather risk-taking yachtsman, whose forms of relaxation, even late in life, were those containing an element of loneliness and danger.

[9] The storm of overseas criticism which followed publication of the article led to assorted statements about the degree to which Dulles himself was responsible for its content, but he did specifically endorse the direct quotations of which the words here quoted are one. See *The New York Times* and *The* (London) *Times*, January 12–20, 1956, for world reaction to the article.

tion, shortly after its accession to office, announced that the U.S. Seventh Fleet would no longer be used to "protect Communist China," i.e., that the embargo which Truman had laid in 1950 upon raids from Formosa against the mainland would be lifted. This announcement was intended principally to indicate to the American electorate that, now that the Republicans had inherited power, a more active policy of "liberation" in China via Chiang Kai-shek's army might be expected. But it was also clearly intended to convey to the government in Peking that a sharper and more intransigent spirit should now be assumed to govern American policy towards China, and that any remnants of the "letting the dust settle" spirit of the 1949 White Paper had been discarded. In fact the "unleashing" made little difference in the U.S. position *vis-à-vis* the Kuomintang forces. Such harassment of the mainland as Chiang's forces were able to mount had been acquiesced in during the Democratic Administration and was no more actively forwarded under the Republicans. The same deliberated conveying of a hint of new bellicosity was behind Dulles's informing Nehru in 1953, in the hope and expectation that the information would be relayed to Peking, that if the truce were broken in Korea, America would resort to atomic retaliation. Nehru has denied that he took sufficient note of this statement to pass it along, and so presumably this particular exercise must be counted abortive, though Dulles himself seems to have assumed otherwise.[1] The point to note is merely the use, as a diplomatic technique, of the hint of threat. The *Daily Worker* portrait of Mr. Dulles as the reactionary straining every muscle to unleash a new war might be said in a sense to have been carefully posed by the subject himself.

It may be argued that there was a painful lack of subtlety in Dulles's mode of emphasizing the non-pacific strain in American foreign policy, and that the most readily discernible result of this

[1] See the debate after the *Life* article of 1956. *The New York Times* and *The Hindu*, January–February 1956. See also *Duel at the Brink*, pp. 111 ff.

policy was to encourage his allies to adapt to their own case Wellington's famous judgment on his troops. But if Dulles's methods seemed heavy-handed to European foreign offices brooding nostalgically on the understatements of traditional diplomacy, they were not out of key with the methods of Khrushchev, as for instance in the missile-rattling of the Suez period. Strength, to be diplomatically effective, must seem to comprehend will as well as capacity, and it is in will rather than capacity that the Western powers have characteristically shown themselves most deficient. (The classic inter-war instance is the period of reoccupation of the Rhineland, when the balance of strength between Germany and the Western powers was very much in favour of the West, but when this strength was absolutely without utility for diplomatic leverage against Hitler, since there clearly existed no will to use it.) Dulles may be said to have seen as his own primary task that of conveying to the other side the West's will to preserve its sphere of power.

One episode of Dulles's diplomacy at least, and it is one that is frequently put down as a major failure on his part, may be reasonably construed as a success for his technique of creating a threatening ambiguity. That was the Indo-China crisis of 1954. It will be recalled that at the Berlin Conference of January 1954 Dulles had rather grudgingly agreed to a conference on Korea and Indo-China, to be held in Geneva in April and to include China. His consent was reluctant because American participation in a conference which tacitly admitted China to the circle of the great powers was bound to incur (as it did) the disapproval of Senator Knowland and a large sector of the Republican Party. But the military situation of the French forces in Indo-China, and the temper of opinion in France, had made it clear that negotiation must be undertaken: the choice was only between France negotiating directly with the Viet Minh (when the weaknesses of the French position would be most obvious) or its negotiating flanked by its allies, as was finally agreed should be done. On the surface, Dulles's contribution to this conference looks unhelpful: it was chiefly to depart from it before the discussions of Indo-China effectively began, and to utter well-publicized background threats of military intervention. Yet one may put the basic question about the conference in this form: what factor induced the Communist *bloc* to sacrifice (at least for the time being) Ho Chi-minh's perceived chance (as a Nationalist as well as a Communist) to inherit power in the whole of Viet-Nam and the strategic advantage for the Communist world that this would have provided, and to settle for half the country? The most reasonable answer appears to be the hectoring uncertainty with which Dulles had enfolded American policy—the crashingly audible manœuvres directed towards setting up a military alliance in Southeast Asia, the loud stage whispers with which he was conducting the quarrel with Britain and bargaining over conditions for military intervention with France. It is impossible to believe that the effect of such episodes as the leak to the *New York Herald Tribune* of May 15, 1954, of the alleged terms for U.S. intervention was not deliberately and carefully calculated. It might of course again be said that the Communists would dismiss these manœuvres as stage thunder, but they could hardly do so with confidence in view of the experience of Korea. If the Americans had been in fact prepared, once the chips were down, to go to war for what the Secretary of State had said was *not* a part of their defence perimeter, how could it be assumed that they would *not* go to war about an area that the Secretary of State kept saying was essential to their whole position in South Asia?

It is true that Eden is not inclined, in his memoirs, to concede much effectiveness to Dulles's role in this conference. He admits that "noises off" may be helpful in negotiations but says that he did not think that the threat of U.S. intervention would incline the Chinese to compromise.[2] However, in view of the personal friction between the two men at this time and later, it would be inhuman to expect from Eden a dispassionate appreciation of Dulles's points as a diplomatist.

---

[2] Op. cit., p. 120.

The point at which Dulles's theory of international politics was most at odds with what might be called the standard liberal assumptions about this field was in his rejection of the view that the relaxation of tension was necessarily a good thing. We have seen in the Indo-China crisis an example of artificially contrived tension as a source of diplomatic leverage in a negotiation. In a more general sense he clearly believed that the sustaining of tension was necessary for some Western purposes. In *War, Peace and Change*, for instance, he notes that "the creation of a vast armament in itself calls for a condition midway between war and peace. Mass emotion on a substantial scale is a prerequisite. The willingness to sacrifice must be engendered. A sense of peril from abroad must be cultivated."[3] That is to say, international tension was the only force through which the Western powers could be induced to modify their normal preoccupation with consumer goods in the direction of allocation of a sufficient portion of their national product to the means of national strength (interpreted chiefly as military power) to stay in the power competition.

There is, of course, some evidence to back this view. A satisfied and essentially non-militaristic power, like the United States, has no psychological motive to accept the taxes necessary for an ambitious military establishment, other than a sense of danger. And only a considerable degree of international tension can sustain a sufficient sense of danger to justify the kind of expenditure required for the military establishment of a contemporary great power. Viewed from this standpoint, the relaxation of tension is not only not necessarily a good in itself, it may even be seen as positively an evil. And since the justification of summit meetings has normally been that they relax tension rather than that they have a prospect of serious agreement, Dulles's policy logically follows from his assumptions.

He was a dedicated pessimist in his general theory of international politics. Though he made formal acknowledgements to the growth of institutions such as the United Nations, he clearly

---

[3] Page 90.

expected the society of states to maintain for the foreseeable future its essentially anarchical nature, and international conflict, and hence international tension, to continue as long as it did so. He was fond of pointing out that wars have occurred, on the average, three times in every five years since 1480: that wars must always be regarded as imminent, that the love of peace is not enough to deter war.[4] Though in his years as Secretary of State he frequently spoke as if the existence of the Communist *bloc* was the source of all evil and all conflict in international politics, it is clear from an examination of his writings before 1939 that he believed conflict to be intrinsic to the nature of international society.

To this normal expectation of conflict as the inevitable outcome of the existence of a system of sovereign states, one might say that Dulles added a concept that is oddly an echo of Leninist/Stalinist thought, or perhaps not so oddly, since states—and statesmen—in conflict do tend to adopt each other's stances. At his first NATO meeting he said the Western powers must be prepared to be strong for an entire historical era. This phrase, and his general vision of an unrelenting though subdued conflict indefinitely drawn out, suggests that he was much affected by what Beal assures us was his bedside-book and aeroplane companion, Stalin's *Problems of Leninism*. At any rate, his view and Stalin's of the nature of international politics were more like each other's than either was like the liberal-optimist view of the same process.

All in all, if the Secretary of State's views were the only factor to be taken into consideration, one would have to conclude that in so far as negotiation from strength was ever a policy of the U.S. Government it was suspended during Dulles's term of office. But other factors entered the situation, and though he cannot be said to have pursued the idea of negotiation, even from strength, it can be said to have pursued him, and indeed to have overtaken him at one point. It is to that process that we must now turn.

---

[4] Cf. Introduction to the second edition of *War or Peace*.

New Demands for Negotiation

Between the middle of 1950 and the early months of 1953 the project of negotiations with Russia had few sponsors in official positions in any of the NATO countries. In America the Administration was preoccupied in late 1950 with the war in Korea, in 1951 with the MacArthur crisis and later the Korean truce talks and the E.D.C., in 1952 with the approach of the Presidential elections. In Britain the election of October 1951 restored Churchill to power, but in circumstances which rather reversed his 1950 situation *vis-à-vis* the Labour Party on the question of peace-making. The election was held at the height of the Anglo-Iranian crisis over the Abadan refinery: the Conservatives charged the Government with a "policy of scuttle" and implied that they themselves would have taken more action, presumably military, against Iran. This Conservative fire-breathing was astutely used by Labour speakers as evidence of a dangerously belligerent Tory disposition, not only in the Middle East but in foreign affairs generally. In the later stages of the cam-

paign Churchill himself was represented as a warmonger: on the
eve of the poll, the *Daily Mirror* (whose sympathies were with
the Labour Party) devoted its front page to photographs of him
and Attlee with an enormous headline "Whose Finger on the
Trigger?" The association of the Conservative Party with the
fear of war perhaps diminished its majority,[1] and moved Churchill
to re-emphasize at his first major speech after the election, at the
Guildhall on November 9, that his great purpose was to stop the
giants of his age from colliding and to expatiate on the necessity
of restoring Britain's diplomatic influence *vis-à-vis* America by
rebuilding its economic strength.[2]

But the times were not propitious for negotiation, as was made
clear by a conference at the Palais Rose of the Foreign Ministers'
Deputies of the United States, Russia, Britain, and France, which
wrangled doggedly from March 5 to June 21, 1951, merely over
an attempt to draw up an agenda for a Foreign Ministers' Conference of the same powers. This meeting grew out of a Russian
protest against the proposals for German rearmament. The
length of the conference perhaps owed rather more to the imminence of general elections in France and Italy than to any per-
sistent hope of agreement.

The whole idea of negotiations with Russia took on at this
period, in American eyes, a strong Left-wing political colouration
that made it automatically suspect. This was partly because of its
connection with what Acheson called the "Trojan dove" technique, the Russian-sponsored "peace movements." The use of
the concept of international co-operation for peace as a device of
Russian foreign policy dates from an earlier period and may be
seen, for instance, in the congress of intellectuals at Wroclaw in

---

[1] The then editor of the *Daily Mirror* told the author that a Conservative
member had estimated the cost of the "warmonger" campaign to the party
as a hundred seats. Churchill sued the *Mirror* for libel after the election: the
case was settled out of court for a payment to a charity. See generally on
this election D. E. Butler: *The British General Election of 1951* (London:
Macmillan & Co.; 1952).

[2] *The* (London) *Times*, November 10, 1951.

August 1948. But the pace was stepped up after the Stockholm meeting of the World Committee for Peace in March 1950, which devised the Stockholm Peace Appeal. The Second World Congress for Peace, meeting in Warsaw in November 1950,[3] demanded a five-power conference, including China. The Third Congress, meeting in Vienna in December 1952, demanded negotiations for a peace treaty with Germany and an end to the arms race. The central proposition of this movement—"We hold that there are no differences between states that cannot be settled by negotiation"[4]—was unexceptionable enough, but its Russian sponsorship was so blatant as to endow the whole notion of diplomatic bargaining with a disreputable fellow-travelling air.

As far as the Labour Party in Britain was concerned, attitudes to negotiation with the Russians were by this time inextricably intertwined with attitudes towards the rearmament of Germany. The original Bevanite revolt in 1951 against the social costs that the proposals for Western rearmament imposed on Britain was strongly reinforced from the section of the party—probably a majority among the rank and file—which had deep qualms about German rearmament, and at best distrusted Germany rather more than Russia. There was, of course, distrust of a rearmed Germany on the Right as well as the Left of British politics: the most impassioned public denunciations of the project were from the Beaverbrook press. And not all the Labour leaders who were actively against German rearmament were Bevanite: Dalton and Shinwell, for instance. But most of those who had been in the Labour Cabinets of 1950 and 1951 were too conscious of having committed themselves to the principle of German rearmament at that time to be able to oppose it with any vehemence as the moment came actually to put the proposals into operation. So that on the whole opposition was concentrated on the Left of the party, and thus the idea of negotiations with Russia, presented as

---

[3] After permission to hold it in Britain had been refused. See *Survey* (R.I.I.A.) 1949–50, pp. 57–60.

[4] *New Times*, No. 1, January 1, 1953, supplement, pp. 3–4.

an alternative to German rearmament, could not but appear in America as a policy of British socialist extremists in league with the compromised "partisans of peace." The idea of an attempt at diplomatic settlement was further damaged by seeming no more than a rationalization of a distrust of Germany, and thus judged less on the basis of the negotiating balance of the time, than on whether one was for or against assuming a change of spirit there. This development was reinforced by Soviet policy, which timed its offers of negotiation to each stage of the Western effort to provide the necessary legal and political conditions for beginning the process of German rearmament, and produced at each stage an "alternative bid" to delay it.

Arguments will be adduced later to the effect that 1952 and early 1953 were in fact the nearest approach in the ten years under consideration (and probably in the whole post-war period) to an actual "position of strength" as far as the Western powers were concerned. It may be noted in passing that there is, as it were, confirmation of this view from the Soviet side, in the Soviet note of March 10, 1952, proposing an urgent four-power conference to produce a peace settlement for the whole of Germany. The note envisaged the ultimate emergence of a unified, rearmed, and neutral Germany within the Potsdam frontiers, and the question of whether the electoral arrangements looking to the creation of an all-German government could be of a sort satisfactory to the West was left indeterminate. The occupying powers were to "examine the question of conditions favouring the earliest establishment of an all-German government expressing the will of the German people."[5] The Western powers replied with pious talk of what a "backward step" it would be to have a German national army, and with an indication of their preference that elections should be supervised by a United Nations commission rather than the occupying powers. Clearly the Soviet proposals were in fact unacceptable to the West German Government

---

[5] Text in Cmd. 8501, and *Soviet News*, March 15, 1952. See Cmds. 8551, 8610, 8663.

because of the mention of the Potsdam frontiers, to America and Britain because they meant neutralization, and to France because at this time the French Government was unwilling to contemplate the idea of a reunified Germany with a national army. Moreover, since the E.D.C. treaty was within a few weeks of signature at the time, the note was inevitably judged chiefly a device to delay signature.[6] No doubt it was so intended, but it seems arguable that it was also the maximum Soviet diplomatic bid against the military integration of Germany into the Western camp, and that the Western powers were, in effect, blinded to the negotiating strength of their own position at this point by their insistence on avoiding any move prejudicial to the chances of the E.D.C. On the normal assumptions of bargaining in power politics, one would expect the maximum Soviet bid against the remilitarization of Germany to mark the point at which the Soviet assessment of future Western strength was at its maximum. This period in 1952, when the ambitious Lisbon goals for NATO had just been announced, the disparity in conventional strength appeared to be on the way to being redressed, the American advantage in means of delivery of atomic weapons was still very marked, and the American H-bomb was foreshadowed, has as good a claim as any to be accounted such a point. In the choice for the U.S.S.R. between maintaining the military and economic advantages that accrued to it from its

---

[6] The note created enough interest in West Germany for Dr. Adenauer to make an effort to offset its impact. The speech at Siegen on March 16, 1952, quoted on the epigraph page is part of his reply. "Our Policy must be to help make the West strong enough to induce the Russians to want to compromise. . . . I believe the latest Russian proposals [the note of March 10] are a proof that if we continue to do this the point will soon be reached when the Russians are ready to negotiate sensibly" [*Frankfurter Allgemeine Zeitung*, March 17, 1952]. He also said at an interview in Paris that the "Soviet proposal was just aimed at delaying the integration of Europe [*Telegraph*, March 24, 1952]. For accounts of German popular reactions at the time, see *Manchester Guardian*, March 26, 1952; *The New York Times*, March 30, 1952; and for a later German critique, based on the same view, Paul Sethe: *Zwischen Bonn und Moskan* (Frankfort: Scheffler; 1957).

East German satellite, and denying to NATO such increment of military strength as Western Germany represented, the latter must have looked a better bargain than it could do at any time after the middle of 1953. The military importance of German troops and therefore the price that Russia would deem worth paying to prevent their recruitment to the Western camp must be held to be reduced from the moment air atomic power to match America's was in clear prospect for Russia, that is, by August 1953.

Since the Soviet negotiating position of March 1952 was never really explored, it is not of course possible to identify the note with certainty as a true "bargaining bid," rather than a "delaying bid." And the question of whether it was in fact in the Western interest to trade the West German increment of strength for the sake of a revised *status quo* in Germany ought not to be prejudged. It will be argued later. The point being made here is simply that, suspending judgment for the moment as to whether this bargain was desirable from the viewpoint of Western power interests, this appears the point at which the best terms ought theoretically to have been obtainable. It is no argument against this to say, as is sometimes done, that the exploration of the Russian position at the Berlin Conference in January 1954 revealed nothing hopeful for the West.[7] The gap of almost two years between the note of March 1952 and the Berlin Conference was a period of marked change in the prospective future relationship of strength between Russia and the West, and one would expect the Russian negotiating terms to harden in such a period. They had certainly done so with a vengeance by the following year. One might say that Russia has had three successive policies on Germany in the post-war period: the "occupied Germany"

---

[7] Molotov's main proposal at the Berlin Conference was for the formation of a provisional all-German government by the existing governments of East and West Germany (see speech of February 4, 1954, in Cmd. 9080, pp. 125–6). Grotewohl also was insisting at this time that negotiations between the two German governments was the first necessity. See *Le Monde*, January 19, 1954.

policy, the "neutralized Germany" policy, and the "two Germanies" policy. The note of March 1952 seems to initiate the "neutralized Germany" policy: by the Berlin Conference, with its stress on the existing governments in East and West Germany, one is beginning to see a foreshadowing of the "two Germanies" policy, thought it is not fully developed until later. None of this is incompatible with an assumption that Russian policy envisaged as an ultimate objective the absorption of the whole of Germany into its sphere of power. But the U.S.S.R., like other powers, has a range of diplomatic objectives and will logically choose its immediate one in the light of its bargaining position for the time being.

It was not until the theoretically "preferable" bargaining period for the West, on this thesis, was nearly at an end that the project of negotiations with Russia was in fact seriously renewed, in Churchill's notable speech of May 11, 1953. Perhaps the most important function of that speech was that it changed the political colour attributable to the idea of such negotiations. The occasion of the speech was the first major foreign-affairs debate in the Commons after the death of Stalin. It seems clear that, though Churchill had been a proponent of negotiations with Russia even during Stalin's lifetime, his lively intellectual curiosity had been aroused by the prospect of meeting the two men in the Kremlin. "It would be a mistake," he said, "to assume that nothing could be settled with Soviet Russia unless or until everything is settled." The settlement of two or three problems such as Korea or the Austrian treaty would be important gains. He regarded the internal manifestations in Russia and the apparent change of mood as far more important and significant than anything that was happening outside, and he was anxious that nothing in the presentation of foreign policy by the NATO powers "should, as it were, supersede or take the emphasis out of what may be a profound movement of Russian feeling." He believed that the problem of reconciling the security of Russia with the freedom and safety of Western Europe was not insoluble, and that "the master-thought which animated Locarno might well play its part between Germany and Russia in the minds of those whose prime ambition it is to consolidate the peace of Europe as the key to the peace of mankind." He wanted to see a conference "on the highest level," "without long delay," of "the smallest number of powers and persons possible," "not overhung by a ponderous or rigid agenda or led into mazes or jungles of technical details zealously contested by hordes of experts and officials drawn up in vast and cumbrous array."[8]

This speech, like that of March 1950, was one of Churchill's major post-war triumphs in the Commons: it was greeted with enthusiastic approval from almost the whole House, and press reaction in Britain and on the Continent was substantially favourable.[9] In America, however, reaction to the Churchill speech was soured and confused by reaction to Attlee's reply. The dangers of public essays in interpretation of an ally's constitution have seldom been better illustrated than by this episode. Attlee was not, as he carefully indicated, criticizing the U.S. system of government, but trying to explain it. However, his reflections on the division of power between the Administration and Congress included the remarks that the Government in America "was not really master in its own house," that "pressure groups and interests were very strong," and "one policy was run by the Treasury, another by the State Department, and perhaps another by the Pentagon," that "the American constitution was framed for an isolationist state and was not particularly well suited when America had become the strongest state in the world and had to give a lead," and that "one wondered sometimes who was more

[8] H. C. Deb., 5th Series, Vol. 515, cols. 896–7.

[9] Though the French were a little irked by some Churchillian remarks in passing on their system of military service, and Dr. Adenauer was said to be displeased with the mention of Locarno in case it implied an agreement to regard present boundaries as settled. (See *Le Monde*, May 13, 1953; *Suddeutsche Zeitung*, May 13, 1953; *Hindu*, May 14, 1953; *Survey* [R.I I A.], 1953, p. 53.)

powerful, the President or Senator McCarthy."[1] There was nothing much in this which had not been said a hundred times by Americans themselves during those years of Senator McCarthy's ascendancy, but coming from the British Leader of the Opposition it had a sharper sting, increased by the circumstance that at first only a headline summary of the speech was available for publication in America, and in this form, without the qualifying clauses with which Attlee characteristically muffled his asperities, the speech seemed more acid in tone than it actually was.

Senator McCarthy was not one to overlook so tempting an opportunity for unpleasantness: in a reply on May 14 in the Senate he called Attlee a Communist and a traitor; said that many ships flying the British flag were really under the control of the Communists; that Attlee was trying to blackmail the United States into a Korean settlement and that "the team of Attlee and Acheson had been doing an excellent job working towards Communism and its spread until President Eisenhower's inauguration."[2] Not many of McCarthy's Senate colleagues followed him in his general attack on British policy, but Senator Dirksen made threatening sounds on the subject of foreign aid, and the majority leader, Senator Knowland, said that Britain was preparing a Far Eastern Munich which would make a third world war inevitable. A Democrat, Senator Paul Douglas, accused Churchill of "nudging the United States into a position where we will have to acquiesce in the main features of Communist proposals." On the whole, both parties cast their comments in accents of dismay, anxiety, and indignation.[3] Comment from the Administration was polite but very cold. The President said at his press conference on May 14 that he had no objection to the proposal for a conference, but the dignity and self-respect of the United States

---

[1] H. C. Deb., 5th Series, Vol. 515, cols. 1063–6.

[2] *Congressional Record*, May 14, 1953, pp. 4909 ff.

[3] See speeches by Senators Short, Vorys, Ferguson, Judd, and Ellender: ibid.

demanded some evidence on Russia's part that such a meeting would be worthwhile.[4] Press reaction was angry on the Right, and dubious even among the more liberal organs of opinion. Churchill's proposal was widely treated as a mere sop to Labour opinion, and Attlee's speech as a gratuitous piece of socialist malice.[5]

It is an interesting footnote to the processes of policy formation in democracies to observe that the pressures on the British and American governments at this point, urging them in diametrically opposite directions, came much less from differences of general public opinion in the two countries than from differences of opinon in the two legislatures. According to a Gallup poll published at the time, American public opinion was if anything rather more favourable to a meeting of the sort projected than was British public opinion. The figures were:

	Britain	U.S.
Favour summit meeting	77	78
Oppose summit meeting	4	15
No opinion	19	7[6]

The essential difference in the situation of the two governments was their positions *vis-à-vis* their respective critics in the legislature, the Opposition in Britain being rather more enthusiastically in favour of negotiations than the Prime Minister's own

---

[4] *Manchester Guardian*, May 15, 1953.

[5] See *The New York Times*, May 13, 1953, for a liberal view and David Lawrence's column in The *New York Herald Tribune* of the same date for a Right-wing one.

[6] *News Chronicle*, May 18, 1953. According to the polls of the American Institute of Public Opinion (Princeton), the views of the public concerning the usefulness of the President's meeting the leaders of Russia show little correlation with Administration attitudes. As early as 1948, about two out of three Americans favoured a meeting between Truman and Stalin. At the period of Eisenhower's inauguration, about seven out of ten of the public thought that his meeting Stalin would help to relieve tension. Just before the 1954 Geneva meeting, despite Dulles's expression of foreboding, a majority was in favour of talks.

party, whereas the true "opposition voices" in the American Congress, the Republican Right, were vehemently against. The result of these contrasts of situation was that for the Prime Minister hardly any conceivable outcome of such a meeting could be damaging, whereas for the President hardly any outcome could be fortunate. If no agreement could be reached, the President would come home to the reproach of having let himself be talked into a futile errand by the British, whereas the Prime Minister would come home to the consolatory assurance that he at least had made an effort. On the other hand, if any kind of agreement, however slight, were reached, the Prime Minister would receive redoubled kudos for his initiative, whereas the President would be open to the charge of "one more Yalta." Senator McCarthy was by no means alone in Congress in believing that all intercourse with the Russians was inherently evil. The State Department, moreover, rather liked to have the "hordes of experts and officials" at a conference that Churchill had hoped to avoid, and to prepare a "ponderous and rigid agenda," and they were conscious that the President was comparatively new to high-level diplomatic bargaining, not toughened by Churchill's long experience with Stalin.

The exchanges between the Commons and the Senate appear to have convinced Dulles, despite his distrust of the course of policy towards which Churchill was tending, that a serious deterioration of relations between Britain and America was possible unless some concessions were made, and an offer of a three-power conference was accordingly extended. This original proposal was for a meeting, at Bermuda about June 15, of the President, the Prime Minister, and the French Premier (M. Pinay at the time the proposal was made). Possibly the Secretary of State hoped this would be a substitute for a four-power meeting: Churchill clearly intended that it should be a preliminary to one. Answering a question in the Commons at the time the conference was announced, he said he hoped the three powers "might take a definite step towards a meeting of far graver import."[7] The State Department was reported to be irritated by this, regarding it as an effort to force the American hand, and feeling in general that British pressure for talks with Russia was a kind of competition for the leadership of the Western alliance, since France (at this time) and the smaller powers tended to side with Britain on the issue.[8]

In any event, the plans made for this conference were dislocated by an announcement on June 27 that the Prime Minister had been advised by his doctors to rest. A year later it was revealed that he had been temporarily incapacitated by a stroke. Since Eden was already ill (Churchill had taken over from him in May the duties of the Foreign Secretary), Lord Salisbury was appointed Acting Foreign Secretary, and a meeting in Washington on July 10 was substituted for the projected conference in Bermuda.

This conference resulted in a compromise of sorts between Churchill's urging of a meeting of heads of governments, with a broad agenda, and Dulles's distrust of any meeting at all. A plan was produced for a four-power meeting, but at the Foreign Ministers' level and confined to Germany and Austria.[9] Dulles was said to have agreed with some reluctance, and chiefly because Adenauer had previously appealed to him for a new Western initiative (a general election was due in Germany on September 6, and some prospect of negotiation would clearly help the Christian Democrats to face the Opposition's criticisms on foreign policy). Moreover, M. Bidault was reported to have admitted that there was no prospect of the French Assembly ratifying the E.D.C. until the Russian peace offensive was put to the test of negotiations.[1] One may also perhaps set down Dulles's comparative amenability to the proposal in part to curiosity as to whether the fall of Beria (which coincided with the Washington conference)

---

[7] H. C. Deb., 5th Series, Vol. 515, col. 2262.
[8] *The New York Times*, May 22, 1953.
[9] Cmd. 8903.
[1] *The* (London) *Times*, July 17, 1953.

and the riots in East Berlin (which had taken place just before) would produce any change in Russian policy. These events were regarded with a hopeful eye in Washington: Senator Wiley (the chairman of the Foreign Relations Committee) said that the fall of Beria provided "one of the greatest opportunities for the West for exploiting the boiling tensions behind the Iron Curtain,"[2] and Dulles remarked that "an inherent weakness was disclosed."[3]

The substitution of the Washington meeting for the proposed Bermuda meeting had not been readily accepted on the Left in Britain, the less so as the true nature of the Prime Minister's temporary withdrawal from active politics was a matter of speculation rather than public knowledge, and there was apparent in Labour comment from this period until 1955 a tendency to assume that the Conservative Party and the Secretary of State, in sinister combination, were taking advantage of the Prime Minister's indisposition to thwart his plans, and that, as Bevan put it, "the Prime Minister's trouble was that he was trying to ignite a lot of wet flannel around him." This feeling was quite apparent in the Commons debate of July 22 on the results of the Washington meeting. Kenneth Younger remarked that, in the hands of Lord Salisbury, the Prime Minister's policy had been "sunk without trace," and Herbert Morrison that "the Government had thrown over the Prime Minister"; Tom Driberg that the communiqué was "an unconditional surrender to everything that Mr. Dulles had demanded."[4] The question of whether the projected meeting would be an occasion for negotiating from strength was touched on slightly by two Conservatives: Selwyn Lloyd, who said that the West had not yet reached parity of strength with the Russians, and Hamilton Kerr, who said that the policy of peace through strength had alone been responsible for the improved situation in the world.[5] Attlee said that the White Paper on the

[2] *The New York Times,* July 1953.
[3] Ibid.
[4] H. C. Deb., 5th Series, Vol. 518, col. 385 seq.
[5] Ibid., cols. 402, 294–5.

conference was disappointing[6] and that the note to Russia stood too rigidly on position.[7]

However, the conference did result in a proposal to Russia for a meeting of Foreign Ministers at the end of September. The fact that no meeting actually eventuated until the beginning of 1954 owed rather more to Russia than to the Western powers. Russian policy *vis-à-vis* East Germany betrays a good deal of uncertainty between May 1953 and the end of that year, and this uncertainty may reasonably be expected to have diminished Russian enthusiasm for discussions with the Western powers. The screw was, as it were, turned too tight in May with the raising of workers' norms in Berlin: this touched off the protest meetings, first in Berlin and then elsewhere, which turned rapidly into a political demonstration against Russia and the East German Government, on such a scale that Russian troops had to be used to suppress them. These events (with which the fall of Beria appeared obscurely connected) led to some hasty concessions to nationalist feeling in East Germany and must presumably also have led to a hasty discounting of any belief that "the gains of the revolution" in East Germany were sufficiently popular to take care of themselves in the competition of free elections.

Russian policy in the next three or four months has a temporizing quality to it. The Soviet reply to the Western proposal for a conference raised the question of the participation of China and the issue of American bases in Europe in so strong a form that some Western comment was inclined to believe that Russia was deliberately damaging the prospect of a conference. When the Western reply suggested Lugano and October 15 as the place and date for a meeting, the Soviet rejoinder reverted to the proposal of a five-power conference to discuss Far Eastern questions, and tensions generally, as well as a four-power conference to discuss Europe, and implied that the five-power conference should be first.[8]

---

[6] Cmd. 8903.

[7] H. C. Deb., 5th Series, Vol. 518, col. 227 seq.

[8] Cmds. 8945 and 8979.

It seems clear from this exchange that Russia was not at this time prepared to take any risks on Germany and that therefore the Western powers might have chanced more radical proposals, if only from the point of view of the propaganda battle, especially as the Western hand had been strengthened by a substantial victory for Dr. Adenauer in the September elections, a pointed contrast to the Russian necessity of maintaining control by bloody repression in the Eastern zone. One of the inconsistencies of the Western position has been a reluctance to trust to some genuine "positions of strength" in the social and political battle of the two Germanies.

But the Western position on the nature of the conference that should be sought was by no means monolithic. There was a statement from 10 Downing Street on September 28 that the Prime Minister still wanted a summit as against a Foreign Ministers' conference. These indications of conflict between Churchill and his party, and even his Cabinet, run strongly through the whole period from 1953 to his resignation in 1955. They were, of course, emphasized by the Labour Party. Douglas Jay, for instance, accused Lord Salisbury of not having pressed Churchill's plan on Dulles at the Washington meeting.[9]

As far as France was concerned, the sharp worsening of the situation in Indo-China, and the conviction that it would be hardly possible to obtain any sort of settlement there without negotiations with China, was beginning to present itself as a reason for a five- rather than a four-power conference. The French press of the non-Communist Left and the Centre was becoming insistent on this (Humanité, of course, had long been so), and the Cabinet was reported split on the prospect.[1] Churchill reiterated on October 20 that he still believed in a four-power conference at the highest level.[2] When Eisenhower replied at his press conference of October 28 that such a meeting would be

---

[9] Observer, October 4, 1953.
[1] Le Monde, Combat, New York Herald Tribune, October 9, 1953.
[2] The (London) Times, October 21, 1953.

hopeless without prior evidence of honest intentions on the part of the Russians, even Right-wing papers in Britain began to contemplate the idea that the Prime Minister should meet Malenkov alone if necessary.[3]

The Soviet reply of November 3[4] to the Western note of October 18 must be regarded as further evidence that at this time negotiations on Germany were not particularly welcome to Russia; not only did it make no reference to the proposed meeting at Lugano, but it reverted to the subject of a five-power conference, and was couched in language so bleak, obscure, and hectoring that it was widely (though inaccurately) treated in the Western press tantamount to a refusal.[5] Even *Le Monde* remarked that the note might have been written in Stalin's prime, and that Russia was giving up trying to prevent the ratification of the E.D.C. treaty.[6] Eisenhower said at his press conference on November 4, 1953, that Russia was preventing a conference by imposing impossible conditions.[7]

Mr. Molotov was apparently disturbed by the propaganda losses entailed in this reception of the Russian note: at any rate, he took the course, very unusual with him, of holding a press conference, on November 13, to correct the impression of refusal.[8] The Western allies again, in their note of November 16, refused a five-power conference, and Mr. Molotov, in one of his characteristic tactical shifts of position, abruptly accepted the Western invitation to a four-power conference, though with the proviso that he would put forward a proposal for a five-power

---

[3] *Daily Telegraph, Daily Mail,* October 29, 1953.

[4] Cmd. 9008.

[5] *The* (London) *Times,* November 5, 1953; *New York Herald Tribune,* November 4, 1953. See also, in *New Statesman and Nation,* "The Great Powers and the Lie," and reply by *Manchester Guardian,* November 24, 1953.

[6] *Le Monde,* November 6, 1953. See also *Daily Telegraph,* November 5, 1953.

[7] *The New York Times,* November 5, 1953.

[8] *The* (London) *Times,* November 17, 1953.

conference. Agreement was finally reached on Berlin as the place, and January 25 as the date.[9]

While these arrangements had been going on, the demand for a summit conference had revived in various directions. Both Churchill and Eden returned recovered to the House of Commons when it resumed in October, and the project of the Bermuda Conference was revived, the new date being December. Churchill made it clear that his views had not changed, remarking at his Guildhall speech on November 9, 1953, that "many people think that the best we can do is to get used to the Cold War like eels are said to get used to skinning" but the policy of Her Majesty's Government was "peace through strength together— and mark this—with any contacts, formal or informal, which may be thought to be helpful.[1] Churchill urged on Eisenhower the merits of a meeting of heads of government at Bermuda, but without success.[2] The idea was doubtless even less appealing to Dulles in view of the imminence of the Berlin Conference.

As has been said, the Berlin Conference revealed a hardening of Russian terms on German reunification from the apparent position of March 1952, whose precise intention must remain uncertain. The main Soviet proposal still envisaged a reunified, rearmed, and neutralized Germany within the 1945 frontiers but with much more stress on proceeding through the existing East and West German governments. On the other hand, the Western powers were equally clearly not interested in any settlement involving the neutralization of Germany. The comparatively amicable diplomatic tone of this conference, despite its absence of agreement on anything save the convening of a five-power conference on Korea and Indo-China, may perhaps be ascribed to the fact that neither had at this time any urgent reason for dis-

---

[9] Cmds. 9022 and 9037.

[1] *The* (London) *Times*, November 10, 1953.

[2] Drummond and Coblentz: op. cit., p. 93. These two diplomatic correspondents, who are well endowed with informants in the Republican Party and the State Department, maintain that the Bermuda Conference was the most contentious of the post-war Western policy meetings.

satisfaction with the *status quo* or the direction in which each conceived it as likely to change.[3]

The next bout of pressure by Churchill for summit talks, like the first enunciation of the notion of "negotiation from strength," was a kind of by-product of a development in nuclear weapons. On February 17 Sterling Cole, the chairman of the Joint Congressional Committee on Atomic Energy, gave some details of results of a test of an American hydrogen bomb in November 1952.[4] This speech was not on a particularly major occasion (it was to a meeting of the National Sand and Gravel Mixers' Convention) and it did not receive any very wide publicity in Europe, but the details of the new weapon's performance struck the Prime Minister very sharply: he said in a speech in the Commons in April that he had been astonished at how little reaction there had been in Europe to the speech, and at the gap in European knowledge of this new weapon, and had decided that further talks on the question of nuclear weapons were necessary.[5] There was a larger impact on the public mind at the end of March, when a great surge of disquiet arose through the mischance of some Japanese fishermen, the crew of the fishing boat *Fortunate Dragon*, who had been accidentally caught in the fall-out of an American H-bomb exploded eight miles from their boat on March 2. Churchill's brooding preoccupation with the dangers of nuclear warfare and the necessity of making some effort to arrive at a less perilous mode of living with the U.S.S.R., expressed with his incomparable weight and simplicity, helped to produce a whole climate of opinion in Britain from this period onwards—a climate rather more congenial to the Left than to the Right in British politics but ironically in the long run more disruptive to the Labour Party than to the Conservatives. Churchill remarked in March that the subject of nuclear weapons

---

[3] For texts of proposals at the conference, see Cmd. 9080.
[4] *The New York Times*, February 18, 1954.
[5] H. C. Deb., 5th Series, Vol. 526, col. 47.

filled his mind "out of all comparison with everything else."[6] These early months of 1954 offered few agreeable vistas in international politics, with the war in Indo-China blowing up in March–April to the sort of crisis that seemed to hold a prospect of general war; with the Berlin Conference confirming the East-West stalemate on Europe; with Dulles's announcement of the principle of "massive retaliation," creating an impression that American policy was entering a still more dangerous phase; with the chances of the E.D.C. looking poorer every month; and with the prospect of a forced cutting of Western losses in Indo-China. The sharp differences of opinion between America and Britain as to the course of the Geneva Conference and the mode of procedure on Southeast Asia provided further reasons for British insistence on another meeting with the President only a few months after Bermuda, in April 1954.

It is clear from subsequent events that Churchill again pressed upon Eisenhower at this meeting the desirability of a summit conference with the Russian leaders, but the auguries were bad for the project from the first. The negotiations on Indo-China which were taking place at Geneva were being represented in America as a disastrous prelude to the fall of the whole of Southeast Asia. Eden had made a speech in a Commons debate on Indo-China, just before his and Churchill's departure for America, in which he had again used the ill-omened word "Locarno" in respect to a possible treaty settlement in Southeast Asia.[7] He seems to have meant by this no more than a multilateral guarantee of the agreed partition line, but in America the word evolved not only the usual wincing away from any formal acceptance of a frontier that conceded a Communist gain, but also some reasoning that, as the original Locarno was followed by the entry of Germany into the League of Nations, an Asian version of it might be intended to do as much for China with regard to the United Nations.

An offended reaction came from the Senate: Senator Know-

---

[6] H. C. Deb., 5th Series, Vol. 525, col. 1052.
[7] H. C. Deb., 5th Series, Vol. 529, cols. 427–41.

land said that he would resign his position as Republican leader
on the day that Communist China was admitted to the United
Nations and devote his full efforts throughout the country to ending American membership in that organization and financial
support of it.[8] The impulse behind Churchill's visit to America,
the impression made on his mind by Sterling Cole's account of
the nuclear explosion of November 1952, and his resulting sense
of the importance of seeking a better basis for relations with
Russia were pleaded in a luncheon speech to Congressional leaders
on June 26, and at a press conference on June 28, during which
he somewhat baffled his auditors by remarking idiosyncratically
that "jaw-jaw is better than war-war."[9] But obviously neither the
President nor the Congressional leaders were converted to his view
on the desirability of a summit meeting.

The American rejection of the proposal for talks in the immediate future which Churchill encountered at this meeting had
a consequence which did not become public knowledge for about
nine months. In the course, apparently, of his return journey by
ship, the Prime Minister made a proposal for a meeting between
himself and Malenkov "in a friendly fashion, without agendas,
with the sole purpose of trying to find a sensible way of living side
by side in an atmosphere of growing trust, ease and happiness."
Molotov replied on July 5 expressing sympathetic interest in the
idea, but the next letter from Churchill marks a retreat on his
part, stating that though he had intended proposing a meeting at
the end of August or the beginning of September, he felt that
continuation with his project would be incompatible with the
suggestion made meanwhile by Russia, in a note of July 24, for a
general conference on European security. It is clear that when the
Prime Minister reached Britain he—or his Cabinet—had second
thoughts about the timing of such a meeting, and its impact on
American and French opinion, especially as the E.D.C. debate
was now approaching its crisis. The exchange between Churchill

---

[8] *Manchester Guardian*, July 2, 1953.
[9] *The New York Times*, June 28, 1954.

and Molotov was made public in March 1955, when a reference to it by the Prime Minister in a Commons debate led the Russians to publish the correspondence.[1]

It seems clear that between July and the end of the year the Prime Minister yielded to the pressure of other people's conviction that the time was not ripe for talks with the Russians. The hasty improvisation of the W.E.U. as a substitute for the E.D.C., and the question of its ratification, fully occupied the time of the Western foreign ministers from August until the end of the year. The Prime Minister was pressed on the subject of summit talks by a number of Labour members, still forlornly hoping to avert the rearmament of Germany, but until early in the new year reiterated the view that the time was not appropriate for talks.[2]

The next initiative for negotiations with Russia was taken by the French Prime Minister, M. Mendès-France, who, during a speech on November 22 in the United Nations General Assembly, proposed a four-power conference in May.[3] The reaction of the British and American Governments to this move on his part was reported to be rather cool, since each had now taken the position that ratification should precede any further moves towards negotiation. On the other hand, the prospect of negotiations before German rearmament actually got under way was believed likely to aid M. Mendès-France in getting the W.E.U. treaties through the Assembly. So an intransigent attitude in Washington would have been pointless, and President Eisenhower remarked in his press conference of November 23 that he would agree to a four-power conference after the ratification of the treaties, "provided there was evidence of a sincere desire for negotiations on the part of the Communist world, for example,

---

[1] Texts of the letters were published in Soviet News, March 1955. Molotov was apparently irked by Churchill's implying that measures of Russian policy prevented the meeting. The Prime Minister handsomely withdrew this implication in a later speech. See H. C. Deb., 5th Series, Vol. 537, cols. 1894–1905, and Vol. 538, cols. 2268–9.

[2] H. C. Deb., 5th Series, Vol. 538, col. 967.

[3] The New York Times, November 23, 1954.

the Austrian peace treaty."[4] M. Mendès-France was thus able to present the prospect of negotiations as one of the arguments in favour of the treaties. They were approved by the Assembly on December 30, though the final approval in the Council of the Republic was not given until March 27, 1955.

By the beginning of 1955, therefore, the convening of a summit meeting had become almost inevitable. The French Government was committed to negotiating, as were both parties in Britain. The prospect of an election in May helped to convince those on the Right wing of the Conservative Party who had previously been sceptical. Dr. Adenauer was under strong pressure from the German Social Democrats for negotiations before the entry into force of the Paris agreements. The State Department thus faced the need of foreshadowing a change of American position, and when on March 21 Senator George, the chairman of the Senate Foreign Relations Committee, urged the President to take the initiative in seeking a meeting of the heads of government of America, Britain, France, and Russia to avert a third world war, observers were inclined to believe that this was a trial balloon for the Administration.[5] Some feeling also existed in Washington that a *détente*, in preparation for a conference, would ease the situation in the Far East and reduce the possibility of immediate conflict with China over Quemoy and Matsu. Already at this period the Russians were conspicuously more interested than the Chinese in *rapprochement* with the Western powers: indeed, Soviet policy in the first four months of the year appeared intent on the virtuous demonstration of peaceful intentions and reasonable behaviour through disarmament proposals, a visit to Marshal Tito to eat humble pie, an effusively welcoming reception of Mr. Nehru, and especially the conclusion of the Austrian peace treaty. The contrast between the production of this forest of olive branches *after* the conclusion of the W.E.U. treaty, with the Soviet warnings *before* the treaty that it would make amicable

---

[4] Ibid., November 24, 1954.
[5] *The* (London) *Times*, March 24, 1955.

relations between East and West impossible, is a striking example of the ability of the Russian Government to disregard any necessity for consistency between words and deeds in foreign policy.

The question must arise, however, whether the one item of the Soviet "peace offensive" which could be held to represent a substantial concession, the Austrian peace treaty, ought to be seen in the light of an actual Soviet "price" paid for the summit conference with America. Dulles was inclined to maintain that it was, and that it could be claimed as evidence of the wisdom of his own policy.[6] On the whole, there seems not much basis for this claim. The Russian Government must have known that there was little reason to pay any particular price for a summit meeting: the omens had been set fair for it from the beginning of the year, and certainly since Senator George's remarks in March. It appears far more likely that the Soviet Foreign Ministry, perceiving that the signature of the W.E.U. treaty was not merely the end of one round of the battle for Germany but the beginning of the next, perceived also that the gesture most likely to impress German opinion with the feasibility of a neutral status was to see it in operation for their Austrian kinsmen. In any case, the neutralization of Austria was by no means an unmixed blessing for the Western powers: it ended their ability to run the NATO supply line from Italy to Germany through that country. There was, however, one sense in which the Austrian treaty made a summit conference more desirable to the Western powers: it necessitated some kind of counter-initiative *vis-à-vis* German opinion, some effort to demonstrate that Russian hints at peaceful reunification for Germany were not likely to be substantiated in acceptable terms when it came to actual negotiations.

The main point at issue as far as Britain was concerned was not whether the conference should be held, but whether it should be at the level of Foreign Ministers or heads of governments. This was a matter of the relative positions of Churchill and Eden. A

---

[6] In a television interview of May 18, 1955.

campaign, not confined to Conservative back-benchers,[7] was waged vigorously at this time to induce the Prime Minister to resign on the grounds of his allegedly failing capabilities. Churchill had been throughout, as has been shown, an advocate of the heads-of-government level: Eden's attitude appeared to vary with his own status. On March 28, as Foreign Secretary, he said that negotiations would be best at the Foreign Ministers' level: a month later, as Prime Minister, he said that either level would do, and in May, with an election projected and the opinion polls showing a close contest likely, he had firmly adopted the summit idea.[8]

As May approached, Dulles, though reported to be still somewhat hesitant, had strong reasons from the part of his allies to settle on an early date. His relations with Eden were by no means good, but on the other hand, a Labour victory in Britain would increase the degree of Anglo-American friction over China policy. Moreover, Dr. Adenauer needed a gesture to help convince German opinion that the Austrian road was not open to them. In terms of the American domestic situation also, conditions could hardly have been more propitious. The President's popularity with the electorate was still immensely high, whereas the Republican Party itself was not in the same happy position. There was no other certain—or even probable—"winning" Republican candidate for 1956. The President had thus no reason to make much effort to placate the Right wing of his party. Indeed, the Right wing was by then itself split for various reasons: there were strong disagreements between McCarthy, Knowland, and Jenner. The only real attack on the projected talks came from Senator McCarthy, who introduced a resolution asking that no such conference should take place until there had been *prior* agreement that "present and future status of the nations of East Europe and Asia now under Communist control should be a subject for discus-

---

[7] See, for instance, the *Daily Mirror* and *Punch* for the first few months of 1955.

[8] See H. C. Deb., 5th Series, Vol. 540, cols. 21–4, 545–6, 1063–6.

sion." This resolution was defeated 77–4 on June 22, 1955, after McCarthy had been refused permission to withdraw it. Only two extreme Right-wing Republicans, Senators Jenner and Malone, and an old-fashioned isolationist, Senator William Langer, voted with McCarthy. There is an agreeable irony in the difference between the crowded gallery and degree of like-mindedness in his colleagues which surrounded McCarthy when he was making his attack on the 1953 proposal of negotiations, and the severity with which he was handled by his Senate colleagues in 1955, when those proposals were at last reaching fruition. His fall was faster than his rise.

In fact, since the Democrats had a majority in both House and Senate from the beginning of 1955, Dulles had to make appropriate adjustments to a new Congressional situation. He had rather offended Democratic feeling at the beginning of the year by the publication of the Yalta papers. This was interpreted in Europe as yet another effort to discredit the idea of top-level negotiations, but in America as a manœuvre dictated by party malice and hardly consistent with the President's appeal in his state-of-the-union message for bipartisan co-operation in foreign policy. Dulles had therefore a special incentive to show readiness to listen to Senator George's suggestions about negotiation.

Some degree of conscious symbolism may be seen in the choice of the NATO meeting in May for the despatch of the Western invitation to Russia for a summit conference. This meeting, inducting Western Germany as fifteenth member of the organization, marked a peak of a belief widespread at the time, especially in America, that the Western powers had in fact reached a point at which they would be negotiating from strength. Few Western statesmen could fail to feel, as the ratifications of W.E.U. came in, that at least *that* round in the struggle for Germany had gone to them. German divisions were in prospect: the Algerian troubles had hardly begun to make inroads on French strength: the Cyprus dispute was just beginning to cast a fraction of its later shadow: the Balkan pact still looked as though

it might function to some effect. The belief induced by consciousness of all this that the West would be in a favourable
negotiating position at Geneva was enhanced by an exaggeration
of the Soviet agricultural troubles of 1955 and by speculation as
to a further struggle for power after the fall of Malenkov in
February.

A somewhat wishful-thinking attitude to the Russian troubles
was heavy-handedly dwelt upon by Washington in the period
just before the summit. Dulles said in a television interview on
May 18 that the Austrian treaty was the first Soviet retreat since
the war and that "Czechoslovakia and Hungary may find freedom
contagious,"[9] and Eisenhower maintained at a press conference
that "we are approaching this thing (negotiations) from a greater
position of strength than ever before."[1] American newspaper
comment took its tone from these statements, enlarging on the
"intolerable pressure" which Western economic and political
successes represented for the Soviet system.[2]

This imprudent vaunting produced a rejoinder from Mr.
Khrushchev. At an American garden party in Moscow just before
the Geneva meeting, he said: "We want an agreement on an
honest basis. Some people would like to wait until our legs are
broken. There will be no such time. That is a fantasy of stupid
people."[3] President Eisenhower replied at his press conference of
July 7: "So far as I know there is no individual in the Government
that has ever said that the Russians . . . are coming to any conference weak. Of course we recognize their great military
strength."[4] Unfortunately, two days later the House Appropriations Committee released the text of testimony given a month before in secret sessions by Dulles, in which he remarked, *inter alia:*
"(The Russians) have been constantly hoping and expecting our

[9] *The New York Times,* May 19, 1955.
[1] Ibid.
[2] See *Christian Science Monitor,* July 18, 1955.
[3] *The New York Times,* July 5, 1955.
[4] *The New York Times,* July 8, 1955.

economy was going to collapse in some way, due to what they regard as inherent defects in the capitalist system. . . . It has been
their system that is on the point of collapsing."[5] In the context of
his testimony as a whole this statement does not appear as ludi-
crous as it seems when isolated: he was clearly not in fact predicting any imminent collapse, only using an unwise degree of
hyperbole in an account of the agricultural difficulties in Russia,
and making in general the point (not necessarily a sound one)
that it was economic difficulties which had produced the Soviet
mood of mildness. According to *The New York Times,* a good
deal of Dulles's testimony had been edited off the record of these
hearings before they were released, and the remarks about "collapsing" had been left in by some oversight.[6] It would be charita-
ble to suppose that Dulles's attitude was based on the assumption that the rosier the view he took on the Western position in
Geneva, the less likely would it be that Congress should make any
serious resistance to the meeting, but it must be conceded that his
alternation, in this period, from discounting the pospects of the
conference (which alienated European opinion) to stressing the
alleged strength of the Western hand (which irritated the Russians) was not calculated to enhance the prestige of American
foreign policy and represented at best one of the least justifiable
examples of his tendency to sacrifice all else to keeping Congress
sweet.

The press treatment in America of Khrushchev's protests
against the assumption that Russia was being driven to a conference by internal weaknesses was tediously facetious in the
"methink the gentleman doth protest too much" vein, and the
protest was even taken as a confirmation of the assumption which
evoked it. For instance, the *New York Herald Tribune* remarked
blandly, apropos of Khrushchev's garden-party disclaimer of weakness: "And if Russia wants a truce, those terms may be forthcoming."[7]

---

[5] *Time,* July 18, 1955.
[6] *The New York Times,* July 12, 1955.
[7] July 6, 1955.

This American insistence that the Western powers were now decisively in the ascendant may have owed some inspiration to a State Department arguing position *vis-à-vis* Britain and France. According to *Time*, the French and British were contending at this stage that the Russians would be negotiating from a position of equality: the State Department was maintaining that the Russians were talking peace only because they had to, citing as evidence for this the instability of the regime, satellite discontent, agricultural troubles, and Chinese demands. "Behind the U.S. position was the firm conviction that the U.S. does not have to trade concession for concession with Bulganin at Geneva."[8] Some *arrière pensée* of this sort may have existed among policy-makers, but on the whole the evidence is to the effect that early 1955 was quite genuinely regarded in America as an actual Western position of strength—more than a position, indeed, a plateau of strength—and as such, presumably presenting the moment when Acheson's original policy of negotiation from strength might be put into operation. Dulles implied this in his press conference of May 24, 1955, though of course without acknowledging Acheson's role in the matter. "It is clear we are seeing the results of a policy of building unity and strength within the free world. . . . This policy has produced a radical change of Soviet policy, illustrated by new Soviet attitudes towards Austria and Yugoslavia."[9]

Moscow radio protested against such views, saying that the Western statesmen who thought that the new Soviet attitude towards Austria, Yugoslavia, disarmament, Western Germany, and Japan was the result of the "bankrupt policy of positions of strength" were quite wrong; that the Soviet moves had, in fact, checkmated this Western policy, which *Pravda* described as "in the throes of a profound crisis brought about by the new Russian diplomacy."[1] There was more than a little truth in this claim, but it carried no conviction at the time in the West, where the general

[8] July 18, 1955.
[9] *The New York Herald Tribune*, May 25, 1955.
[1] Quoted in the *Economist*, June 25, 1955.

assumption echoed Paul Hoffman's ". . . after a decade of costly struggle we are finally winning the peace. . . . If the Russians, for whatever reason, are willing to let the Cold War simmer down to competitive co-existence, I do not see how our free society can fail to win the competition."[2] Even the more cautious kind of British opinion was inclined to believe that the worst patch in the Western road had been passed. "The position of equality, which the West so long sought as an essential basis for negotiation, has been achieved in more than one respect. For the first time in a decade, Western representatives can sit down without the nagging knowledge that time is wholly on the Soviet side. Even the bluff Mr. Khrushchev cannot disguise the strain now imposed on the whole cumbrous Soviet system by the ever more costly burden of arms, by China's demands for aid, and by the Russian people's own newly articulate desire for a less bleak life. The real significance of the summit is that the slope is no longer against the free nations."[3] The most notable exception to the general optimism about Western achievements was the military correspondent of *The New York Times*, Hanson Baldwin, who was sceptical not only as to whether the West had in fact achieved a "position of strength" in the Cold War, but even as to whether a stable balance of power had been reached.[4]

One of the most remarkable things about this pre-summit glow of optimism about Western strength is that it vanished with the speed of a stage illusion almost as soon as the conference got under way—leaving the observer, as it were, rubbing his eyes and wondering, in the hard light of common day, precisely why the international landscape had looked so different a moment past. Optimism did, it is true, survive experience in a few commentators for a short while: *Fortune*, for instance, wrote in a post-summit editorial entitled "The Smell of Victory" that "the summer of 1955 represents the moment when the ratio of Soviet

[2] *Life*, July 18, 1955.
[3] *The Economist*, July 16, 1955.
[4] *The New York Times*, July 3, 1955.

weakness to Western strength became very plain to them and assumed practical military, political and economic meaning."[5] This is one of those statements which require, like dreams, to be interpreted by contraries, for though the summit meeting did re-define the relationships of power, it did so in precisely the oppo-site sense.

By the middle of the conference it was quite clear that the Russians did not share the West's assumption of a Western advantage in negotiating position. They were not negotiating from weakness in the shape of fear of Germany, or in any way interested in a guarantee against her. Bulganin dismissed Eden's offer of a security pact with the observation that strong states do not need sponsors, though, he added blandly, small powers like Britain and France may find themselves in need of them. The confidence of Russian policy-makers that their writ could be made to run in Central Europe, so obvious in 1956 in relation to Hungary and Poland, was apparent also in their stand on Ger-many in 1955. They were no longer interested in any scheme for the unification of Germany that did not maintain intact their advantages in Eastern Germany, or offer a *quid pro quo* as sub-stantial as the breaking-up of the Western alliance and the exit of American troops in Europe. There may have been a time when the Russians were prepared to barter their position in Eastern Germany against the exclusion of Germany from NATO, but it was clear at Geneva that the minimum price by 1955 was the demolition of NATO and the exclusion of American forces from Europe. Khrushchev made the reduced importance of any settle-ment with Germany in Russian foreign policy quite clear. "The peace of Europe does not depend on German reunification," he said, and he has repeated this statement, with variations, a num-ber of times since.[6] In the words of *The* (London) *Times*: "What was striking at Geneva was the firmness with which the

---

[5] August 1955.

[6] See, for instance, the Lippmann interview in *The Observer* of April 23, 1961.

Russians announced that Germany could not hope for unity on the present European setting. They did not even press forward their old plan of unity for a neutralized Germany."[7] And *The Economist* remarked later: "The outstanding feature of the talks was the Soviet leaders' frankness. More openly and flatly than ever they declared their aims: to destroy the Atlantic alliance, to push the Americans out of Europe, to reshape Germany to their own design. They proclaimed their intention of blackmailing the Germans by withholding reunion until NATO itself had been scrapped. Those Germans who believe (as do, curiously enough, some people in Britain) that Russia has shown itself ready to grant the Germans reunion in freedom now if they merely 'weaken' their links with NATO can maintain this belief only by shutting their eyes tightly as to what Marshal Bulganin actually said at the Summit."[8] The leader went on to quote *Pravda* of the previous week as saying: "Not only on a European but on a world scale the balance between the two systems has for a long time been in favour of Communism."

In justice to Dulles, one must concede that there was a point on which his expectations about a summit meeting were well-founded. He believed that it must involve a tacit recognition of the *status quo* in Eastern Europe, and was therefore inconsistent with even the faint remaining pretensions of his policy of "liberation." This proved to be the case. There is an indefinable sense, after the "summit," that Eastern Europe had been conceded to be Russia's bailiwick. Macmillan's remark, coming away from Geneva, and lapsing into the superannuated joviality of a cant phrase of the 1930's, "there ain't gonna be no war," underlined this point. War had become less likely, not because the two dominant powers had reached a negotiated accommodation, but because there had been an unspoken recognition of spheres of influence and the prospective penalties of disturbing them.

One can hardly call the heads-of-government meeting at Ge-

---

[7] See also *The New York Times*, July 21, 1955.

[8] October 22, 1955.

neva a "negotiation," since that word properly implies the
putting forward of detailed practical propositions on which agreement might conceivably be reached, whereas the heads-of-government dealt, in fact, in generalities and proclamations. They
could hardly do otherwise in the discussion time available to
them.[9] The meeting of Foreign Ministers which took place at the
same time managed some substantive discussion of the issues of
German reunification, European security, and disarmament. As
James Reston said, if it was sunny at the top, it was chilly down
below.[1] That is, when discussion left the realm of reassurances for
that of practical accommodation, the continuing reality of the
Cold War immediately made its presence felt. One might liken
the situation to those areas of Siberia where the earth a few inches
below the surface is always permanently frozen, but where the top
soil, thawed briefly each year, produces for the occasion a short-
lived but showy efflorescence. Working on the diplomatic top
soil, the heads of government appeared to be producing results,
but the Foreign Ministers working on the permafrost below made
no visible progress. The atmosphere when the Foreign Ministers
resumed in October was not, as far as they were concerned, very
much different from July: the realities were merely more bleakly
visible. If there had been any doubt in July about the question of
whether the Russian Government was prepared to see the East
German regime vanish, Molotov was adamantly firm in October
that the reunification of Germany must wait on the demolition of
NATO and the evacuation of American troops from Europe.

What reasons may be assigned for the failure of the Geneva discussions to approach actual bargaining? Let us clear a few minor
considerations away first. The summit meeting was certainly not
on the pattern that Churchill had wanted. He had suggested it
should be confined to the smallest number of powers and persons
possible, and should meet with informality, privacy, and seclusion.
In fact, of course, the proceedings were formal, the advisers

---

[9] They met each day at 4 p.m. and talked until about 8 p.m.
[1] *The New York Times,* July 23, 1955.

numerous, and the publicity overwhelming. But these factors had only a marginal influence on the situation. Even in the mid-twentieth century, if political leaders are determined that a bargain can and must be struck, they can secure privacy to strike it in.

Were the statesmen's hands tied by the pressure of opinion in their respective countries? There is a sense, of course, in which the area in which negotiations may be conducted is always delimited by assumptions in the countries of the statesmen concerned about the nature and meaning of their respective foreign policies. But, subject to this qualification, one can say that the Western statesmen concerned were in a comparatively favourable situation. This was particularly true of Eisenhower, who in 1955 was at the peak of his prestige and popularity with the American electorate, and in a much more commanding position *vis-à-vis* his party than either earlier or later. Nor would almost any conceivable kind of bargain with the Russians have damaged the domestic political position of the British or French participants. Whether the domestic political position of Khrushchev would have been damaged by a bargain with the Western powers (Bulganin may presumably be regarded even in 1955 as a figurehead) is a question on which there is less evidence: since his rise to power was clearly not complete at this stage, he may indeed have been more delicately balanced on competing forces within his own party than any of the Western participants.

Let us then consider the substance of the questions at issue. In essence they were three: German reunification, European security, and arms control. On German reunification, as has been said, the chief outcome of the conferences both in July and October was to make it clear how strong the Russians felt themselves to be *vis-à-vis* Germany and her Western friends, how little incentive they felt to give up their position in Eastern Germany for any prize short of the retreat of American power from Europe, how little pressure they felt under in Europe, even from a NATO grown to its probable maximum strength with the addition of West Germany. Those theories of Russian foreign policy which lay heavy stress on fear of German revanchism have some colour of plausibility for the period up to 1955, but not after that date. At least this would be so if one could assume that foreign-policy issues were always judged by policy-makers in the logical terms of present and prospective relationships of power. But, in fact, *past* relationships of power probably contribute almost as much to the attitudes of political leaders as they do to the attitudes of those they lead. The most ironic nemesis for Germany as a power would be a Russian policy in which a rational appreciation of the present margin of Russian advantage was attended by an emotional bias derived from Germany's formidable past: that is, a present relationship which says "we need not make concessions" compounded with a past relationship which adds "and we ought not either."

There has not been much evidence, since Germany began to play a relatively active diplomatic role *vis-à-vis* Russia in 1955, of any other impulse in Russian policy. Germany's diplomatic leverage in Moscow, judged by results, is not high. Moreover, its diplomatic leverage in the West must partly be a sort of extension of its leverage in Moscow: the basic component is the ostentatiously renounced idea of "a new Rapallo." But the theory of the "new Rapallo" simply neglects the change in the power relationship between the two countries: it amounts to assuming that someone who has once found it profitable to play pat-a-cake with a tiger cub will judge it desirable to do so again with a full-grown (and conspicuously sabre-toothed) tiger. The prosperous, Catholic, conservative bourgeoisie who are the dominant political element in Dr. Adenauer's Germany have not shown much enthusiasm for emulating the young lady of Riga.

Dr. Adenauer's concept of "positions of strength," which governed the whole relationship of Germany to the West (particularly America) on the one hand, and to Russia on the other for the period of this study, must be said to be based on the assumption that German reunification and other national diplomatic objectives could only be safely pursued in firm company with the NATO powers. The results of the 1955 conference may perhaps have shaken this assumption, or dispelled an earlier optimism,[2] but subsequent events did not do much to encourage a German belief that any alternative mode of procedure offered a better hope of pulling the national chestnuts out of the fire. Even the Left in German politics has become progressively less optimistic on this point, as witness the Social Democrats' abandonment of their earlier offer of neutrality for reunification.[3]

The mood of Russian confidence in its own military and diplomatic strength revealed at Geneva dominated not only the discussions of German reunification but those of European security. The schemes which offered guarantees against aggression by European powers were not received with much interest, except in so far as their real impact was on American power.

There remained the question of arms control, to be understood for the moment as including schemes of disarmament and arms reduction. The most spectacular negotiating bid in this field was Eisenhower's "open skies" proposal, the suggestion that America and Russia should each open its territories to photo reconnaissance by the other. This proposition made a more immediate appeal to Western public opinion than any other notion put forward at the conference and must be accounted a major psychological success for the West, but the Russian refusal to take

---

[2] Shown, for instance, in his speech of October 2, 1952: "I believe that when Western integration has been achieved and the Atlantic military alliance is strong Stalin will realize that the Cold War no longer plays off, and will be prepared to enter into negotiations with the West." (*Manchester Guardian*, October 3, 1952.)

[3] At least one acute observer, Claus Jacobi, implies that the Federal Government would have been unofficially willing, from about 1957, to make the same bargain if the Russians had shown signs of offering attractive terms. See his article, "German Paradoxes," in *Foreign Affairs*, April 1957, pp. 436 ff. The policy change on the part of the Social Democrats was made official at the S.P.D. party congress of November 1958, which adopted Brandt as Shadow Chancellor and declared that the party would accept the NATO obligations of the Federal Government.

it seriously as a basis for negotiation was not surprising. Arms control is a field in which, to interest both sides, any scheme must be so constructed that it is possible to envisage its operating *without altering the relationships of power.* This was clearly not the case with regard to the "open skies" proposal, since the ability to maintain secrecy about military installations is an important element in Russian power, but nonexistent in American power.

However, there was one proposition put forward in the field of arms control that may be said to have passed, on first inspection, the test of potential equal advantage. That was the idea, suggested by Eden, of a zone of arms limitation in Central Europe. As developed at the October meeting, this proposal provided for a zone 100 to 150 miles wide along the Eastern frontier of a re-united Germany. In this form it was clearly unlikely to have much appeal for the Russians, but the central notion, that of widening the space between the opposed forces in Europe, offered at least a promising element in the common stock of bargaining propositions, and one capable of development in various directions.[4]

There were some possible NATO objections to any sort of movement of Western troops away from their forward positions, such as that it would shorten the warning of enemy attack, reduce the troops' ability to manœuvre, and raise acute problems of barrack space. General Gruenther was said to regard his space as already too confined, and to doubt whether it would be possible to fight effectively unless his troops were already in Germany in peace-time.[5] On the other hand, the military advantages for

---

[4] The assorted schemes of arms limitation and disengagement produced since have had many differing strategic and political meanings. See Eugene Hinterhoff: *Disengagement* (London: Stevens & Sons; 1959). For the Foreign Ministers' discussions, see Cmd. 9663.

[5] *Manchester Guardian*, July 14, 1955. But this position may have been based on political rather than strictly military considerations. General Clyde Edellman, the commander of the American forces in Europe, admitted later that Western forces could be withdrawn behind the Rhine without much strategic disadvantage, though at some administrative inconvenience. (*The* [London] *Times*, May 8, 1959).

NATO of a Russian departure from East Germany had to be balanced against these inconveniences. The belief that NATO, as such, was not among possible negotiating counters, and that neither were the American bases in Europe, was of course common ground to all the NATO powers. But the Atlantic alliance itself was not necessarily impossible to divorce from the strategy it had earlier adopted in Europe, a strategy which was in any case in process of change. But the prospects of such a divorce, and the reasons why in 1955 the Western powers found their diplomatic leverage *vis-à-vis* Russia rather less than had been hoped, were connected with a development that must now be examined, in the relations between diplomacy and military establishments.

[5]

New Constituents for Strength

THE ORIGINS of the military balance whose effect on negotiation made itself understood at the summit conversations of 1955 must be traced to an event that took place a few days before the election which brought President Eisenhower to office. The first week of November 1952 marks the real end of the original post-1950 phase of military strength building in the West. A new government and a new weapon were to mean the "new look" in the American military establishment and eventually the new diplomatic relationship of 1955–60. Though, of course, it was the Democratic decisions of early 1950 that produced the bomb and so presented the Republican Administration as it entered office in 1953 with the necessity of making choices as to how the bomb's existence should modify the strategic doctrines and the foreign-policy attitudes of the United States Government. One may indeed say that of the two decisions made by Truman and Acheson in early 1950, the results of the first (concerning the H-bomb) ultimately vitiated the results of the second (concerning conventional forces).

Shortly after the election, in December 1952, the President-elect visited Korea, fulfilling a promise made during his campaign. His return journey, aboard the U.S. cruiser *Helena*, was the occasion of crucial post-election policy discussions for the incoming Administration. Those on board included Dulles; Charles E. Wilson, who was to be Secretary of Defence; George M. Humphrey, who was to be Secretary of the Treasury; Admiral Radford, who was to be Chaiman of the Joint Chiefs of Staff; and Joseph M. Dodge, a banker who was to be Director of the Office of the Budget. According to a Republican journalist with privileged access to information, Charles J. V. Murphy: "The most important part of the discussion aboard the *Helena* had to do with balancing what we came to call the Great Equation—how to equate needed military strength with maximum economic strength."[1]

For "maximum economic strength," in this company, one may read "tax cuts and a balanced budget." At a post-nomination meeting with Senator Taft in September 1952, Eisenhower had already promised to reduce federal expenditures to about $70 billion for the fiscal year 1954, and $60 billion for the following year.[2] Given that defence and defence support absorbed the lion's share of the budget, and that most of the rest went in the essential running expenses of the state, and social services which even the extreme right of the party conceded it would be electorally embarrassing to reduce, a decision to cut the budget became almost automatically a decision to buy a less expensive defence establishment.

The new President was already committed to this policy by the

---

[1] Murphy's account is in a series of articles in *Fortune*, January–March 1956, a sort of official encomium of the Eisenhower Administration written obviously with the 1956 election in view. This particular sentence is from the January article, p. 87.

[2] Senator Taft's participation in the election campaign was thought essential, and Eisenhower's agreement on a number of policy points was in the nature of a *quid pro quo*. See Donovan: op. cit., pp. 103–9, and Rovere: *The Eisenhower Years*, pp. 102–6.

memory of his own compaign promises and undertakings to the
party stalwarts who had helped elect him. The men who made up
his Cabinet ("eight millionaires and a plumber," as Washington
comment put it)[3] were identified with a sector of the community
which had not been backward in making the same demand.
But this should not be taken to mean that Eisenhower was forced
into a course of action uncongenial to him. The clearest impression that emerges from his own utterances, aside from a generalized good will, is a staunch economic conservatism. His press
conferences sometimes gave the impression of his having encountered no economic idea more radical than the rules of thrift
appropriate to a soldierly household, and of his believing that
these rules, writ large, were enough to guide the complex choices
of the enormous and overwhelmingly productive society he was
now called upon to preside over.

The desire to cut taxes was not the only politically urgent
pressure on the incoming Administration. Reaction at the popular
level against the whole Korean involvement was also important,
not only on the question of ending the Korean war, but also
because it was one fountain-head of the wave of emotion that
brought Eisenhower to power. Resentment that Americans should

----

[3] The "plumber" was Martin B. Durkin, Secretary of Labor, actually the
president of the United Association of Journeymen and Apprentices of the
Plumbing and Pipefitting Industry. "Eight millionaires" is only a mild exaggeration. Wilson (Defence) and Humphrey (Treasury) represented industrial and financial empires of enormous magnitude. Weeks (Commerce),
Summerfield (Postmaster General), McKay (Interior), and Mrs. Hobby
(Health, Education, and Welfare) all controlled very substantial business
interests, though not on the scale of the first two. (Weeks distinguished
himself shortly after his appointment by calling for the resignation of the
director of the National Bureau of Standards, who had pointed out that a
certain battery additive being marketed was in fact worthless: the new Secretary of Commerce felt that such tactless truth-telling indicated an attitude
unsympathetic to business.) Dulles and the Attorney General, Brownell,
were both very prosperous lawyers, associated with firms connected with the
world of international finance. Only Benson (Agriculture), an apostle of the
Mormon Church, was a man of modest means. See Merlo J. Pusey: *Eisenhower the President* (New York: The Macmillan Company; 1956), pp. 47 ff.

be stuck, apparently interminably, in Korean foxholes and should be unable to use their undoubted technological superiority over the Chinese to exempt themselves from this sort of ordeal was a powerful political force. Some of the resentment at Attlee's visit to America at the end of 1950 was due to a belief (ill-founded) that only the pressure of the allies against the use of the atomic bomb prevented America from emancipating itself from this situation.

So one may say that the two strongest political pressures bearing on the incoming Administration both urged it in the direction of change in the military establishment. And there had existed for almost half a century a theory of warfare which enticingly promised greater security at less expense and with a lower human cost *at least as far as combat forces were concerned* than conventional war. This was, of course, the theory of the strategic as against the tactical use of air power. Though the general outlines of the claims for air power have been widely known since the writings of Douhet in the 1920's,[4] it is often overlooked that the whole debate between the proponents and the critics of "massive retaliation" is a variation of the much older debate about the limits of the air strike. There are three points to note. The first is that the concept of air power alone as a war-winning weapon dates almost from the first use of military aircraft. A report by Smuts to the War Cabinet in 1917 put it thus: "The day may not be far distant when aerial operations . . . may become the principal operations of war, to which military and naval operations may become secondary and subordinate."[5] The second point is that up till 1952 this expectation by what we may call the "innovators" in the theory of war was constantly falsified by

---

[4] His chief work, *The Command of the Air*, published in 1921, was translated into English in the early thirties and distributed to officers of the U.S. Air Force, but there had been an earlier influence through military missions of the First World War. See Bernard Brodie: *Strategy in the Missile Age* (Princeton: 1959), pp. 71 ff.

[5] Quoted in Asher Lee: *Air Power* (London: Gerald Duckworth & Co.; 1955).

events and rejected by what we may call the "traditionalists," i.e., military and naval officers, chiefly, who were not prepared to concede the more ambitious of the airmen's claims. As one strategist has put it: "Ever since Douhet's doctrine of victory by air power alone, a doctrine proposed when the aeroplane was hardly capable of destroying the huts of a command headquarters on a bright and sunny day, there has always been a group of devoted 'futurists' who often evaluate future expected capabilities of a new weapon system, within the present-day framework, with everything except their new weapon system remaining at today's state of development."[6] In the Second World War the effectiveness of bombing was consistently overrated and the resilience of the economy and the population consistently underrated. This is fairly well known as regards conventional bombing, especially of Germany. Sir Charles Snow has revealed that the original night-bombing operations against Germany were undertaken on a mis-estimate by a factor of ten of their probable effectiveness.[7]

What is less appreciated, since the results never reached the popular level, is that something of the same process of discounting earlier claims took place among strategists as regards atomic bombing. When the post-war U.S. bombing surveys came to assess the damage done at Hiroshima and Nagasaki against that done by conventional bombing at Tokyo or in Germany, they were inclined to reject the more apocalyptic claims for it, and to point out, for instance, that a conventional raid with 120 Super-Fortresses at Nagasaki or with 210 at Hiroshima (and these would be quite ordinary-sized raids by the standards of the last year of the war) would have done the same kind of damage. The postwar tests at Bikini and in New Mexico further contributed to discounting the first claims for atomic bombing: it was even

---

[6] Lee: op. cit., p. 99.

[7] *Science and Government* (London: Oxford University Press; 1961), pp. 48–51. These were Lord Cherwell's estimates: those of Sir Henry Tizard and Professor P. M. S. Blackett were more modest, but still assumed greater damage than actually resulted.

estimated that against certain types of resistant targets of con-
crete and steel the atomic bomb might be less effective than
a series of rocket or armour-piercing bombs.[8] These reassessments
made no impact on the public image of atomic warfare, perhaps
because it was to no one's interest to spell out their implications.
The Western powers, whose only substantial weapon between
1945 and 1950 was the atomic bomb, had obviously no reason to
publicize its limitations. The lay critics of Western military
policy tended to concentrate their denunciations on the in-
humanity of atomic weapons rather than their possible ineffectiveness.[9]

The evolution of the hydrogen bomb, of course, shook the
scepticism about the military efficiency of strategic bombing of
even the most determined of the traditionalists, since the leap in
yield of destruction from atomic to hydrogen bombs was much
greater than that from conventional to atomic bombs. It did not,
however, silence them, and their rear-guard action will be described later.

The point to note at present is that the extra emphasis on air
power decided on at the beginning of the Eisenhower Administration was no new idea. It had been the dominant Western
strategic notion for the whole period from 1945 to 1949. In fact,
the three years of the Acheson-inspired drive to rebuild conventional military forces, from the drafting of N.S.C. 68 to the
end of the Democratic Administration, represents the only deviation from the norm of Western reliance on air-power concepts
in the period before 1961. The outcome of the effort to build a
hydrogen bomb had of course been uncertain for the whole of
this three-year period, and some of the most eminent scientists
had been sceptical for much of it. It was not until a meeting of
scientists in Princeton in June 1951, when Dr. Teller explained

---

[8] Lee: op. cit., pp. 20 ff.
[9] A notable exception was Professor P. M. S. Blackett, whose *The Military
and Political Consequences of Atomic Energy* (London: Turnstile Press;
1946) showed an early appreciation of this point.

a new device, that the project looked "technically sweet";[1] the proof of success, and the awe-inspiring scale of success, were fully apparent only with the explosion of November 7, 1952, releasing five million tons of T.N.T. equivalent and entirely destroying the atoll on which the H-device had been placed. Though some reservations about the prospect of getting the bomb into a reasonably transportable form may have remained even after this explosion, it had become abundantly clear that a quite new dimension of "threatenable destruction" could now be built into the American military establishment.

Finally, it should be borne in mind that Western dependence on strategic air power is not to be solely identified with America. One of its most energetic and able exponents was Marshal of the R.A.F. Sir John Slessor,[2] and his views seem to have been shaped by Churchill, at least temporarily. A few months after Churchill's return to office, Slessor was sent to Washington, apparently to sound out the American Joint Chiefs of Staff on the possibility of more military reliance on air power. Presumably this was Churchill's first reaction to the economic stringencies involved in continuing with the military budget he had inherited from the Labour Government. Acheson and Truman were unreceptive to the idea.[3]

Let us now examine more closely the nature of the air-power theory. The conventional theory of war has assumed it to be the business of the armed forces of one country to overcome or destroy the *armed forces* of the country it is fighting, this being taken as a necessary antecedent to imposing the political will of the country whose armed forces most nearly remain intact on the country whose armed forces have gone to the wall. But, as the air-power theorists have pointed out, this is, so to speak, doing it the hard way, since the armed forces are almost by definition the toughest and most resistant-to-attack element

---

[1] Oppenheimer transcript, pp. 242 and 251.
[2] See his *Strategy for the West* (London: Cassell & Company; 1954).
[3] Murphy: op. cit.

within the polity. In the past there has been no chance of avoiding this preliminary to the imposition of political will since the armed forces have been normally so deployed as to protect the frontiers or the seat of government. Thus, the capitulation of the armed forces has come to be regarded as an end, when it is in fact only a means: the true end is the political capitulation of the other government, and this may be secured by forms of pressure other than the destruction of the armed forces, for instance the destruction of industries and centres of population, which are far more vulnerable and less easy to hide or protect. This theory of warfare obviously makes nonsense of those rules for the protection of civilians which have been formalized in various stages since the time of Grotius, but which existed even before then. It represents, as Schelling has pointed out, a reversion to a much older mode of military sanctions, "a massive and modern version of an ancient institution: the exchange of hostages. In olden times, one committed oneself to a promise by delivering hostages physically into the hands of one's distrustful 'partner'; today's military technology makes it possible to have the lives of a potential enemy's women and children in one's grasp while he keeps those women and children thousands of miles away. So long as each side has the manifest power to destroy a nation and its population in response to an attack by the other, the 'balance of terror' amounts to a tacit understanding backed by a total exchange of all conceivable hostages."[4]

In the later elaboration of the theory of deterrence, as sophisticated distinctions began to be made between "counter-force" and "counter-city" strikes, a reversion may be noted to the traditional view of armed forces as the proper object of military attack, at least in so far as the counter-force strike is concerned. Moral discomfort at the implications for civilians of the strategic airstrike theory is obvious in some of its advocates,[5] and accounts

---

[4] Thomas C. Schelling: "Surprise Attack and Disarmament," in Knorr: op. cit., p. 189.

[5] See, for instance, a correspondence that developed in *The Listener* February–March 1954, after Sir John Slessor first outlined his concept of Western defence by strategic air strike in a series of broadcast talks.

perhaps for a portion of the later refinements in the metaphysics of deterrence. Ironically enough, the budgetary incentives which during the early years of the strategic revolution, in the American inter-service competition for the lion's share of the defence dollar, originally made the Air Force the prime advocate of strategic reliance on nuclear strike against cities (since that strategy then maximized the Air Force budget as against those of the Army and Navy) now operate to the reverse effect. The Army and Navy have become identified with the "finite deterrent/counter city" strategy, which requires fewer missiles and planes, and thus has the incidental merit, from their point of view, of leaving more funds for Army and Navy requirements. The Air Force is now identified with the "counter-force" strike, which requires much greater numbers of missiles and planes than the "counter city" strike (since bases are harder to hit than cities) and which might seem to have the incidental merit of directing policy away from reliance essentially on the mass slaughter of civilians, except that the notion of "pre-emption" is ineluctably associated with that of the "counter-force" strike.[6]

However, these developments belong to the period from 1957. To return to the situation at the end of 1952, one may say that there were four factors at work on the President-elect and his chief advisers as they made their preliminary policy formulations: a party pressure to cut taxes, the consciousness of popular revulsion against the Korean involvement or another like it, the H-bomb's promise of a new dimension of destructive power, and the already influential air theorists' view that security could be obtained by means other than conventional forces. One must also bear in mind that these were decisions by an administration that had not as yet actually entered office, or encountered its difficulties.

The decisions taken on board the *Helena* included apparently a decision that the defence establishment could be geared more specifically towards the notion of meeting general war, that the

---

[6] See articles by Hanson Baldwin in *The New York Times*, January 12–18, 1961.

armed services could count on being able to use nuclear weapons whenever necessary, and possibly an agreement as to the level to which the Army should be reduced. At least General Ridgway, who as Army Chief of Staff was later to engage in public dispute with Eisenhower, remarks in his memoirs that he believed the future size and strength of the Army was decided in these discussions.[7]

Of the men on board the *Helena* when the decisions were made, only Eisenhower and Dulles could have been expected to have devoted much time to the relationship between a foreign policy and a defence establishment: that is, to the connection between the kinds of diplomatic leverage America was likely to want to exert and the kinds of military sanctions that might be required to back it. Eisenhower had of course been personally confronted in his earlier career with the question whether it was not desirable to bear one's political ends in mind when making strategic decisions—but there is not much evidence that he remembered the arguments of 1945 in 1953.[8]

Dulles, on his earlier pronouncements, was decidedly more identified with the impending line of change than the President. Before it was certain that Eisenhower would be the Presidential nominee, in the spring of 1952,[9] he had begun to develop a foreign-policy platform related to the ideas expounded by Taft in

[7] Matthew B. Ridgway: *Soldier* (New York: Harper & Brothers; 1956), p. 288.

[8] The arguments that the author has in mind are those with Churchill over the direction that the Western advance should take in Germany and whether British and American forces should seek to reach Berlin before the Russians. See Herbert Feis: *Churchill, Roosevelt, Stalin* (Princeton; 1957), pp. 600, 609. In both cases the essential question before Eisenhower was how far the political objectives of the West should determine its military choices. But the General was faced with cost expressed in his men's lives and the President with cost in legal tender.

[9] See his article in *Life* published in May 1952 and presumably written in March or April. It was not formally certain that Eisenhower would be the candidate until after the Republican Party convention. Even informally, there was some doubt until the primaries had produced substantial evidence of his superiority over Taft as a vote winner, about the end of May.

his 1951 book, *A Foreign Policy for Americans*, in which he had
set forth the notion that economic considerations precluded the
idea of creating armed forces adequate to meet every form of
attack, and that there should instead be an emphasis on air
power, and a refusal to be involved with land forces either in
Europe or Asia. According to Murphy, Dulles had begun to move
towards the ideas later presented as "massive retaliation" (which
was the diplomatic correlative of these strategic decisions) as
early as his negotiation of the Japanese peace treaty in 1951.[1]

On June 24, 1952, Eisenhower specifically rejected any idea
that "all we had to do was sit at home and have an Air Force to
suddenly dispatch off into the wild blue yonder, and that we
would have all the influence we needed."[2] Even the phrase "new
look" belonged to Taft, who had demanded a "new look" by the
new Chiefs of Staff at the military establishment.[3]

On the whole, comparing the Truman-Acheson decisions with
the Eisenhower-Dulles decisions, one receives the impression that
the vital differences are those between the Secretaries of State
rather than between the Presidents. It is an interesting illustration
of the way in which the bipolarization of power tends to turn
foreign policy into a mere superstructure of defence that the most
important distinction between two successive Secretaries of
State was perhaps their respective attitudes towards armed forces.
In part this must be attributed to differences in diplomatic experience: Acheson had been in conduct of policy through the
Korean crisis, which (especially in its initial stages) was an
object lesson in the importance of conventional forces as against
atomic weapons, particularly in a situation in which policy had
to be conditioned by the necessity of maintaining an alliance.
But in any case Acheson was altogether more alliance-oriented
than Dulles: the great achievement of his period as a policy-
maker was the American alliance system in Europe, to which,

---

[1] Op. cit. (March), pp. 111–12.
[2] *The New York Times*, June 25, 1952.
[3] The *New York Herald Tribune*, May 18, 1953.

from his first foreshadowing of the Marshall Plan in May 1947, he certainly contributed more than any other single individual. Dulles had a temperamental affinity for "absolute solutions": large unsubtle answers to complex problems. He was a congenital cutter of Gordian knots, a process that in diplomacy tends to lead to a good many loose ends. There is an inescapable hint in such attitudes of an emotional conviction (however overlaid with intellectual subtleties) that the conduct of foreign policy can be reduced to the dealing out of summary vengeance to the wrongdoer. Possibly this is the normal outcome of a feeling, rooted in the long security of the American past, that one is not only morally right but also invulnerable, as the judge on the bench is invulnerable to the criminal in the dock.

However, the decisions taken aboard the *Helena* about the future direction of policy were of course of a preliminary nature only. The military budget for 1953 was already determined by the existing defence establishment and the plans of the outgoing Administration: the new Administration decisions did not much affect policy until fiscal 1954. During the summer of 1953, when the budget for 1954 was under consideration, the Administration again subjected its policies to scrutiny, in two major studies, known respectively as the "Solarium" study and the "Sequoia" study. Both studies were secret but some information is available on each.[4]

The "Solarium" study (so named after the White House sun-room, in which a preliminary meeting was held) was concerned with examining three political-strategic policies which might be assumed to be open to the United States in its relations with the U.S.S.R. The first policy assumption was a continuation of something like containment, more or less as implemented by the

---

[4] The author's information is based chiefly on interviews in America in 1959, but some details of this policy-making have since been published in W. W. Rostow: *The United States in the World Arena* (New York: Harper & Brothers; 1961) and there were earlier journalistic leaks; see Alsop: op. cit., pp. 225 ff.

Democratic Administration; the second was a more dramatic variant of the containment idea—a cross-the-line-at-your-atomic-peril version; the third assumption was a radical change of approach, on the lines of requiring the Russians to negotiate under a two-year ultimatum (somewhat the sort of policy that Khrushchev was to adopt later in the first stage of the Berlin crisis). A separate report was made on the prospects of a favourable outcome for America of each of these lines of policy. The full membership of the National Security Council listened to the reports early in October 1953.

The report on the third of these policy assumptions (which would have amounted to an actual attempt of sorts to negotiate from strength) was not sanguine, apparently stressing the exposed position of Western Europe and the idea that it must be regarded as a hostage to Russia. The first Soviet H-bomb explosion had been detected in August, about the time the study group was sitting, and it had presumably entered their calculations. The reports on the first and second policy possibilities were more favourable: Dulles's public unveiling of the Administration's alleged new policy, in the famous "massive retaliation" speech three months later, seems to represent a blend of the first and second sets of assumptions.

However, several of those who had worked on the "Solarium" study were astonished and disconcerted by the "massive retaliation" speech, and other influences appear to account for various of its aspects. The Joint Chiefs of Staff were at this period engaged on the "Sequoia" study (named after the Navy Secretary's yacht, aboard which their discussions took place). They had been instructed to reach agreement upon the fundamental defence needs of the country for a period extending into mid-1957.[5] Reportedly, the results of this study, when put to the National Security Council on October 13, produced objections on the score of the costs involved, whereas the chairman of the Joint

---

[5] Murphy: op. cit., May 26, p. 102.

Chiefs of Staff, Admiral Radford, told the Council that the civilians must advise the military what sort of war to get ready for.[6] There certainly appears to be an echo of such a demand in the "massive retaliation" speech in the passage which reads:

So long as our basic policy concepts were unclear our military leaders could not be selective in building our military power . . . we needed to be ready to fight in the Arctic and in the tropics; in Asia, the near East and in Europe; by sea, by land and by air; with old weapons and with new weapons. . . . But before military planning could be changed the President and his advisers, as represented by the National Security Council, had to take some basic policy decisions. . . . Now the Department of Defence and the Joint Chiefs of Staff can shape our military establishment to fit what is our policy instead of having to try to be ready to meet the enemy's many choices.[7]

The chief witness as to how the decision on the military budget for 1954 was finally worked out is General Ridgway. A certain degree of reserve should perhaps be applied to Army evidence on this question. As a comment current in Washington at the time put it, the Administration throughout its tenure of office was looking for an Army Chief of Staff who would preside over the liquidation of the Army. What it acquired instead were two Army Chiefs of Staff who fought vigorous rear-guard actions against this, not only in office but more especially in their memoirs—General Ridgway in *Soldier*, General Maxwell D. Taylor in *The Uncertain Trumpet*.[8]

Ridgway's account is blunt:

When I presented my estimates of cost to Mr. Wilson [the Secretary of Defence] expressing the view that any lesser budget would dangerously weaken the Army's capability of meeting what I considered its part of United States Government commitments, his answer, in substance, was that he disagreed with my interpretation of what

[6] Alsop: op. cit., p. 226.
[7] Text in *Documents* (R.I.I.A.) 1954, p. 265.
[8] London: Stevens; 1960.

constituted commitments. Subsequently, I was informed that the money available would be reduced by some two billion dollars, and the men proportionately.

To me there was no logic in this reasoning. My bewilderment was increased by the fact that at the same time these reductions were being ordered in the Army's budget, economists, with the blessing of the Administration, were hailing the country's greatest boom, predicting that within the next five years the national production was going to rise from $360 billion to $500 billion. If that were true, then I was not greatly impressed with the argument that $2 billion more in the Defense Department budget was going to bankrupt the country.

The real situation then dawned on me. This military budget was not based so much on military requirements, or on what the economy of the country could stand, as on political considerations.[9]

The Defence Department made its final decision on future force levels just before the Christmas of 1953.[1] Included among them was the general decision that the Army should be cut by half a million men by the summer of 1954.[2] Further cuts were to come later. The impact of the eight years of the Republican Administration on the Army offers a neat refutation of any view that military men (in politics) are necessarily militarists. When President Eisenhower took office, the Army amounted to 1,533,-000 men, including twenty combat divisions. In 1961, when President Kennedy succeeded him, the Army stood at 856,000 men. This included fourteen nominal divisions, but the disposable forces were less than this would seem to indicate. Five divisions were in Germany, two (under-strength and partly recruited from Koreans) in Korea, one was in Hawaii, and three were training divisions manned by recruits, so that the strategic reserve in the United States comprised only three divisions.[3]

As has been pointed out in a previous chapter, the build-up of

[9] Ridgway: op. cit., p. 272.
[1] Ibid., p. 303.
[2] Ibid., p. 288.
[3] The *New York Herald Tribune*, March 3, 1961.

conventional forces among the European members of NATO had already begun to mark time during 1952, and by the end of that year the Lisbon goals, adopted in February, appeared unlikely to be attained. If the military plans foreshadowed by the new American Administration had been of a different sort, this tendency might have been reversed, but, as it was, the American decisions strengthened and sanctioned the trend already apparent. The NATO meeting of May 1953, the first that Dulles attended as Secretary of State, may be regarded as an agreed abandonment of the Lisbon goals. In the euphemisms used by Dulles in his television report of the discussions, "at this NATO meeting we put our emphasis on getting greater strength by less costly methods."[4] The phrase used to cover the new expectations was "the long haul." General Norstad has implied that the concept of a smaller force armed with tactical nuclear weapons was adopted as the working basis for NATO strategic planning during 1953,[5] though the change was not fully avowed until December 1954.[6] The recasting of requirements was done by a "New Approach Group" set up under the chairmanship of General Gruenther when he succeeded General Ridgway as Supreme Commander in July 1953. The views reached by this group as to the nature of any future war in Europe (assuming that Russia and America were engaged) governed NATO planning until 1961. It was held that such a war would inevitably be nuclear, that the peak of destruction would occur in the first few days, that the outcome of the conflict would be determined by forces in being, and that first strikes would be at potential retaliatory forces rather than centres of population.[7]

As far as divisional numbers were concerned, the cut in strategic requirements was not, as is usually supposed, in those

---

[4] *The New York Times*, April 30, 1953.
[5] NATO Letter, December 1, 1956 (Vol. 4., No. 12).
[6] In a North Altantic Council Communiqué. *See Survey* (R.I.I.A.), 1954, p. 115.
[7] *The New York Times*, July 25, 1954.

to be held in readiness on the Central Front but in those
mobilizable in the first thirty days. The earlier strategic plan had
required only 24–25 divisions in readiness, the rest to be available
by D+15 or D+30. The divisions to be actually in readiness
were in fact slightly increased in the new plans, to 30, but much
less emphasis was placed on divisions in quasi-readiness.[8] This
was a natural consequence of the change in the time scale envisaged for war. To quote Norstad: "Today with atomic weapons
the time-factor is entirely different. Months and years may have
been compressed into days and weeks."[9] This view in turn was
partly dictated by questions of supply and reinforcements. The
problem of supplying and reinforcing troops in Europe from
across the Atlantic with a large Soviet submarine fleet in operation and ports liable to be knocked out by atomic weapons was
almost enough in itself to rule out a conventional campaign
by the West. On the other hand, Soviet supply lines would be
almost equally subject to interdiction by Western atomic weapons
(presumably in Poland and East Germany) so that the difficulties
of prolonged military action did not apply only to one side.

Not much of the evolution in military arrangements which has
been described here was known to the general public at the time
when Dulles made his speech about "massive retaliation" to the
Council on Foreign Relations on January 12, 1954. It will be
recalled that the main point of this speech was to announce a
"basic decision" by the Administration to place its military dependence "primarily upon a great capacity to retaliate, instantly,
by means and at places of our choosing," that is, to place more
reliance on deterrent power, and less dependence on local defensive power. This would, he assured the electorate, provide
"more basic security at less cost, even though at some times and
some places there may be setbacks to the cause of freedom."[1]

---

[8] Norstad does not specify the numbers required in each category, but see
Hilsman and Mikschc: ops. cit.

[9] Op. cit.

[1] Text in *The New York Times*, January 13, 1954.

The fact that the speech represented a public unveiling of a military model whose shaping had begun as long before as December 1952 explains why it struck so many commentators at the time as being obsolescent even as it was announced. A policy debatably appropriate in a world still lit by the glare of the first American H-bomb looked a good deal less reasonable in a world that contained a Soviet weapon of the same sort. In the few weeks that followed Dulles's speech there was much comment and many demands for clarification from American and allied political leaders, and the Administration in response backtracked a good deal and maintained soothingly that there was no revolutionary intent, just an evolutionary change. In the upshot, press comment was inclined to dismiss the whole thing as merely a little fresh window-dressing applied to old stock. But this was not an adequate judgment. As had been pointed out, Acheson's notion of strength, in the decisions of 1949–50 with which this study began, comprised two elements: that of nuclear power, which represented a stepping-up of the 1945–9 policy of the atomic strike, and that of an effort towards near parity in conventional forces, an effort which originated in the desire to readjust the U.S. defensive stance to the loss of the American atomic monopoly and was reinforced by the traumatic experience of Korea. The real significance of the "massive retaliation" speech was that it brought political doctrine into line with the process, already under way for almost a year, of abandoning or reducing the effort at this second kind of strength. In effect it was an avowal that the Western powers, for reasons of economy, had decided to reduce the number of military options open to themselves, to try and make their last-ditch sanction look convincing for ditches that everyone knew were less than final and hope to supply conviction by verbal ferocity. Acheson's own criticism of the Dulles policy[2] emphasized this point: "Strategic atomic bombing is not our first but our last resort. . . . If it is said, as it sometimes has been, that we cannot afford another

_____

[2] In an article in *The New York Times*, March 28, 1954.

war like Korea, the answer is that such a war is the only kind that we or anyone else can afford." Dulles's words were more dramatic than his policies in many aspects of his Secretaryship of State. In this particular instance one may say that his weakness for the forceful phrase led him into two over-simplifications: an exaggeration of the element of newness, of radical departure in the policy as a whole (on this question he had progressively to eat his own words for the rest of the year), and an implication that the "all or nothing" policy, the maximum-stake policy, had been extended from Europe to Asia. The crisis period of the Indo-China war, only four months later, was to prove that this was not in fact the case. If a final criticism of the speech may be made in terms of the relationship between the Administration and the electorate, one might say that it misrepresented a situation in which actually something was being *subtracted* from U.S. defence potentialities (to wit, the effort at effective conventional forces in Europe) as a situation in which something was being *added*. It is ironic to reflect that the period of effort to redress the conventional balance, 1950–2, was a period of substantial remaining atomic advantage for the West, whereas the period abandoning this effort was one of rapidly vanishing atomic advantage.

Let us now consider the precise diplomatic and political meaning of the new NATO strategy in Europe—the kind of diplomatic or political ends for which it could provide a military sanction. There is one political claim for it which has application to diplomatic relationships within the alliance rather than *vis-à-vis* Russia: that is the claim that, despite the reduction of its forces, NATO's new strategy would enable it to defend a more easterly line than the old one. In Norstad's words: "By basing our plans on the full use of these (atomic) weapons we found we could carry out a forward strategy instead of falling back to the line of the Rhine."[3] It is, of course, obvious that the integration of Germany within the Western alliance could

---

[3] Ibid.

hardly appear a satisfactory bargain from the German point of view if all it promised in the event of hostilities was the preservation of the small fragment of German territory lying West of the Rhine. In a sense, therefore, the decision on the necessity of incorporating German troops in the NATO forces implied the adoption of this forward-line concept (it was implied but not actually stated that the line would be close to the zonal boundary), which in turn involved the use of tactical nuclear weapons. However, the NATO claim, if it is to be taken seriously at all, must be considered in conjunction with the time concept previously mentioned. Time is indeed the key element in the forward strategy, whether one is considering it *vis-à-vis* Germany or *vis-à-vis* Russia. As many critics have pointed out, thirty divisions is a figure that seems to fall between two stools. If it is thought of as a basis for any prolonged resistance to the Russians, it appears rather small, even on the assumption of atomic tactical weapons. The Russian Army is also equipped with such weapons, and though it has been argued that they have an inherent tendency to favour the defensive (since activities in the nature of massing for attack will make the army highly vulnerable to battlefield atomic weapons), there seems not much reason to suppose that a small atomic force could indefinitely hold off a larger atomic force. Some military authorities have indeed argued that atomic warfare will make more rather than fewer troops necessary since the combat zones will be so much wider and the casualty rate may be expected to be so much greater.[4]

On the other hand, the view is often taken that the role of the NATO conventional forces is purely diplomatic or political—that is, that they have a mere "plateglass" or "tripwire" function, serving chiefly as a visible and non-repudiable token of American commitment to Europe, as much to reassure the European members of NATO as to inhibit Russian adventurism. No doubt there

---

[4] It is interesting to note that Russian strategists have adopted this view. See below, p. 175. General Ridgway argued to the same effect; op. cit., pp. 286 ff.

has been some truth in this version of NATO's functions during the years in which the actual forces on the Central Front have been well below the planned thirty divisions. But if one assumes the thirty divisions to have actually been created, they may seem rather over-substantial for this kind of token role.

General Norstad's account of the political and military function of his forces is rather more complex than either of these views. Testifying before the Senate Foreign Relations Committee in June 1957, he put it thus:

> I propose to hold long enough to force the Soviets to consider the effect of this retaliatory force which will lead to their destruction, and if they start the war I think we can hold until the effect of our retaliatory force is felt. . . . I am confident that given the forces we have indicated we require [security deletion] we can hold for this purpose.[5]

There are two purposes indicated here: "to hold long enough to force the Soviets to *consider*" [the effect of nuclear bombing] and "to hold until the effect of our retaliatory force is felt." These two functions, though they may seem deliberately blurred together in this and other official statements, are in fact quite distinct. The first is the concept of imposing a pause for negotiation during which NATO forces would prevent the penetration of the Red Army into Europe. The assumption obviously is that in this period both sides would refrain from strategic nuclear exchange, and would balance the costs of raising the war to the pitch of nuclear exchange against their minimum diplomatic objectives in the crisis situation. This is the function for NATO foreshadowed by Churchill in his statement in 1954 that there would be a pause for "an alert and an alarm," bringing the use of nuclear weapons into "discussions of a decisive character by the heads of all the great states that are involved."[6] Some comment has tended to assume that the negotiating time provided

---

[5] *United States News and World Report,* July 5, 1957, reporting testimonies of June 7, 1957.

[6] H. C. Deb., 5th Series, Vol. 535, col. 177.

in this fashion by the NATO forces would be quite short. Alastair Buchan has suggested that even with the full complement of thirty divisions it would only be a matter of a week.[7] But official circles have maintained that, given the use of battle-field atomic weapons on both sides, the holding time would be about a month.[8]

This official doctrine of the "pause" was reported to have been further elaborated in a NATO document known as MC70, a strategic appreciation for the five years 1957–62, based on the concept that NATO forces should be designed to balance only that portion of Russian forces maintained in East Germany, Poland, and Hungary and that tactical nuclear forces would necessarily be used to prevent their reinforcement. (It was assumed that the Russians could bring up an additional fifty-five divisions in fourteen days if their lines of communication, which run principally through Poland, were not thus disrupted.)[9]

That is, the pause is envisaged not as being between the outbreak of hostilities and the use of atomic weapons, but between the outbreak and either the strategic nuclear exchange or a truce for negotiated settlement. (The respective negotiating strengths of the parties at this point would turn on a delicate balance between their fortunes at the time in the semi-conventional battle, their first-strike capabilities, and their ability to provide shelter for their peoples.)

This concept of the role of the NATO forces is obviously designed to meet the ambiguities of a situation in which the distinction between a negotiable border clash and the prelude to general war would not necessarily be immediately apparent. The second half of General Norstad's sentence, concerning the role of the NATO forces during the waging of the nuclear battle, has perhaps now become outmoded by the development of technology. With present bomb sizes, the decision, once the

---

[7] *The Reporter,* June 13, 1957.
[8] *Daily Telegraph,* August 4, 1961.
[9] *The New York Times,* August 8, 1961.

strategic nuclear exchange is under way, is regarded as likely to come in hours or a very few days, and any action taken by conventional forces will be irrelevant. Bernard Brodie has pointed out that the earlier picture of the Red Army rolling across Europe, even after the centres of organized society and political command in Russia had been destroyed, was without much basis in historical experience or psychological probability. Under such circumstances armies tend to disintegrate, and while a problem of guerrilla bands would no doubt exist, it would be, as Sir John Cockcroft once said of genetic damage, a minor element in the over-all disaster. Indeed, even the rudimentary degree of political organization represented by bands of *condottieri* would possibly prove useful rather than pernicious in a post-nuclear-war period.

There is a third possibility aside from the "hold for negotiation" case and the "hold during nuclear strike" case in which the NATO forces would be involved: that of limited and strictly conventional war in Europe. One must assume that in this case such a war would be limited not by any agreed ground rules, but by each side's perception that it could not afford to win too much, since the other side could not afford to lose too much—though each side would of course only be guessing at the other's tolerance of loss. It seems probable that, if this restraint in fact operated effectively, some of the old pre-nuclear possibilities for the West might return, including that of a slow build-up of strength. This would of course depend on Western ability to hold, with conventional weapons only, for an adequate period. But the disparity in strength was not based on factors so permanent and irreversible as to make necessary continuance of the flat official negation of such a possibility which was standard doctrine during the Republican Administration, and was exemplified in President Eisenhower's remark in the early months of the Berlin crisis that he did not propose to fight a limited war in Europe.[1]

Admittedly, official spokesmen have been caught in a cleft stick

[1] *The New York Times*, March 12, 1959.

on this issue. Since the first priority in Western political strategy after 1953 (and indeed before then) was to maintain the *credibility* of the deterrent, any statement laying stress on NATO's capability in conventional warfare or even limited nuclear war was subject to the disadvantage that it would be instantly interpreted by commentators in the West and perhaps by more important circles in the East as evidence of hesitation and ambiguity in official attitudes to the deterrent strategy. Even the NATO tendency to rather exaggerate the advantage of Soviet conventional strength over that of Western forces, and to play down arguments such as Liddell Hart's on the relationship between strength necessary for defence and that necessary for attack,[2] may be considered part of the technique of maintaining the credibility of the deterrent, though it had the unfortunate side effect of making it seem useless to build up Western forces.

On the indications of his first year of office, President Kennedy's policy was based on the assumption that conventional resistance, at least for a time, must be among the options open to the West in Europe. In thus reversing the decisions of early 1953, he may be said to be reverting to a development of the policy of N.S.C. 68.[3] There is therefore considerable interest in analysing the reasons for the shortfall of NATO forces in the period 1953–60, though they represent in part a continuation of the factors already mentioned as affecting the situation in 1951–2. The deficiency was substantial: the highest point reached by 1960 was 21⅓ divisions of the planned thirty.

The causes provide a sort of paradigm of the difficulties of coalition diplomacy. Two of the Central Front powers, the United

---

[2] The ratio suggested is of the order of two to three between defending and attacking forces as providing a reasonable margin of strength. See B. H. Liddell Hart: "A Shield Force for NATO," *Guardian*, February 16, 1960.

[3] The appointments of Paul Nitze, who drafted N.S.C. 68, as Assistant Secretary of Defence for International Security Affairs, and of General Maxwell D. Taylor as the President's personal adviser on military questions and later Chairman of the Joint Chiefs of Staff, are significant of the direction of his policy.

States and Britain, were in the process, during the years concerned, of adapting their armed forces to the concepts of the
strategic revolution. The reduction in the sizes of their respective
armies that this entailed did not necessarily much impair their
ability to meet their commitments to NATO, since these commitments were very small anyway—five and four divisions respectively. Britain's strategic changes were the more radical of
the two: the 1957 Defence White Paper envisaged the cutting
of the combined strengths of the three services, at that time
about 690,000, to little more than half this number, and their
stabilization on an all-regular footing at a strength of about
372,000 men by the end of 1962. This allowed for an army
strength of only 165,000.[4] Given the turn-over from a conscript
system to regular soldiers (conscription was to end in 1962),
this change did not affect the total of combat forces available
in peace-time as much as might have been expected, but the
British Government advised its NATO partners in December
1956 that it proposed to cut forces under NATO command by
22,000 men. In 1960 Britain had eight brigades in Germany, one
of them being in Berlin,[5] though the number of troops, at
50,000, was 5,000 below the promised quota.

It was the political and psychological effect of the British and

---

[4] This was the "floor" figure: there was some official talk of 182,000 as a
preferred or "ceiling" figure. The genesis of the British strategic revolution
of 1955–7 is still a little mysterious. The influence of the 1955 decision to
build an H-bomb is clear enough, and the influence of the economic strain
of conventional defence in a period of full employment and balance-of-
payments difficulties. Macmillan (then Chancellor of the Exchequer) justified the changes in December 1956 on the ground that defence expenditure
adversely affected internal investment and research-and-development efforts
in other areas (*Daily Telegraph*, December 14, 1956). But it is not clear
that the proposed changes were of a sort to improve this situation. Whether
the relative ineffectiveness of the Suez operation had any effect on estimates
of the usefulness of conventional forces remains uncertain, as does the influence of the American attitude at the Suez period on the decision to press
forward with plans for British nuclear weapons.

[5] Institute of Strategic Studies: *The Communist Bloc and the Free World:
The Military Balance 1960* (London; 1961).

American changes on their allies in NATO, rather than the effect on the ability of the two countries concerned to meet their own obligations to the NATO army, that was of significance. When the non-nuclear members of NATO heard Mr. Anthony Head, then British Defence Minister, justify the British cuts by arguing that the new NATO weapons were so expensive that no NATO member could afford both to maintain present numbers and to arm them on the new scale, and that on the other hand they could not afford to accept out-of-date armaments when dealing with the Soviet Union, so that therefore there must be an adjustment in the direction of fewer men equipped with the latest weapons, including tactical atomic weapons,[6] they could hardly fail to reflect that what was sauce for the British and American geese would be sauce for the remaining NATO ganders. The effect of *expectation* of a further and irreversible march of change may be more dramatic than changes actually made. One may see this in the debate occasioned by the reports of the so-called "Radford plan." During the summer of 1956, press stories appearing in America attributed to Admiral Radford, at that time still Chairman of the Joint Chiefs of Staff, sponsorship of a project for the reduction of the U.S. armed forces by 800,000 men as nuclear fire power was improved. This would have entailed the reduction of the Army to half a million men.[7] The report was rather half-heartedly denied by Admiral Radford and the Defence Secretary, Charles E. Wilson; it was said to be "anticipating conclusions which the Chairman had not yet reached,"[8] but was very much taken to heart by Adenauer and created six months' diplomatic strain between him and Dulles.[9] The term of conscription for the German Army, which had previously been set at eighteen months, was reduced to twelve months, ostensibly because of this, though Dulles is said to have believed that Adenauer was merely using

---

[6] *Daily Telegraph*, December 14, 1956.
[7] *The New York Times*, July 13, 1956.
[8] Ibid., July 15, 1956.
[9] Drummond and Coblenz: op. cit., pp. 45 ff.

the outcry over the Radford plan as a pretext to modify his own conscription proposals because of their domestic unpopularity in West Germany.[1]

Other factors than the quarrel over the conscription period operated to delay the growth of the German Army. The original 1955 plan had envisaged the twelve divisions that Germany was to commit to NATO as being ready by 1959: however, by 1960 only seven divisions were actually in being.[2] Germany shared with the other NATO powers in Europe a reluctance to accept the economic cost of large conventional forces. Already in 1955 Herr Schäffer, the Minister of Finance, was asserting that 9,000 million marks was the limit which could be spent on defence without endangering "the financial order and the monetary stability of the Federal Republic."[3] This statement was plainly incompatible with maintaining the original timetable for the armed forces, which would have required the Federal Government to find 16,000 million marks a year from its budget. The 9,000 million marks a year actually expended, which was resented by other NATO countries as not representing a defence burden equivalent to their own, was represented by the Germans as only part of their defence costs, other parts being the 20,000-man frontier defence force, contributions to the West Berlin economy, support and assimilation of refugees, and war veterans' pensions. They claimed that these expenses brought their defence costs to about 14,000 million marks,[4] or about 10 per cent of the gross national product, the "prescribed" level for major members of NATO.[5] On the question of NATO's strategic concepts, there were obvious difficulties in any formulation that was

---

[1] Ibid., p. 47.

[2] Institute of Strategic Studies: op. cit. By late 1961 it appeared probable that the twelve divisions would be ready in mid-1963 and that the German conscription period would be raised to eighteen months in 1962 (*Guardian*, December 9, 1961).

[3] *The London Times*, September 2, 1955.

[4] *The New York Times*, August 31, 1955.

[5] Though on other figures the proportion seemed more like 4.5 per cent on average over the period 1953–9. See table in Hedley Bull: *The Control of the Arms Race* (London: Institute of Strategic Studies; 1961), p. 71.

militarily realistic being also, no matter how carefully dressed up, politically palatable to Germany. During NATO's first strategic period, based on conventional forces, Western strength was never great enough for anything more to be envisaged than a delaying withdrawal to the Rhine,[6] to await a Western build-up of strength and later counter-attacks. Clearly this offered Germany an initial period of devastation during the withdrawal, a period of Russian occupation for most of the country, then further devastation as the Russians were, it would be hoped, pushed back. On the other hand, after 1953, when planning was claimed to be based on a "forward line," it was clear that this must be somewhat west of the zonal boundary, and that the area of Germany both east and west of it would be the main area of tactical nuclear exchange. A NATO exercise called "Carte Blanche," held in July 1955, though it only lasted for a few days of simulated bombing, was reported to have shown that a similar battle in earnest would have resulted in 1,700,000 Germans killed and 3,000,000 injured.[7] The implications of the official strategies produced some alternative proposals from German military commentators, especially from Colonel Bogislaw von Bonin and from Adelbert Weinstein, along the lines of mobile zonal defence by a volunteer army armed with conventional weapons, but official planners were inclined to dismiss these schemes as over-optimistic, pointing out unanswerably that if NATO's main forces, armed with the most sophisticated and advanced weapons available, were thought unlikely to be able to hold in that area, it was curious reasoning to assume that a smaller and less adequately armed force would do so.

In September 1956 the German Government, which had previously resisted the NATO trend to reliance on tactical atomic weapons, reversed its position and has since increasingly com-

---

[6] See interview with General Norstad, *NATO Letter*, December 1, 1956.
[7] See Gordon A. Craig: "NATO and the New German Army," in *Military Policy and National Security*, ed. W. W. Kaufmann (Princeton; 1956), pp. 221 ff.

mitted itself to the strategic concept that nuclear weapons must
be deployed close to the forward line and used early in any
outbreak of hostilities. Thus the question has arisen of the
"nuclearization" of the German armed forces, and some German
share in the political control of nuclear weapons. Like other
NATO forces, the German troops have, of course, some potential
"nuclear capacity" in the sense of having been trained with
missiles that may carry either a conventional or an atomic war-
head, and they were due to be equipped with a support aircraft
(the F104) capable of transporting small nuclear bombs. But
the key of the nuclear closet remained in American hands, and
the right of making atomic weapons of its own was renounced by
Germany in the W.E.U. treaty.

The prospects of a German share in political decisions on
nuclear war depended on the prospects of the "NATO deterrent,"
and Kennedy's attitude to this scheme appeared markedly less
favourable than that of the Republican Administration. When
it was evolved, about the end of 1959, it was thought of chiefly
as an offset to the reduced credibility of the American deterrent,
in a situation of increasing American vulnerability, as a guarantee
against attack in Europe. But either the difficulties inherent in
the notion of fifteen fingers on the trigger (and the safety catch)
or the rising tension of 1960–1 seems to have persuaded Kennedy
against it. Norstad said at the end of 1961 that the idea was
dead, and Kennedy remarked bluntly in the interview he gave
to the editor of *Izvestia* that he would be reluctant to see Ger
many with nuclear arms, and that if it ever developed a nuclear
capacity of its own it would be appropriate for America and
Russia to consider the situation together,[8] a frank implication
that the two powers might have a common interest against
Germany.

One may see Kennedy's policy in 1961 as intent not only on
reducing Western dependence on nuclear weapons, as for in-

[8] For a transcript of this interview, see *The New York Times*, November
29, 1961.

stance in the decisions to reinforce American troops in Europe and to raise two new American divisions, but as intent also on modifying the public image of the relationship of conventional strength in Europe. This might be called the "Russians are not ten feet tall" campaign: speeches and inspired press stories pointing out that the previously used conventional figure of 175 Soviet divisions could be discounted, that Russian divisions were in any case much smaller than American divisions, many of them at skeleton strength and probably only about thirty at full strength, that the satellite forces were unreliable and the Soviet rear would be endangered—in a word, using as much endeavour to prove that conventional resistance was possible as had once been used to prove it was impossible.[9]

One might say that, as Stalin was the real architect of NATO in the Berlin crisis of 1948, so Khrushchev was the agent through whose efforts in the Berlin crisis of 1958–61 NATO came at last within reach of its forces target of thirty divisions. Most of the resistance in Europe to the new direction of American policy appeared to be British, stemming perhaps from dislike of the idea of incurring larger support costs in Germany, or of jettisoning the concepts of the 1957 White Paper, but rationalized as a fear of reducing the credibility of the deterrent. France, of course, had avoided having the structure of her military establishment modified by the concepts of the strategic revolution, though this was due less to strength of traditional conviction on the part of her generals than to the fact of her solid engagement through-

---

[9] See especially the speeches by Gilpatric on June 6 (*The New York Herald Tribune*, June 7, 1961) maintaining that the United States had almost as many men under arms as Russia, and by Roger Hilsman on August 24 (*The* [London] *Times*, August 25) maintaining that NATO strength was roughly equivalent to what the Russians had on the forward line in Europe. According to *The* (London) *Times* defence correspondent, who was sceptical about these claims, it was maintained in American administrative circles that it would be possible for NATO forces to hold for up to sixty days. See also a series of obviously inspired news stories in *The New York Times* and the *Christian Science Monitor* from August 4 to 13, 1961.

out the post-war period in colonial wars for which the *poilu*
appeared the most useful instrument. Her army in 1960 was
nearly as large as that of the United States (812,000 men as
against 870,000 of a population a quarter the size)[1] and certainly
contained a higher proportion of men with recent combat experience than any other Western army. Only two French divisions were at the disposal of NATO for most of the period
1955–60, and even these were said to have had their ranks
stripped of experienced troops and filled with green conscripts
or elements which it was thought unwise to leave in North
Africa. The NATO command neither approved nor contested
the withdrawal of French NATO troops for service in Algeria.
Its attitude in the matter was based on an interpretation of the
Paris treaties that appeared to permit any member of the alliance
to withdraw troops at will for use in areas outside the command,
and in any case the defence of Algeria was specifically covered
by the North Atlantic Treaty. However, it is worth noting that
an end to the French military action in Algeria, and the return
of the French Army to metropolitan France, though conceivably
dangerous to French political institutions, could substantially
change the situation of NATO's conventional forces. In conjunction with the formation of the five remaining German divisions, it could nearly double troops available on the Central
Front, as against the position in 1959.

But, of course, the meaning of the thirty divisions in 1963 was
not what it would have been in 1952 or 1953. For the reasons why
this was so, one must look again at the other component of
military strength, nuclear weapons and their means of delivery.

The most notable and obvious contrast in the period under
review is that between the Western failure to match the U.S.S.R.
in conventional forces and the Russian success in matching the
West in air atomic power. Whereas in 1950 the Russian superiority in conventional forces was still balanced by a substantial
Western superiority in (though no longer a monopoly of)

---

[1] Institute of Strategic Studies: op. cit.

atomic weapons, and a very large lead in the means of delivery, in 1960 the Russian advantage in conventional forces was not decisively diminished, the Western lead in atomic weapons was replaced by saturation stockpiles on both sides, and the erstwhile Western advantage in the means of delivery had been so much reduced as to have come for a time under the suspicion of actual inferiority.

The debate over why this happened must necessarily centre around the size of, the reasons for, and the significance that should be attached to the "missile gap"—though the question of whether one could be said to exist at all is a matter on which election to office appeared to have changed the convictions of some Democrats. In a sense this question was for the Republicans in 1959 what the charge of "losing China" was for the Democrats in 1952. So many reputations, so many possible political futures, and so many vested interests became involved in it that almost any statement, whether from Republican defender or Democratic attacker, needed to be weighed with a careful scepticism. Even President Eisenhower, normally a paladin of private enterprise, once hinted that the effort to obtain larger appropriations in this field was not unconnected with private profits.[2] One can say at least that two Republican Secretaries of Defence, Neil H. McElroy and Thomas S. Gates (whose political interests would not have been served by exaggeration), implied in 1959 and 1960 respectively that Russia held a considerable lead in this field, and that assorted Democrats and commentators of both parties maintained that the lead was greater and more damaging than was officially admitted. But, early in 1961, reports appeared from Washington, based on an off-the-record speech by the new Secretary of Defence, Robert McNamara, that studies made by the Kennedy Administration after its inauguration showed that in fact no such gap existed, though this interpretation of his speech was later denied.[3] In a sense, the mechanics of democracy

[2] *The New York Times*, July 14, 1959.
[3] See *The New York Times*, February 7 to 13, 1962, especially February 9, for the development of this controversy.

made it inevitable not only that the Democrats out of office should attack the Republican record on this issue, and enlarge the size of the missile gap—as for instance when Senator Stuart Symington maintained that McElroy's admission of a three-to-one lead for the Russians was really an attempt to minimize their lead, and that the real ratio was more like six-to-one[4]—but that they should also, when in office and therefore charged with responsibility for maintaining the credibility of the deterrent, find it necessary to discount their earlier warnings. Gilpatric's speech of October 1961, claiming that American second-strike capacity was at least as great as Russian first-strike capacity, was an extreme example of how much rosier a military situation can appear from an inside than from an outside view.[5]

But even if the "missile gap" was as mythical an entity as the unicorn, and of no more military significance than the halberd, there is no doubt that the debate about its existence and significance was in itself damaging to American diplomatic leverage. "The battle is the payoff," as the American Army adage has it; but until the battle national power is what it is deemed to be, and whatever affects estimates of the relative power of America and Russia must affect their diplomatic leverage *vis-à-vis* each other, and *vis-à-vis* other states. So whatever the military significance of the apparent Russian advantages in this field, no one can doubt its psychological, political, and diplomatic importance. But in any case more solid evidence than the testimony of political witnesses—to wit, a number of circling sputniks and cosmonauts—existed to indicate some degree of Russian superiority in rocket technique, and it is of interest therefore to ask how and why America incurred the appearance of disadvantage.

Dr. Werner von Braun has testified that the lost years were those of Truman's Administration; he has said that from 1945 to 1951 the United States had no ballistic-missile programme worth mentioning.[6] On the other hand, the real "crash pro-

---

[4] *The New York Times*, July 14, 1959.

[5] *The New York Times*, October 22, 1961.

[6] *The New York Times*, November 10, 1957.

gramme" in missiles was not begun until late 1955, i.e., three years after the Republicans came to office, and well after they had had substantial warning of Russian successes. According to Trevor Gardner, who was Assistant Secretary of the Air Force in charge of Research and Development (including the Air Force's missile programme) for three years of the Eisenhower Administration, and who resigned in February 1956 in protest at that Administration's policies, adequate research funds for the project were not provided even after 1955. In articles written after his resignation, he asserted that the temporary increase in Research and Development funds made available in 1951 because of the Korean war were promptly reduced in 1953, and that after that year Air Force Research and Development funds were maintained essentially constant at a figure 20 per cent lower than the 1953 cut.[7]

Among the other reasons he gives for the lagging of the American intercontinental-missile development were rivalry between the Army, Navy, and Air Force guided-missile programmes and the civilian satellite project, the "administrative nightmare" of committees and sub-committees competing with each other for influence and appropriations, and the fact that the project, though given top-priority status, shared it with many subsidiary missile projects, with the result that there was "no such thing as top priority." Moreover the executive personnel of the missiles programme, according to him, was "notable for its preponderance of management experts recruited from private business, and for its poverty of full-time scientists who qualify as missile experts and know what they're talking about."[8]

The programme was perhaps damaged, or certainly not conspicuously aided, by the Administration's inability to resolve the main rivalry, that between the Air Force and the Army. The Air Force had on the whole less success with its Thor missile than

---

[7] "Must Our Air Force Be Second Best?" and "Our Guided Missile Crisis," *Look*, May 8, 1956, pp. 77 ff, and May 15, 1956, pp. 46 ff.
[8] Ibid.

the Army with its Jupiter. The service rivalry was exacerbated by the fact that the Thor was developed by private contractors, and the Jupiter in a "socialistic" government factory system. Truman has blamed the lag chiefly on investigations of the politics of scientists.[9] The Fort Monmouth Army laboratory, whose work in 1954 Senator McCarthy disrupted almost single-handed in his investigations, was engaged in electronic work for missile development, and Dr. Edward U. Condon, who had been working on problems connected with the re-entry of missiles, was forced out of classified work in 1954 on the direct insistence of Vice-President Nixon, who claimed this success for himself in an election speech in that year.[1] And the Administration appears to have shied away, in security-haunted distrust, from the obvious model for the crash programme, that used for the atomic bomb. As C. J. V. Murphy (an assiduous apologist for the Republicans) delicately put it: "Marriages of the military and scientific temperaments are always subject to strain, and another project of the Manhattan District type, with scientists in effective control, was not deemed desirable."[2]

On the whole, however, the relative rates of progress were less a matter of blameable misjudgment in America than of conspicuous success by the U.S.S.R. Soviet strategic doctrine and the Soviet defence establishment went through an evolutionary process between 1953 and 1960 that was in some ways fascinatingly similar to that in the U.S.A., despite the dissimilarity of the results. Stalin's theory of war, enunciated in February 1942,[3] seems not to have been open to question or review during his life-time. It was a doctrine that necessarily tended to discount the importance of new weapons, since it held that the outcome of war must be determined by five "permanently operating fac-

---

[9] *Washington Post*, November 5, 1957.

[1] See Marquis Childs: *Eisenhower: Captive Hero* (London: Hammond & Company; 1959), p. 169.

[2] Murphy: op. cit., p. 248.

[3] It was embodied in Order No. 55 of February 23, 1952.

tors"—stability of the rear, the morale of the army, the quantity and quality of divisions, the army's weapons, and the organizing ability of the commanding officers. This list is, of course, rather a recital of the obvious, but there was a political point in emphasizing these factors in 1942, since at that time the very notable and striking military advantage which the German Army had gained through surprise needed to be set in the framework of a theory which could colourably maintain that the outcome of the war was nevertheless not in doubt. The indifference with which Stalin at Potsdam received the news of the atomic bomb has usually been attributed to his having been told of it earlier through information passed to Russian agents by Dr. Klaus Fuchs. Without doubting this prior knowledge, one may point out that his attitude was consistent also with a determination to maintain, or a real conviction, that the "permanently operating factors" were still decisive.

Between 1945 and 1949, in the period of American atomic monopoly, and to a lesser extent between 1949 and 1953, in the period of markedly inferior Soviet means of delivery of the new weapons, the potentialities that might be held to lie in surprise obviously conduced to the advantage of the Americans rather than the Russians, and therefore debate over the role of the new weapons and of the surprise attack with which they might be associated was conspicuously lacking in Russia. (It might be observed, incidentally, that Russia as well as America had traumatic experiences with surprise in World War II, the initial strategic advantage of the Germans being hardly less than that of the Japanese, though surprise was achieved in both cases in the teeth of intelligence warnings.)

At the time of Stalin's death, the first Russian test of a hydrogen bomb was only five months in the future, and the Russian stockpile of atomic bombs had been accumulating for three and a half years. Yet there had been no published analysis by military theorists of the effect of the new weapons on the conventional

Stalinist theory of war. One authority attributes this silence to a
cult of secrecy which would have kept most strategists from any
knowledge of their potentialities.[4] Whether there was in fact no
speculation among strategists for lack of the knowledge to base
it on, or whether it was merely prudently kept under cover while
Stalin lived, a process of debate on the Stalinist theory began six
months after his death and resulted within two years in a significant reassessment. One can distinguish in this debate, as in that
in the West, schools of thought describable as "traditionalists"
and "innovators," with Marshal Vasilevsky occupying somewhat
the position of General Ridgway in the American discussions.
The first shot of the "innovators" came in September 1953 with
the publication in *Military Thought*, the organ of the Soviet
General Staff, of an article by Major-General Talensky rejecting
the rigid dogmatism of the Stalinist theory and insisting on the
identity of the principles of warfare for both sides.[5]

In the following month, an article by Colonel Ncnakhov
pointed out that the advantages and dangers of surprise attack
had become sharper through the evolution of weapons of mass
destruction: "Surprise can bring great advantage to the aggressor
and enormous loss to the victim of the attack."[6] These views
aroused a sharp reaction: Talensky was described as anti-scientific
and anti-Marxian, and at one stage relieved of his editorship of
Military Thought. But in March 1955 a victory for the innovators
became evident with the publication of an article by Marshal
Rotmistrov entitled "On the Rôle of Surprise in Contemporary
War." Marshal Rotmistrov ventured the assertion that surprise
could be decisive not only in a battle but in a war.

In certain cases surprise attack with the mass use of new weapons
can provoke the quick collapse of a state whose capability for resist-

---

[4] Raymond L. Garthoff: *The Soviet Image of Future War* (Washington:
Public Affairs Press; 1959), p. 9.

[5] Herbert S. Dinerstein: "The Revolution in Soviet Strategic Thinking,"
Foreign Affairs, January 1958.

[6] Garthoff; op. cit., p. 62.

ance is low as a consequence of the basic failures of its social and economic structure and also of an unfavourable geographic location.[7]

With this article there also emerges in Soviet doctrine the distinction made in Western strategic doctrine between "preventive war" and a "pre-emptive strike": Rotmistrov concludes that the U.S.S.R. must always be ready for "pre-emptive actions against the cunning of aggressors."[8]

Dinerstein connects the Soviet debate over strategic change with the struggle between Khrushchev and Malenkov in 1954, which led to Malenkov's being ousted from the Prime Ministership in 1955. Malenkov's proposals for a radical redirection of Soviet economic policies in the direction of light industry and consumer goods was, he holds, connected with Soviet development of an H-bomb and a belief that America was now effectively deterred, that war was no longer inevitable, and that therefore there was a possibility of cutting the military budget and reducing the emphasis on heavy industry. These views would necessarily have tended to bring him into conflict with the military. It is notable that Zhukov assumed the post of Minister of Defence in February 1955, at the time of Khrushchev's victory over Malenkov (which would be consistent with Khrushchev's having found the Army a useful ally at this point), and that Shepilov at the time lumped Malenkov with the "economists" whose views would have resulted in Russia's being left without rockets.[9]

A recent reformulation incorporating the changes made to suit the new strategic position (and Khrushchev's 1956 criticisms of Stalin) is this one:

The thesis on the permanently operating factors was at that period (1942) a new word in Soviet military science. Under the influence of the cult of the individual, however, this thesis began to be turned into an infallible dogma. . . . As a result of the unprecedented progress of contemporary weapons, and above all of nuclear weapons, jet

---

[7] Ibid., p. 65.
[8] Dinerstein: op. cit.
[9] Dinerstein: op. cit.

aviation and missiles, surprise is now in effect turning into a permanently operating factor, and that circumstance must be taken into account by military science. Under contemporary conditions the role of science and technology grows enormously; without them it would be impossible to advance any field of endeavour, including the military. Hence, science too should be added to the list of permanently operating factors determining the fate of war.[1]

It must be noted that Soviet strategists have not by any means adopted air-power doctrine in its more wholehearted sense. The basic strategic concept remains the destruction of armed forces and the occupation of enemy territory. They still hold to the concept of a lengthy war, and the size of their Army and submarine fleet reflects this. They have not, unlike the Western powers, discarded the concept of the "broken-backed" period.

Moreover, the use of these weapons (atomic and hydrogen bombs, and ICBM and IRBM missiles) by both sides will more likely lead to extending the duration of the war than to speeding it. Hence, while in the past major wars could be short or long, in our time all major wars inevitably assume a quite drawn-out character.[2]

As far as the means of delivery were concerned, there were several reason why the Soviet switch to rockets rather than manned aircraft should have occurred earlier than in the U.S.A. The Russians had a considerable early tradition of experimentation with rockets: they were using crude short-range military rockets early in the nineteenth century, and a Tsarist scientist who lived on into the Soviet era, Konstantin Tsiolkowsky, produced, in 1903, the blueprint of a rocket burning hydrogen and oxygen.[3] The truck-mounted artillery-type Katyushka rocket was

---

[1] Colonel P. Sidorov: "The Creative Character of Soviet Military Science," *Soviet Fleet*, December 11, 1958. Reproduced in translation in Garthoff: op. cit., Appendix C.

[2] Article in the *Soviet Army Journal*, June 1958, quoted in Garthoff: op. cit., p. 24.

[3] Asher Lee and Richard E. Stockwell: "Soviet Missiles," in *The Soviet Air and Missile Forces*, ed. Lee (London: George Weidenfelt and Nicolson; 1959), pp. 147 ff.

used to some effect in the Second World War, at the battles of Moscow and Stalingrad. But they had no long-range rockets, and one must assume that their capture of the German experts and research facilities associated with the V-2 installations at Peenemunde and in Thuringia and Czechoslovakia were a major asset in this field. Many German scientists and technicians were shipped back to Russia in October 1946.[4]

The development of the Russian aircraft industry appears to have been at least as vigorously forwarded as that of rocketry until 1953. The successive development of particular types of aircraft is in itself an interesting indication of the kinds of military necessity to which priority was being given. The first stage was the production of fighter aircraft: the Mig 15 and its successors, in the period from 1945 to about 1949. The second phase, light bombers and ground-support aircraft, overlapped with this. It was not until about 1950 that the effort to build long-range heavy bombers got under way. The fruits of this effort, the Bison, Badger, and Bear aircraft, were first shown publicly about 1954, notably in the May Day parade of that year, and created something of a sensation in the West. Until that time the only long-range heavy bomber was the T-U 4, modelled on the U.S. wartime Superfortress, not a very formidable threat in comparison with post-war Western aircraft, especially as its range was comparatively restricted.[5]

After 1953/4 the effort to create new models, or large numbers of very long-range bombers, suitable for attack on the U.S.A. itself, appeared to have been somewhat damped. The estimate in 1960 was that only 60 Bear and 100 to 120 Bison bombers, of a

---

[4] Though some of the most eminent went to America. There seems little basis for the popular American conviction that the later Russian successes were due primarily to their having been luckier on the draw, so to speak, on this occasion—a conviction informally expressed by an American comment after the first sputnik. "So what? All it proves is that their Heinies are better than our Heinies."

[5] Air Chief Marshal Sir Phillip Joubert: "Long Range Air Attack," in Lee: *Soviet Air and Missile Forces*.

range adequate to inflict damage inside the U.S.A.,[6] were in
service, as against a U.S. and British force of over 450 B52's, 1,250
B47's, and about 200 British V-class bombers, all capable of
striking targets within the U.S.S.R. This would seem to confirm
the reports that the first major Russian successes in the field of
intermediate-range ballistic missiles came in 1953/4. It was said
to be intelligence reports to this effect which led to the setting-up
in 1955 of the NATO radar-tracking system in Turkey to monitor
Russian missile firing.[7] In May 1955 the Russians were sufficiently
confident of the succession of missiles to aircraft for the publication of a pamphlet by the then chief of the Soviet Air Force,
Marshal Pavel Zhigarev, announcing the obsolescence of the
strategic bomber and the coming reign of the intercontinental
rocket, and claiming that Russia had already successfully fired
one. The Russians could the more readily switch from bombers to
missiles because when they began to build a long-range strike
force in serious quantities, about 1952, they did not have a substantial already existing efficient modern air force as the Americans did, and were therefore not, as it were, involved in writing
down a large existing investment. And the intermediate-range
ballistic missile was strategically immensely important to them,
since it offered a prospect of knocking out the European bases
on which a large element of the strength of S.A.C. was dependent.

The American dismissal, from 1961, of earlier estimates of
the "missile gap" as politically inspired alarmism[8] rested chiefly
on new Intelligence analyses said to show that the Russians had
not translated their advantage in rocket-thrust (demonstrated by
a substantial time and weight lead with both the sputniks and
the astronauts) into actual rocket stockpiles. One interpretation
of this failure or restraint would be that they were not interested

---

[6] Institute of Strategic Studies: op. cit. The medium bomber Badger
(range 3,500 miles) could possibly be used on one-way strikes at the United
States, but would be more suitable for use against European targets.

[7] The *New York Herald Tribune*, October 9, 1957.

[8] See *The New York Times*, November 27, 1961.

in building a "counter-force pre-emptive" deterrent but only a "finite counter-city" one. Diplomatically, an American conclusion of this sort conduced towards a *détente*, since it waved out of the circle of immediate consideration the most dangerous spectre that haunts it, that of the successful surprise attack, the nuclear "Pearl Harbor." Yet, for the immediate future, this spectre could not be made to retreat farther than the corners of the room, for whether or not there was ever a "missile gap" there are certainly an "information gap" and a "decision gap," both intrinsic to the nature of the two societies. In any case, the uncertainties generated by a period of rapid technological change, plus indications from the Russian nuclear-test series of late 1961 and the consciousness of earlier Russian successes in substantiating claims made in this field,[9] endowed their position in "the state of the art" with an ambiguity as effective as demonstrated power.

Whatever the military significance of that power, its psychological and diplomatic significance was most astutely used, especially through the sputniks and the cosmonauts—almost unique in diplomacy in the manner in which they managed to combine a hint of military threat with the fascination of human adventure. Sabres have been effectively rattled often enough in diplomacy, but seldom with so deft an accomplishment of the siren song of scientific progress. The balance of power now sways more visibly to technical change than to political change, and the unknown Soviet physicists and engineers who beat America to the rocket that put up the first sputnik altered the power map of the world more than most of its eminent statesmen could do. To adapt a Churchillian phrase, never before in the history of human combat has the destiny of so many depended on the relative intelligence and training of so few.

---

[9] For Russian claims in the now-decisive field of missile defence, see speeches by Marshal Malinovski (*Guardian*, October 25, 1961) and Khrushchev (ibid., July 7, 1962).

[6]

"Summitry": Phase Two

THE North Atlantic Council meeting of December 1957, the starting point for the climb to the disastrous summit meeting of May 1960, offered in some respects the sharpest juxtaposition of the idea of negotiation and the idea of strength since the original Acheson and Churchill statements of 1950. And, as on that occasion, both the American anxiety about the rebuilding of strength and the British preoccupation with a resumption of negotiations arose from evidence of a success for Russian military technology. One may say indeed that in these seven years the wheel came full spiral, since the situation of 1957 was a direct parallel to that of 1950 but at a higher level of deadliness in weapons.

The *détente* associated with the 1955 summit meeting had continued to exert some influence on the general climate of international politics until July 1956, even though the Western powers had become increasingly concerned with the direction of change in the Middle East, and the Russians with changes equally disturbing from their point of view in Eastern Europe. One might liken the atmosphere from mid-1955 to mid-1956 to a spell of uneasy warmth before the violent and destructive storms of November–December 1956. During this period there was little public pressure in the West for negotiations with Russia. An inadequately examined assumption existed that, because the "balance of terror" would operate in such a way as to direct the struggles of competitive co-existence towards economic and political means, therefore old-fashioned considerations of relative military strength and the way in which a particular *status quo* was expressed in territorial frontiers had become almost irrelevant. This belief was influential enough to inspire an attempt to mitigate the military aspect of NATO by giving the organization non-military functions. The President of Italy, Signor Gronchi, voiced a general European feeling when he addressed Congress during a state visit to Washington at the end of February 1956:

The Atlantic Pact as conceived and operated thus far was appropriate and sufficient so long as there was a fear of imminent armed aggression, intensified by an unbalance of strength. . . . However, it should be brought into line with today's realities, when the military unbalance has been reduced and there have been so many changes of situation in the world.[1]

This optimism about the reduced importance of the military activities of the alliance resulted in the appointment, at the May 1956 NATO meeting, of a committee charged with looking into non-military functions it might assume in order to avoid any danger of desuetude. The committee duly reported in December, but not much except some fellowships and scholarships came of its efforts. Most of the possible extra functions that might have been suggested for NATO were either unacceptable to member governments jealous of their sovereignty, or already being performed by other agencies. In any case, events at the end of 1956 in Hungary and at Suez made it clear that military strength might

---

[1] Quoted in *The United States in World Affairs, 1956* (New York: Council on Foreign Relations; 1957), p. 156.

be of some continuing importance even in the world of the
nuclear stalemate.

The first Russian return to the subject of negotiations after the
tensions of late 1956 was in a speech by Bulganin in May 1957,[2]
but it was not until later in the year that a pressure wave of feeling
about the idea became noticeable in Western Europe. The
launching of the first Russian sputnik in October and the growth
of appreciation of what it indicated concerning Russian progress
in the field of ballistic missiles were of course a main inspiration
of demand for negotiations after that time. However, during the
whole of 1957 there were forces at work in Britain which would
in any case have tended to move government policy in that
direction, and which accounted for the substantial divergence
between the British and American attitudes after October.

The most notable of these forces was the organization of the
movements first against the testing of nuclear weapons and then
against nuclear weapons generally. This movement, known from
1958 as the Campaign for Nuclear Disarmament, gained most of
its initial impetus from reaction to British rather than to American or NATO policy. Some degree of organized protest against
atomic weapons of course existed from the early post-war period,
and a first, very small and unpublicized "Aldermaston March"
took place in 1952, but its members were mostly adherents to
actual pacifist groups. Even after the announcement, in the 1955
Defence White Paper,[3] of Britain's intention to manufacture
hydrogen bombs, the volume of protest was not great enough to
be of political importance, and Sir Richard Acland, who resigned
on the issue, lost his seat at the subsequent general election.
Only towards the end of 1956, with the prospect of an actual
British test of a hydrogen weapon in May 1957, did the movement
gather momentum. It was formally constituted, under the name
of the National Council for the Abolition of Nuclear Weapons
Tests, in February 1957, and rapidly acquired the support and

---

[2] Text in *The New York Times*, May 17, 1957.
[3] Cmd. 9391.

sponsorship of a number of people who were by no means novices in the arts of publicity—Bertrand Russell, Canon Collins, Kingsley Martin, J. B. Priestley, and A. J. P. Taylor. It is not necessarily an adverse judgment on the movement to say that it functioned throughout 1957 and in succeeding years as a very competent pressure group, with a sophisticated understanding of techniques and a sharp eye for maximum effect. Its use of marches, public meetings, letter campaigns to M.P.'s, and later the conversion of constituency Labour Parties and strategic trade unions, was notably efficient.[4] During 1957, when its official objectives stressed only the prevention of nuclear-weapons tests, it was less identified with the political Left than it became after 1958, when its name was changed to the Campaign for Nuclear Disarmament and it set its sights (without losing much of its membership) on the more ambitious objective of promoting the renunciation of nuclear weapons either unilaterally by Britain or the West, or multilaterally by a process of negotiation with the Russians. It is hardly possible to define the objectives of the rank-and-file of the movement more specifically than this, since it covers a spectrum of political opinion, from those who merely maintain that Britain could more usefully put its resources into conventional arms than into atomic weapons (a view also taken by many American academic strategists, including Henry Kissinger and Albert Wohlstetter) to those whose real objective is British renunciation of NATO and the American connection, and the adoption of a neutralist position, or even a revival of the Anglo-Russian alliance.

However, though the nuclear disarmers were to find the Labour Party more sympathetic, and to concentrate their attentions there from late 1958 (somewhat to the damage of the party, which suffered three years' internecine warfare over defence policy), in 1957, its official policy was to avoid close identifi-

---

[4] An account of the composition and techniques of the C.N.D. as a pressure group may be found in an unpublished M.A. (Econ.) thesis of Manchester University, R. A. Exley: *The Campaign for Nuclear Disarmament* (1959).

cation with either party,[5] and from the class origin of its members
it must have seemed to party organizers to contain at least as
many potential Conservative as potential Labour voters. The
people who went on the Aldermaston Marches and took part in
the meetings and demonstrations were students, teachers, clerks,
civil servants, journalists, scientists, and suburban housewives: in
the 1959 march only 4 per cent of the marchers were estimated
to be of working-class origin.[6] The active membership was also
predominantly very young: 41 per cent on this occasion were
estimated to be under twenty-one, and J. B. Priestley remarked
that the audiences at C.N.D. meetings were usually composed of
those under twenty-five and those over fifty.[7] The leadership of
the campaign was with the generally eminent, particularly in the
arts, rather than with party political figures. Especially in 1957
and early 1958, therefore, one can say that the movement was
sufficiently non-partisan, and interested enough potential Conservative voters to be of some influence on the Right as well as
the Left of British politics, and that it channelled a very wide-
spread sort of uneasiness that could fill the correspondence
columns of *The Times*[8] as well as the *Tribune* or the *New Statesman and Nation.* This uneasiness was kept simmering throughout 1957 by the issue of the British nuclear tests and the pub-
licizing of the fact that American aircraft on flights from British
bases actually carried nuclear weapons.[9]

Though the *political* significance of the two movements was
quite different, one might say that active membership of the anti-
nuclear campaign offered the same *emotional* outlet in the Britain
of the late 1950's that joining the Communist Party had done in

---

[5] This was a hard-fought decision within the movement. See Exley: op.
cit., pp. 293 ff.
[6] Ibid., p. 218. The estimate was made on a 10 per cent random sample
interviewed by the journal *Perspective.*
[7] Ibid.
[8] See a publication by *The* (London) *Times*, "The Nuclear Dilemma"
(Letters to the Editor originally printed early in 1957).
[9] *The* (London) *Times*, November 29, 1957.

the 1930's. To clamber on to a Polaris submarine, or sit on a pavement in Whitehall waiting to be removed in a police wagon did not entail the same degree of risk as the war in Spain, but it allowed the same chance of feeling that one had made a gesture of protest against a purblind and malicious Establishment, wedded to Gadarene policies. In a word, it was a movement in the classical tradition of middle-class radicalism in Britain and thus had a pervasive influence on articulate political opinion generally.

There were, however, other initiatives which directed opinion in Britain towards alternative diplomatic and defence policies to those the West was engaged in. The Labour Party's official leadership was preoccupied with the concept of disengagement. Like the protest against nuclear weapons, this was something that had existed in embryonic form in the earlier post-war period. Schemes associated with the names of Dr. Pfleiderer and Colonel von Bonin had been aired in 1952 and 1954. Marshal of the R.A.F. Sir John Slessor had made proposals in 1954, and Sir Anthony Eden in 1955, which revolved around the idea of separating or interposing a zone of reduced armaments between the forces of the West and the Communist *bloc* in Europe.[1] Gaitskell developed a somewhat more radical scheme than these in lectures that he delivered at Harvard early in 1957,[2] arguing for a "disengaged zone" which would cover Germany, Poland, Czechoslovakia and Hungary, and perhaps Rumania and Bulgaria, within which armed forces would be subject to inspection and control. A European security treaty would provide guarantees by the Great Powers for the neutral-zone states. This plan was further elaborated by Denis Healey in a pamphlet, *A Neutral Belt in Europe*.[3] The Reith lectures broadcast by George Kennan in November and December 1957 gave wider popular cur-

---

[1] For details of the various schemes and a general discussion of the idea, see Michael Howard: *Disengagement in Europe* (London: Penguin Books; 1958).

[2] Later published under the title *The Challenge of Co-existence* (Harvard; 1958).

[3] Fabian Society; 1958.

rency to the notion of some form of withdrawal from direct confrontation between Western and Communist forces in Europe, and a sharp sense of the essentially unsatisfactory and unstable nature of the *status quo*, and of the self-defeating quality of the current official Western responses to the security dilemma.[4] Finally, one might say that British opinion in 1957 still benefited or suffered from the trauma of late 1956, with its severe diplomatic defeat and its lesson that British policy must seek to find a *modus vivondi* with the dangerous new forces in the world rather than hope to vanquish them. And some benevolent sentiments were directed by Khrushchev specifically to Britain, in his reply to an open letter from Bertrand Russell in the *New Statesman and Nation*, though their reception was not wholly uncritical.[5]

Thus, the debate following the Russian sputnik, from October to December 1957, took place in Britain against a background of eighteen months' sharp division and general unrest over foreign and defence policy, and with an already strong consensus that the position of the West had been critically weakened, especially in the Middle East, and was continuing to deteriorate. In the circumstances, the sputnik itself appeared chiefly as yet another reason for seeking some better *modus vivendi*. Labour speakers in the Commons raised the question of further summit nego-tiations shortly after it was launched,[6] and a speech by Khrush-chev on November 6, proposing a meeting to talk about "ruling war out as a means of dealing with international issues",[7] made a substantial impression.

In America, the public mood and the pressures on the Govern-ment were quite different from those in Britain. A movement of

---

[4] Lectures republished as *Russia, the Atom and the West* (London: Oxford University Press; 1958).

[5] See the *New Statesman and Nation*, November 23 seq. The corres-pondence was republished by MacGibbon and Kee in 1958. Dulles also re-ceived an open letter from Russell at the same time, and the State Department managed a comparatively adroit reply on his behalf.

[6] H. C. Deb., 5th Series, Vol. 578, col. 1280.

[7] *The* (London) *Times*, November 7, 1957.

protest against nuclear weapons did exist, but it was less wide-spread and excited less general public sympathy than that in Britain. This was perhaps a natural outcome of the climate of opinion about the Cold War in the two countries. Whether one regards the effects of the C.N.D. movement as helpful or damaging, on the whole, to the prospects of peace,[8] one must concede

---

[8] Any estimate would have to take into account on the debit side the argument that, so to speak, Khrushchev would not have had much incentive to shake the tree without some indication that the fruit was ripe. That is, from his point of view a movement of mass dissent from government policy in a Western bourgeois society, especially one important to the working of the NATO alliance, was a clear incentive to step up tension in the hope of further splitting the society or the alliance. Moreover, from the point of view of the other decision-maker chiefly concerned, the American President, the movement could not but appear as a faint question mark over the future reliability of what had been the most influential of America's European allies, and thus inevitably a reason for reinsurance in the form of strengthening American bonds with the two chief alternative allies, Western Germany and France. Thus, on the Western side of the power balance, the movement had a clear tendency to shift diplomatic leverage (i.e., influence over decisions) from the most compromise-oriented of America's European allies (Britain) to the most intransigent and revisionist (France and Western Germany). And for the Communist side of the balance it provided an indicator of the profitability of raising the general level of world tension and hoping in the Trotskyist manner to appeal to the peoples over the heads of their governments. Thus, insofar as it could be held to influence at all the two governments on whose decisions the prospects of peace really depended, the influence was in the opposite direction to what members of the C.N.D. hoped. There remains the question of its influence on decisions of the British Government. Here the general impetus of the movement was towards a position of neutrality for Britain. But this objective also, if achieved (which appeared profoundly unlikely), would demonstrably tend to endanger rather than enhance the prospects of peace. For Britain's defection from NATO would produce the sharpest swing in the balance of power since 1949, and it is precisely such swings in the balance which tend to precipitate major wars, as for instance the Soviet shift of position to alliance with Germany in August 1939.

Against these considerations there is really only one argument that can be used in favour of the movement—that is, that it might in some fashion so arouse and transform public opinion that all governments would be effectively restrained from any action endangering the peace. Clearly, if this were in fact likely to happen, it would provide an immensely preferable substitute for the whole balance-of-power system, and most of the apparatus

that it expressed among other things a lively moral concern about the means through which Western purposes might justifiably be promoted.[9] In America, unlike Britain, general moral enthusiasm in the conflict with Russia was strong enough to discourage much sensitivity about means. Other factors promoting dissatisfaction with the trend of Western policy were also less present in America than in Britain. The second Eisenhower Administration, in its first year of office, was not precisely a hive of new ideas. The Democratic opposition, still very much under Acheson's influence, based its criticisms on the inadequacy of the drive towards strength rather than on any demand for genuinely new initiatives in policy. The influence of Dr. Adenauer's dislike of any scheme of disengagement that hinted at neutralization for Germany, or for any part of it, was much more influential in inhibiting American than British interest in such proposals.

All these influences ensured that the American reaction to the sputniks in October and November was quite different from that in Britain. The confused anger produced not so much by the Russian successes as by the American failure for several months to put up a satellite of its own alongside the Russian ones issued

---

of traditional international politics could and should go into the discard. But the belief that this was in any way likely rested on faith rather than evidence. For, as has been pointed out, the effective decision-makers in this matter are Khrushchev and his successors on the one hand, and Kennedy and his successors on the other. And though each is no doubt susceptible to pressures transmitted upwards from the bases of their respective societies, those societies are themselves both so confident of their own national virtues and purposes as not to be fertile ground for movements of this sort. The C.N.D. and its offshoots are in fact (though they appear unconscious of this historic succession) relying on that standby of liberals and progressives in the interwar period, the force of "enlightened world public opinion," which was then to be the lance upholding the rule of law and of the League of Nations in international politics—and which proved so broken a reed even when it was tried on national societies far less adequately armoured in the consciousness of virtuous national purposes than America or Russia.

[9] See Robert W. Tucker: *The Just War. A Study in Contemporary American Doctrine* (Baltimore: Johns Hopkins Press; 1960) for a distinguished discussion of American moral attitudes to war.

diplomatically in a sense that something must be done to stiffen the NATO alliance. This was the mood in which the decision was taken that the North Atlantic Council meeting of December 1957 should be at the level of heads of governments, with President Eisenhower attending, and that agreement should be sought on the stationing of American intermediate-range ballistic missiles in Western Europe. The general tone of editorial opinion on the first two Russian sputniks is conveyed by *The New York Times*[1] comment that the main purpose of the sputnik was political rather than scientific: it was a device to compel the United States to deal with the U.S.S.R. separately as a way of breaking up the American alliance system. The *Christian Science Monitor* wrote that "military—and diplomatic—logic today is posing one single desperately essential task for the United States. That is to catch up, at whatever cost, with the Soviet Union in missile development."[2] A wave of even greater alarm was created by the size and weight of the second sputnik, in early November. There was talk that America's loss of the lead in this field was a defeat equivalent to Pearl Harbor.[3] At the time, a mysterious and inconclusive little war scare existed between Turkey and Syria, and Khrushchev's missile-rattling technique in this crisis was itself regarded as a sign of Russia feeling her new diplomatic strength.

So, when the North Atlantic Council convened for its head-of-government meeting in December, it was clear in advance that it would be preoccupied with reaching some reconciliation between a mainly British-sponsored move for a new round of negotiations with Russia, at the summit or elsewhere, and an American anxiety that some gesture of political solidarity and recruitment of military strength should be made. In terms of specific issues, this involved on the one hand discussion of intermediate-range ballistic missile bases and nuclear stockpiles in Europe, the terms under which they should be controlled, and who had the right

---

[1] October 10, 1957.
[2] October 15, 1957.
[3] *The* (London) *Times*, November 4, 1957.

to "pull the trigger" in an emergency, and on the other hand
what sort of response should be made to the Russian suggestion
of a new summit meeting (repeated in diplomatic notes from
Bulganin to Western governments on December 11).[4]

The results of the North Atlantic Council meeting were treated
in some Western European comments as a defeat or rebuff for
Dulles[5] on the ground that he failed to obtain from all his allies
firm agreements on the installation of American intermediate-
range ballistic missiles on their respective territories. It is true
that there was an agreement only in principle on this question,
that Norway and Denmark showed themselves unequivocally
opposed to bases on their territories, that Germany and France
were reserved about the conditions under which they might accept them, and that the European attitude generally was one of
caution rather than enthusiasm. Moreover, the European members of NATO, even Dr. Adenauer, showed a considerable tendency to agree with the British proposition that the Russian bids
could not be passed off with a debating reply, but must be treated
seriously. But it would be wrong to represent the caution over
missiles as putting a damaging crimp in the plans of the Pentagon. On the contrary, the American Government would have
been embarrassed by a general European enthusiasm for their
installation, since very few were expected to be available for
about two years. In November the Secretary of Defence, Neil
McElroy, put the best probable operational date for the missiles
which it had been arranged in the previous March[6] should be
delivered to Britain as soon as possible, as the end of 1958, and
missiles for other bases in Europe, if they should be accepted,
were not likely to be available until well into 1959. Moreover,

---

[4] Cmnd. 381.

[5] See "Europe in Revolt," by Paul Johnson, in *New Statesman and
Nation*, December 28, 1957. For communiqué, see *The* (London) *Times*,
December 20, 1957.

[6] At the Eisenhower-Macmillan meeting in Bermuda. The acquisition of
these missiles was essentially part of the 1957 revolution in *British* strategic
doctrine, not part of the American adaptation to the post-sputnik world.

the missile type in question, the Thor, was not regarded as particularly satisfactory, except as an interim weapon. Fifteen months later, in May 1959, General Norstad made it clear in a television interview that I.R.B.M.'s were still in very short supply,[7] and in fact, by the time they were more readily available, further strategic changes had reduced their importance so that the only installations decided on other than those in Britain were in Italy and Turkey.

Thus, Dulles's purpose at the December 1957 meeting should be construed not as that of making firm arrangements for sowing the territories of his European allies with missiles, but as that of obtaining a sort of gesture of non-intimidation as a psychological offset to the world-wide sense that the balance of power had tilted in the Soviet direction. The agreement in principle on missile bases was the most that could be done at the time to this end. And if the agreement on missiles was no more than "in principle," so was the agreement to seek negotiations with the Russians. Indeed, of the two, the agreement on bases eventuated in an actual installation, at least in Britain, three months earlier than the agreement on negotiations eventuated in a meeting. Therefore, if one judges this meeting purely in terms of tactical skill in obtaining agreement to his country's policy, it should be accounted a success rather than a failure for Dulles, though whether the missile gesture itself was a well-considered one is a different matter. As Walter Lippmann pointed out at the time, it contrived an appearance of provocation for the Russians without any extra protection for the European members of NATO.[8] Dulles himself does not seem to have expected a great deal from the decision. His main speech of the meeting, on December 19, shows him in one of his most sober moods. The strategy of

---

[7] By March 1960 the last of the sixty Thor missiles to be installed at the four missile bases in England had been delivered, and three of the four bases were operational (The *New York Herald Tribune*, March 10, 1960; see also *Guardian*, February 12, 1960, for description of bases).

[8] The *New York Herald Tribune*, December 22, 1957.

victory, he said, involved "combining our military, economic and moral assets" to meet Soviet strength: steadfastness on this course would lead in time "one year, five years, ten years, twenty years—I don't know"—to a change of attitude by the Soviet rulers towards their own people and the world.[9]

The European tendency to interpret the December meeting as a defeat for the United States had its real basis in a sense of changed power relationships within NATO. The balance of power within an alliance depends on its members' positions as "net producers" or "net consumers" of security. Probably no state in an alliance is ever purely a producer or purely a consumer of security. If it were purely a producer (i.e., if the alliance could add nothing to its safety), it would have no motive (other than altruism) for being in the alliance; if it were purely a consumer, the other members would have no motive (other than altruism) for receiving it into the alliance. In the case of NATO one may for instance say that even Iceland, despite its lack of armed forces, is to some extent a "producer" of security because of the importance of the base at Keflavik. If one were arranging the members of NATO along a producer-consumer scale, one might put nearest the "consumer" end Denmark, with its very tempting and exposed strategic position and almost negligible forces. Such claim to the position of a "producer" of security as it has, comes chiefly from the importance of its situation as a check on the deployment of Russian submarines. Germany perhaps represents the middle of the scale, important for its forces and the deployment that its territory makes possible, but politically very vulnerable, needing the alliance even more than the alliance needs it. America is certainly still closest to the net "producer" end of the scale, even after 1957, contributing far more to the individual security of each of its allies than any of them individually contributes to the security of America. However, the emphasis within the alliance certainly shifts after 1957: whereas before that time NATO was

---

[9] *The New York Times*, December 20, 1957.

chiefly an organization through which America extended a security guarantee to Europe, after 1957 it is almost equally an organization necessary to America's maintenance of the balance of power against Russia.

The change of relationship within NATO was a natural outcome of the growth of Soviet long-range striking power. In an alliance, the more vulnerable members confide their safety in part to the conviction which they hope the potential enemy feels that he cannot "knock out" the least vulnerable member of the alliance, and that therefore, while the alliance is "credible," it is pointless for him to proceed against any other member. But when the strongest member becomes vulnerable, it becomes a more rational target than any other member, since the defeat of the alliance as a whole can be compassed by its defeat.

One may say, on this line of reasoning, that the root cause of decline in the cohesiveness of NATO is not to be looked for in the quarrels of its members among themselves, but in the fact that, as the invulnerability of America is reduced, the real *raison d'être* of the alliance, its convincingness as a deterrent to attack, becomes less. Logically there must come a point when for a minor power it must seem safer to place its bet on neutrality than on its own weight in the balance of power.

Not that this point had been reached, or even approached, in 1957. All that had occurred was that America had become somewhat more a "consumer" of security *vis-à-vis* the European members of NATO than before that time. In a word, the sputniks, and what they indicated about Soviet I.C.B.M.S.'s, raised the importance of NATO for America's *own* defence, as against that of her European allies, at least during the period for which it had to depend on what were officially called "diversified means of delivery." These diversified means included S.A.C. bombers and I.R.B.M.'s from NATO bases, S.A.C. bombers from home bases, and sea-borne missiles. The sense of the greater dependence of America was noted even by the most solidly pro-NATO opinion. *The Economist,* for instance, observed: "Once the Americans possessed a decisive superiority; then they had at least a half share in the balance of mutual terror; now they can avoid a period of perilous inferiority only if they can achieve a wide enough dispersal of the weapons they have."[1]

Four epochs of the nuclear age may be distinguished by 1960. The first, 1945-9, is of American monopoly and unilateral deterrence. The second, 1950-3, is of weakening unilateral deterrence, with a growing Soviet atomic stockpile, but a marked American superiority in the means of delivery. The third, 1954-7, is of bilateral deterrence, with effective parity in stockpiles on both sides, and growing Soviet efficiency in the means of delivery. The fourth, 1958-63 (?) is of saturation stockpiles and ambiguity between American or Soviet margin of superiority in the means of delivery: bilateral deterrence may still exist, but its basis is shaky, especially in the latter part of the period, the "missile gap," and this situation determines the nature of negotiations likely to be undertaken, as the earlier epochs had done in their time.

Between December 1957 and June 1958 discussions of the time, place, and agenda of a new summit conference were conducted without much apparent urgency on either side. Dulles's main insistence was on the necessity of adequate advance preparation of any such meeting either through Ambassadors or through a Foreign Ministers' meeting. This was hardly surprising, since neither President Eisenhower himself nor American opinion generally showed much relish for the idea of his being obliged to meet Khrushchev while the aftermath remained of the slight stroke which he suffered in November 1957. If the President showed in this period of his tenure of office a tendency to flee from policy-papers to the golf course, it was complemented by Dulles's liking for keeping the threads of American foreign policy firmly in his own hands, being negotiator-in-chief as well as policy formulator. In view of these attitudes of the two men, one might say at this time that actual decisions were likely to be made by the Secretary

---

[1] December 7, 1957.

of State rather than the President, and that therefore if the Russians had been anxious to negotiate rather than to make capital from advocacy of negotiations, a Foreign Ministers' conference might have proved the most promising medium. But Dulles had of course somewhat disqualified himself as a negotiator, and Russian diplomatists in Moscow insisted that their dislike and distrust of him was at the root of their objections to a Foreign Ministers' meeting,[2] though Khrushchev was reported to have said at a British Embassy party that it was Dulles himself who was blocking a meeting.[3]

The intensive exchange of unproductive notes at the beginning of the year, the heavy-handedness of the Russian replies, and the fact that they suggested an expansion of the meeting to accommodate Italy as well as the U.S.A., Britain, and France on the Western side, and Poland, Czechoslovakia, and Rumania on the Eastern, damped down the negotiating enthusiasm of the NATO powers a good deal, and the May meeting of the North Atlantic Council showed much less interest in the idea than that of the previous December, issuing a tough-minded communiqué to the effect that summit meetings were not the only, and not necessarily the best, means of conducting negotiations and reducing tension.[4]

Into this situation there erupted in July the *coup d'état* in Iraq, and the consequential American landing in Lebanon and British landing in Jordan. The one-month false start which followed, towards a new summit meeting on the Middle East, is among the most interesting episodes in this diplomatic *salle des pas perdus* since it shows the first working in the Communist camp of the factor which had long embarrassed the West: the intransigence of one member of the alliance.

When Khrushchev on July 19, in the wake of the British and American landings, called for a new summit meeting to discuss the Middle East, he may well have actually believed that inter-

---

[2] *The* (London) *Times*, February 4, 1958.
[3] *The New York Times*, June 14, 1958.
[4] *The* (London) *Times*, May 8, 1958.

vention in those countries might be a prelude to an effort at counter-revolution in Iraq. The tone of his note is of flaunted strength: ". . . you will know that the U.S.S.R. also has atom and hydrogen bombs, an air force and a navy and ballistic rockets of all types, including intercontinental ones."[5] No set of circumstances could have seemed less propitious as a summit background for America and Britain than those of July 1958: they must at best appear as dubiously reformed imperialists suddenly reasserting a demand that their writs should run in the Middle East, and possibly meditating the restoration in Iraq of an *ancien régime* that, whatever its actual merits, was not to the taste of the rising political class there. It was far less acceptable to the Americans than previous summit proposals since it was unprepared and offered very little prospect of successful negotiation. In fact, the prospect was of a summit trial for the West on a charge of "colonialism," with some embarrassing evidence in the shape of British and American troops actually in the countries concerned. The State Department was reported to blame the British for this embarrassment, and obviously "leaked" to selected Washington correspondents the information that "President Eisenhower has agreed to attend what he and his advisers profoundly and unanimously believe to be the wrong meeting at the wrong time and place on the wrong subject."[6] Dulles, after agreeing to a meeting, was reported to have had one of his bouts of second thoughts, and have settled on the view that, given luck and the election of a new President in the Lebanon, the crisis could be weathered without a meeting that would amount to official recognition of Russian interest in the Middle East. He was however obliged to acquiesce by the tone of Macmillan's letter to Khrushchev, and the necessity of avoiding the appearance of another rift with Britain.[7]

Considering how unpromising these circumstances were for the

---

[5] *The New York Times,* July 20, 1958.

[6] *The New York Times,* July 29, 1958.

[7] *The Economist,* July 26, 1958.

Western powers, it is notable how little diplomatic profit Russia was able to make from them. This was chiefly due of course to the attitude of China, but in part it must be put down to the initial Russian rashness of agreeing that the meeting should be held within the framework of the Security Council. Khrushchev had then hastily to withdraw this agreement, having apparently needed to be remainded by his Chinese allies in the course of his sudden visit to Peking at the end of July that in a Security Council meeting the place of the representative of China would be "occupied by the political corpse of Chiang Kai-shek."[8]

The episode was then allowed to peter out in the Special Assembly of mid-August 1958, which the Russians deprived of any summit quality by using Gromyko as their representative, though Eisenhower attended. The meeting had not even, from the Russian viewpoint, the merit of producing a resolution particularly unpalatable to the Western powers, and the final settlement owed less to Russian intervention than to Arab nationalism—a two-edged weapon, not necessarily any more conformable to Russian purposes in the Middle East than to Western ones.

On the whole, this particular episode served as an illustration that Dulles's automatic alarm and despondency when confronted with the prospect of meetings with the Communist *bloc* might be ill-founded. Western statesmen came more happily out of the encounter than Khrushchev. The West's protégés in Lebanon and Jordan were at least temporarily maintained against violent change. President Eisenhower's good-will speech at the Assembly had some success. Macmillan was enabled to face the election of the following year without having provided the Opposition with any electorally-appealing complaint against his foreign policy.[9] Khrushchev, on the other hand, had no cause for satisfaction with

---

[8] Soviet note of August 4, 1958: text in *Soviet News*, August 1958.

[9] See D. E. Butler and R. Rose: *The British General Election of 1959* (London: Macmillan & Co.; 1960), pp. 64–5, 71. Foreign policy was of little importance in the election. Even the mention of Suez came to be avoided by Labour speakers when it proved something of a boomerang.

these events, having allowed it to become clear that a serious
cleavage existed between himself and his Chinese allies and that
the Chinese had some power of veto on his diplomatic manœuvr-
ing, and having rather lost ground to the Arab nationalists in the
Middle East. He had reason to feel that he needed a compensa-
tory diplomatic success, and the drive for one may be seen in his
policy three months later.

There is a decisive difference between the final crisis that produced the summit meeting of May 1960 and all the earlier
"negotiation" pressures considered in the course of this study. It
was the first crisis in which Russian policy can be said to be that
of a revisionist rather than a *status quo* power. Earlier Russian demands for negotiation, whether at the summit or elsewhere, had
been based essentially on the wish to prevent something happening: to prevent the integration of West Germany into the Western camp, to prevent the E.D.C. treaty being ratified, to prevent
the W.E.U. being set up, to prevent Western intervention in
Iraq or Lebanon or Jordan. With the Berlin crisis of 1958–60 the
demand for negotiations arises for the first time from Soviet revisionism, from the Soviet demand for change in the status of Berlin.

It will be recalled that this particular episode began in November 1958 with notes from Khrushchev to the Western powers
calling for the establishment of a free city of West Berlin, and
threatening that if no agreement was reached within six months
he would sign a peace treaty with East Germany which would
terminate Western rights in Berlin. Whether the objective of this
move is judged to be the forcing of recognition of the East
German Government, or the forcing of Western troops and
officials out of Berlin, or the actual incorporation of Berlin into
the Soviet sphere, or if it is seen rather as a preliminary gambit
towards an eventual detachment of West Germany from NATO,
it must clearly be classed as revisionist. The Russians had good
reasons for wanting to end the role of Berlin as (until August 13,
1961) a shop window for the Western way of life, a forward
listening post, an escape hatch for dissentients in East Germany,

and as allowing West Germany something of the prestige of the capital. But aside from this, the geographical position of Berlin provided almost the perfect negotiating squeeze, with means of easy, controllable, adjustable pressure on the Western position through road, rail, and air communications. It was thus a potential lever for exerting pressure for a general settlement. Berlin might be "a bone in our throats" to the Russians, as Khrushchev said, but for the West it was an extended arm, eminently twistable.

In any case, once the "two Germanies" policy had hardened, Berlin was the anomaly most obviously needing to be tidied up, the factor most obviously militating against making any variety of tolerable success, even by satellite standards, of East Germany. Economically, there can be no doubt that the loss of manpower, especially young men of the professional and skilled-artisan classes was damaging to the East German state: Ulbricht claimed later that the training of those who eventually became escapees had cost the community 30,000,000,000 marks.[1] Politically, the effect of the exodus was more ambiguous: the drawing-off of freedom-minded persons, the natural leaders of resistance and revolt, might even be held to make the control of the people as a whole easier for the rulers of the state, but the loss of prestige involved in the sight of 200,000 a year of the citizens of the only people's democracy with an escape hatch voting with their feet for life in the capitalist jungle must be held to have outweighed this benefit.

The sealing-off of the eastern half of Berlin after August 13 may be seen from the Russian viewpoint as a substitute for a political settlement. Bearing in mind that the erection of the wall was begun only a few weeks after the Vienna discussion between Kennedy and Khrushchev, one could regard it as solid evidence that the President on that occasion successfully conveyed the unlikelihood of America's yielding to pressure for change in the status of West Berlin. There was a hint in *Neues Deutschland* about a fortnight before the wall went up that if diplomacy did

---

[1] *The Observer*, December 31, 1961.

not provide a settlement, another solution might be found. It
should be noted that, though the wall more or less ended the
"bone in our throat" aspect of Berlin of which Khrushchev had
complained, it did not modify the "twistable arm" aspect of the
city for the West, since that depends on the Western lines of
communication having to run through East German-controlled
territory or air space.

The wall, of course, reduced the political point of Berlin for
the Federal Republic: it was their advanced "presence" inside the
Soviet sphere, and a presence does rather need to be seen. Both
the morale of the Berliners, which has depended in part on a
lively sense of their own role as a token that Berlin might again
be the capital of a non-Communist Germany, and as a sort of
beacon in the surrounding Russian-dominated darkness, and the
morale of West Germans, to whom the wall has been chilling evidence of the reality and possible permanence of national division,
have been somewhat damaged. Strauss has spoken of the growth
of anti-American feeling.[2]

The usefulness of Berlin to the Russians as a general diplomatic
lever against NATO lies in the cleavage on national interests and
priorities on this issue between West Germany and the whole
of the rest of the alliance, including America. One may see this,
for instance, in attitudes to the proposal that the city might be
given a new status, under international guarantee, as a base for the
U.N. or some of its agencies. For the Western powers some such
arrangement could be useful: it would have at least the minimum
virtue of providing a plausible safeguard for the personal liberty
of West Berliners, which was their chief moral commitment in
the matter, and enabling them to withdraw with minimum loss
of face from a situation which was strategically untenable. But to
West Gemany and particularly to Dr. Adenauer's government,

---

[2] The New York Herald Tribune, October 1, 1961. The chief indication
of the state of morale in West Berlin is the movement of people and capital
from the city, on which the authorities concerned were not communicative,
but see the Sunday Times, October 29, 1961.

such a settlement would represent a staggering political and diplomatic defeat, the loss in effect of one of the *Länder* of the Federal Republic in which much hope and prestige, and a great deal of hard cash, had been invested.[3] Similarly, the diplomatic recognition of East Germany, which to the other Western powers was no more than a possible negotiating card, or a shrugging acceptance of the existing situation, would mean to Bonn the loss of one of the chief benefits of its adherence to the West (a benefit formalized in the 1954 agreements which preceded its entry into NATO), the status of being the sole legal and moral representative of Germany, the one voice legitimately entitled to speak as successor to the historic Reich. Even formal acquiescence in the Oder-Neisse Line, considered as a negotiating card, was attended by embarrassments underrated in the West for any German Government.

However, at the end of 1961 Khrushchev appeared less interested in Berlin from the point of view of its usefulness as a diplomatic lever between Germany and NATO than in the viability of the East German state. His speech to the 22nd Congress of the Soviet Communist Party, lifting the threat of a German peace treaty by the end of the year,[4] may perhaps be regarded as ending the 1960–1 season of this perennial crisis.

To revert to a more general conspectus of Russian attitudes, one may see the growth of a "two Germanies" policy (lightly disguised by talk of confederation) beneath the skin of the "neutralized Germany" policy as early as the Berlin Conference of 1954. Its progressive hardening is marked by statements from Khrushchev, as his remark of April 4, 1956, that German reunification was not necessary for world peace,[5] and his appeal in De-

---

[3] Estimates of the financial subsidy from West Germany to West Berlin vary from $500,000,000 to $1,000,000,000 a year. Of this, about $250,-000,000 was in direct support and $250,000,000 in payments of various sorts to Berliners, the remainder in preferential tax and other treatments for investment there. See *The New York Times,* October 15, 1961; *The Observer,* October 29, 1961.

[4] *The* (London) *Times,* October 18, 1961.

[5] *The New York Times,* April 5, 1956.

cember 1957: "Let us recognize the *status quo*."[6] By 1960, little pretence at interest in reunification, even with neutralization, is made. The Soviet Ambassador in Germany, when asked at a meeting of West German politicians whether Russia would accept a united Germany that was militarily neutral and reconciled to the Oder-Neisse Line, said no—it would have to be "peace-loving and democratic," obviously in the "peoples' democracy" sense. Though the Ambassador did not confirm this interpretation, Khrushchev himself did, in the interview he accorded Walter Lippmann in 1961, saying that he was prepared to see a united Germany—if it was a Communist Germany.[7]

A second factor that distinguishes the Berlin episode from the earlier Russian pressures for a summit meeting was the importance in it of the personal attitudes and political fortunes of the four statesmen most concerned. Macmillan's conviction that the Russian move was profoundly dangerous, perhaps more so than Khrushchev himself realized, shaped the first stage of the crisis. It led to his flight to Moscow in February to point out to Khrushchev that this threat, if persisted in, would create a situation of extreme peril. According to an account of the Moscow meetings given by a member of the British party present, Khrushchev at first refused to take this statement seriously and the Prime Minister had to repeat it three times at separate meetings before it made an impression. When he was brought to understand that his visitor meant what he said, Khrushchev reacted with a display of personal rage, and there occurred the episode which aroused a good deal of press speculation at the time, his abrupt cancellation, on a plea of tooth-ache, of his previously announced plan to accompany Macmillan on a trip to Kiev. But after Macmillan's return from this trip he was in a milder mood and agreed to a meeting of the Council of Foreign Ministers to consider the situation. The Foreign Ministers, meeting at Geneva in August, made enough progress to induce President Eisenhower at the Prime Minister's urging to send a message to

[6] Ibid., December 23, 1957.
[7] Quoted by Lippmann in a television programme, August 5, 1961.

Khrushchev saying that if a summit meeting eventuated, as seemed possible, Canada might be the most appropriate place for it, and that if Khrushchev wanted to visit the U.S.A. on his way back from the meeting, he would be a welcome guest.[8] Khrushchev then disconcerted the State Department considerably by replying blandly that he would be glad to accept this invitation but that there was no need to connect it with a summit meeting: he would come anyway.

Thus he secured, to the undisguised rage of many elements in the U.S. Administration, both the chance of a barnstorming tour of America and the prospect of bilateral talks with the U.S. Government. On the whole, however, the profits to Russia of this excursion were relatively slight. If Khrushchev hoped to practise in America the Leninist technique of appealing to the people over the heads of their government, he must have been disappointed by the results.[9] And the private talks with President Eisenhower at Camp David resulted actually in a concession by the Russians—temporary withdrawal of the time limit for negotiations over Berlin—without any particular reciprocal concession by the Western powers.

On later evidence it would seem that the sharpness underlying these discussions, and the general posture of American Administration opinion, may well have convinced Khrushchev that not much was to be hoped for from direct negotiation with America,

---

[8] This move was rather sourly regarded by the Foreign Office, as preventing an interim agreement.

[9] The author was in America at this time and had a good view both of Khrushchev and of the reaction of the American crowds to him at four points in his journey—Washington, New York, Los Angeles, and San Francisco. As far as a spectator could discern, Khrushchev began his journey ebulliently confident of his ability to make converts, and became progressively aggrieved and disillusioned. The crowds appeared motivated as much by hostility as curiosity, except perhaps in San Francisco, where they were merely curious. There is some confirmation of Khrushchev's disillusionment during the tour as to the receptivity of the American populace in the fact that Russian press treatment of the story grew abruptly colder about half way through the tour. See *The Observer*, October 27, 1959.

or between the four powers, at least until after the American presidential elections. This was not a reason for actually breaking off preparations for the summit meeting, since the attitude of one beseeching negotiations may obviously be far more diplomatically profitable than the negotiations themselves.

And if he had no particular reason to hurry on a summit meeting after Camp David, he was spared any effort to postpone it by the intransigence of de Gaulle, to whom the six months' delay between late 1959 and the final date of May 1960 must undoubtedly be attributed. A French Government spokesman made it clear in October[1] that the President was not only unenthusiastic about the project generally, but determined that the meeting should not be held until after the French atomic test and some consolidation of his position *vis-à-vis* the French Right-wing extremists in Algeria. This further reduced the importance of the meeting from any Russian viewpoint, since it meant that President Eisenhower would come to it at a time when the early stages of the American presidential elections were already under way, his two potential successors clearly visible, as it were, over his shoulder, his active life in politics practically at an end, his personal importance much reduced, and his ablity to make any kind of meaningful commitment for the United States approaching vanishing point.

And as though determined to extinguish any Russian interest in the meeting, Western spokesmen from December 1959 to April 1960 continually reiterated that there was to be no change in the Western position on Berlin,[2] and the press even indicated that there was some hardening of the Western mood as against the Foreign Minister's Conference of the summer of 1959, which had been envisaging an interim agreement with perhaps a limit on the number and armament of the troops, and other concessions. This

---

[1] See *Le Monde*, October 22, 1959.
[2] See speeches by Herter and Dillon in April (*The New York Times*, April 5 and 21, 1960) and a press conference by Eisenhower (*The New York Times*, April 28).

tougher attitude must be put down to the influence of Dr. Adenauer, who was opposed to any kind of new interim agreement on Berlin, regarding it as unlikely to do other than damage the West's position. He did not even want discussion of Berlin, and seems to have felt that the only subject that could safely be discussed at the summit was disarmament.[3] De Gaulle's temperament and France's stake in the role that "Europe of the Six" might play in the future power balance ensured strong French adhesion to the same viewpoint.

This is the situation against which the Russian decision to break off the summit conference must be seen. That is not to say that the U-2 aircraft incident, and the desire to inhibit further flights, were not of importance. Capacity to gather intelligence is now a more vital element in power relations than ever before in history, because of the enormous importance of the "first strike." Russia's ability to maintain secrecy about military movements and installations is thus an important element in the over-all balance of strategic advantage. To reduce the effectiveness of American military surveillance of Russia, by scaring off the allies who provide the bases that made it possible, would in itself have been a more important gain in terms of power positions than any concession at all likely to have been made at the May summit, if it had taken place. The use of political means to check the flights was obviously of particular importance if the military means available to the Russians were not altogether effective.[4]

But flights of this sort had been taking place for five years and had been known to the Russians at least since 1955, as Khrushchev himself said in his speech of May 9, without producing any demand that they be abjured by America before negotiation could take place. The importance given to the flight of May 1 clearly arose from the fortuitous conjunction of its providing a good reason for breaking off the meeting with a decision that the

---

[3] *The New York Times*, November 22, 1959.

[4] Khrushchev's speech of May 9, 1960, implied that on a similar flight a month earlier, Russian interception efforts had failed.

meeting itself offered few prospective advantages, and that its apparent failure would present more difficulties, in this particular instance, for Khrushchev than for the Western powers.

The Chinese dislike of the whole idea of the summit meeting was made obvious well before the U-2 incident. An intensive campaign against it was mounted in the Peking press late in April: the Russians were warned that there was "no change at all, even after the Camp David conference, even on the eve of the summit conference, in the war policy carried out by the United States and by Eisenhower personally" and were asked: "How would it help if this were to be covered up or white-washed?" The claim was repeated that nuclear war would destroy only imperialism, leaving the Communist powers "a truly beautiful future."[5] And aside from those in the Kremlin who thought like the Chinese, or thought at least that maintaining the Chinese alliance in good repair was more important than a *détente* with the West, one must bear in mind the possible influence exerted by representatives of the quarter-million officers who would have found themselves redundant if the more ambitious plans for arms reduction had been put into force.[6] All in all, Khrushchev may have had as little domestic room for manœuvre at this stage as Acheson had in 1952 or Dulles in 1953.

Breaking up the summit meeting was, in a sense, the one clear way to make a Russian success of it, once the U-2 incident had occurred. Adlai Stevenson remarked of this that Khrushchev may have wrecked the conference, but American policy handed him the crow-bar and chisel.[7] One might add that Mao Tse-Tung

---

[5] Quoted in *The Economist*, June 4, 1960.

[6] It may be noted that Khrushchev's speech of July 5, 1961, concerning the suspension of the intended cuts in armed forces, would appear to denote that these officers have won a reprieve, whether because of international events or because of effective internal pressures. Press comment linked Marshal Malinovski's prominence at Khrushchev's side in Paris with dismay of the officer corps at the prospect of being found surplus (*The New York Times*, May 19, 1960).

[7] *The* (London) *Times*, May 21, 1960.

appears to have put the power behind his elbow. In the circumstances, the initial period of the crisis, between May 5 and 12,
when Khrushchev seemed to be offering Eisenhower a handsome
opportunity to escape personal responsibility for the incident,
must be explained either by his clinging to a policy of *détente*
which he had undertaken against some opposition, or, more
cynically, by a determination to spin out the initial stages to the
point at which the *dénouement* could take place with an actual
confrontation of the President in Paris, and with the triumphal
final press conference at the Palais de Chaillot.

It seems more likely, however, that, in the fourteen days or so
between the shooting down of the plane on May 1 and his presenting of the humiliating and obviously unacceptable demands of
May 15 to the President, a genuine tussle took place between
Khrushchev and those who favoured some degree of *détente* with
America on the one hand, and the forces favouring the "hard
line" on the other. In the circumstances, the Russian proponents
of summitry would necessarily have had difficulty in making
it seem more profitable to persist with the meeting than to break
it off. If the meeting went on, no Western concessions on Berlin
appeared likely, and an official deadlock would confront Russia
with the choice of backing down on the threat of a separate
peace treaty with East Germany, which would be a diplomatic
defeat, or going through with it, which would deprive Russia of
the advantage of having the threat in hand for a more fruitful
future occasion, and would create a situation of uncertain dangers.
On the other hand, breaking off the meeting on the issue of the
U-2 not only represented a placatory move towards China, it enabled Russia to maximize irritation with American policy among
her European allies, and appeal emotionally to a good many
people to whom the flight would appear a flagrant provocation
with no basis either in law or necessity.

Thus the situation was prepared which President Eisenhower's
successor was to inherit in 1961. Ought one to assume that the
fact of a Russian approach for talks with President Kennedy the

moment he had been inaugurated[8] indicates a persistence or
revival of the *détente* policy, as against the "hard line," in the
Russian Government? Possibly, but if so the *détente* envisaged is
obviously of a very special sort. From both Kennedy's and
Khrushchev's respective reports on the talks in Vienna in May/
June 1961,[9] and also from reports leaked to correspondents by the
State Department,[1] it is quite clear that Russia was not prepared
to buy such a *détente* with any form of accommodation or concession, even of the most token variety. The very well informed
columnist James Reston conveys the astonishment of the American delegation at the explicitness with which Khrushchev indicates his belief that Kennedy had no alternative but to acquiesce
in the expansion, by means other than war, of the Soviet power
sphere.

This meeting in Vienna, though circumspection about feelings
in France and elsewhere kept it from being officially classed as a
summit meeting, was in fact closer to the original 1953 prescription for the summit than those of Geneva and Paris, since it
did amount to a private and businesslike confrontation of the
effective leaders of the dominant powers. Its nature makes clear
the direction of change in the intervening years. The progress, if
that is the word, is from the hope of negotiation to acceptance
of the necessity of communication. Kennedy's report makes this
point strongly: "I think we reduced the possibility of misjudgment. . . . No advantage or concession was either gained or
given . . . both of us were there, I think, because we realized that
each nation has the power to inflict enormous damage on the
other . . . and that care should thus be taken to prevent our
conflicting interests from so confronting each other that war
necessarily ensued." Even communication is conceded to be diffi-

---

[8] Or even before. The Russian Ambassador in Washington was said to
have begun informal approaches early in January 1961 (The *New York
Herald Tribune*, January 10, 1961; *The* (London) *Times*, January 5, 1961).
[9] The text of Kennedy's report in *The New York Times*, June 7, 1961,
and of Khrushchev's in *Soviet News*, June 17, 1961.
[1] See *Guardian*, June 10, 1961.

cult: "The Soviets and ourselves give wholly different meanings to the same words: war, peace, democracy and popular will . . . we have wholly different concepts of where the world is and where it is going." This difficulty of communications between the spokesmen of two theories of society was even more precisely illuminated by reports of a lunch-time conversation. Khrushchev explained earnestly that when he had remarked recently to Walter Lippmann that the Rockefeller family controlled President Kennedy he was using the Rockefeller name to indicate the American rich generally; Kennedy's effort to dissuade him from this view of American society was apparently to retort: "Not one of those men contributed to my campaign."[2]

It might be noted in passing that the necessity of establishing direct communication with the actual chief decision-maker in Soviet society, and the fear that if this were not done war would arise through miscalculation, appears to have been the dominant impulse behind Macmillan's efforts to promote not only the summit meeting of May 1960, but a whole "range of summits," i.e., meetings "every eight or nine months."[3] He further emphasized in his Guildhall speech of November 15, 1959, that what he chiefly hoped from the May meeting was that it would arrange another: "We should in our parliamentary jargon adjourn and ask leave to sit again."[4] And he told the Kremlin banquet that he addressed in Moscow that the gravest danger of war was from miscalculation.[5]

The sense that change in the relations of power has changed the setting for negotiation is ominous in Khrushchev's report to the Vienna meeting. "Evidently they [the Western powers] forget that times are different now. . . . Even in the past the 'positions of strength' policy was useless against the Soviet Union but now it is more than ever doomed to failure. . . . We have what is necessary to defend our interests."

---

[2] The *New York Herald Tribune*, June 16, 1961.
[3] See an interview which he gave to the *Daily Express*, January 1, 1960.
[4] *The* (London) *Times*, November 17, 1959.
[5] *Soviet News*, June 17, 1961.

Even more visibly than in the case of Berlin, the initial stages of the Cuban crisis of October 1962 showed the Russian transition from a *status quo* to a revisionist negotiating stance, clearly reflecting an assumption that the balance of power had swung far enough to favour such enterprises. Yet in this piece of adventurism the effective power relations between Russia and the West proved precisely the reverse of those in Berlin. The local conventional military balance was overwhelmingly in favour of America: Cuba indeed is deeper inside the American power sphere than Berlin is inside the Soviet power sphere. Thus, once the President had indicated determination to use his local conventional strength (in this case naval forces), Khrushchev was faced with the choice between a diplomatic backdown, an ineffective and dangerous local resistance (by the Russian ships involved), or raising the stakes to general nuclear war. The point of perplexity becomes why he chose ground so disadvantageous. No doubt there are possible answers involving relationships inside the Communist camp. But it may also be observed that the potential winnings must have seemed worth the gamble, even given the odds against success. If it had come off, if the President had been overpreoccupied with the election campaign or slow to react for some other reason, and the missile base had been made complete and operational, the episode would have constituted a triumph for Khrushchev. Even the ranks of Tuscany drawn up in Peking could scarce have forborne to cheer. For it would have meant that he had parlayed the Russian influence in Cuba, in less than four years, into a negotiable asset that could quite reasonably be bargained against the Western position in Berlin, and used to shake the whole American alliance structure. Kennedy once exclaimed to Gromyko: "You have offered to trade us an apple for an orchard!"[6] Cuba may be called the perfect exemplification of how to grow your apple for this kind of diplomacy.

---

[6] *The New York Times*, October 7, 1961.

"*Si Monumentum Requiris*"

Tʜᴇ sᴛʀᴀɴᴅ of historical experience with which this study has been concerned may be interpreted in a number of ways: it may be regarded at one untenable extreme as chiefly an illustration of how two competing alliances may be bound to the policy purposes of their most vulnerable members, or at another extreme as an illustration of the progress of a policy through the stages of ambition, distraction, approximation, and supersession, as a study in cross-purposes and the political uses of illusion, an example of how wide the gap may be between declared policy and what is actually done, and of how much more important in politics than intention is what Fisher called the play of the contingent and the unforeseen. Most of the criticism of "negotiation from strength" as a slogan has been based on the belief that it was no more than a rationalization of a dislike and distrust of negotiation: that negotiation was never seriously intended. This study has hoped to show that it might also have been attacked on the ground that strength was no more seriously sought than negotiation: that no adequate effort was made to provide a military establishment commensurate with the ambitions implied. The search for an ideal military posture is the

enemy of negotiation, as Kennan has said. In this case it has been
the enemy also of an *effective* military posture.

Before attempting a more detailed analysis of the meaning of
this strand in the history of the past ten years, something should
be said of a possible rebuttal of the criticism just made. The most
persuasive justification of the phrase is usually couched in terms
like these. In a Western political system, with an opposition
necessarily seeking at regular intervals to outbid the government
politically, it was impossible for either party to offer the electorate,
in foreign policy, merely the prospect that by running as fast as it
could it would stay in the same place relatively to the Russians,
even if this had in fact been the case (which is doubtful) and
even if it had been perceived to be the case in 1950 (which would
have required an ability to see farther through a brick wall than
most people can). And even if this had been, and had been perceived as, the reality of the power relationship, the electorate
cannot stand very much reality, and alliances work the better for
some official pious hope, even if nobody really pays much heed
to it. It fulfils much the same function for the NATO statesman
as the theory of the last judgment does for the elect: no one expects the actual event to be just around the corner, but even the
sceptic may concede that the impact of the idea on behaviour is
probably in the right direction. Thus one can say that to examine
the phrase "negotiation from strength" in respect to actual negotiation or actual strength is to miss the point, and to set the phrase
in the wrong universe of discourse. The right framework for it is
not the relations between America and Russia but the relations
of government and opposition in a Western electorate. And, the
apologist might add, if you judge "negotiation from strength"
simply as a foreign-policy ideal to put before the electorate, you
must concede that it has had at least the merits, first, of dividing
the NATO alliance less than any other official aspiration would
have done and, second, of reducing the appeal of two far more
dangerous ideas, negotiating from weakness, which means appeasement and which might have left the West's final position

even weaker than it is today, or adventuristic aspirations of the "preventive war" kind. In other words, in an epoch in which negotiation did not offer any reasonable prospects of an actual improvement of the Western situation, a stand-pat attitude was probably the least dangerous one. But this kind of sophisti-cated Micawberism in foreign policy must be presented to the electorate veiled in a hopeful vagueness. Hence the use of phrases like "negotiation from strength."

Some substance must be conceded to the argument about the inevitability of an official myth for NATO, and the difficulty of finding any other phrase that fitted the requirements of the alliance so well. But any justification couched in terms of this sort must be judged against the fact that the central reality of international politics is relative strength and the accommodations (of which negotiation is the formal expression) that it makes necessary and possible. So that even if one dismissed "negotiation from strength" as a harmless, necessary, public-relations-man's phrase, one would be left with the successive variations in the strength relationship, and the consequent modifications of atti-tudes to settlement, as the most significant aspect of the relation of Russia and America in the period under review. And since this central relationship determines other relationships, as that be-tween bowler and batsman determines the placing of the field in cricket, so the variation in strength and the attitudes to negotia-tion of these powers would still be the central element in the history of the period.

In any case, the phrase had an actual correlative in the sphere of policy. As has been pointed out, its evolution corresponded to a period when very important decisions were in fact being made about the process of strength-building in the West. At least as far as strength-building was concerned, the trouble was not so much that there was no such policy as that the policy was not successful. Disregarding for the moment any difficulties inherent in the idea itself as a general concept in diplomacy, and concen-trating on factors peculiar to the ten years under review, we can say that the failure had three parts—failure in two efforts at strength, and in the choice of a time for negotiation.

This view must depend, of course, on an implied assumption that the prospects for actual negotiation were less good at the end of the ten years' process than at the beginning. Further arguments on this point will be adduced later, but for the present an adequate *prima facie* case may perhaps be made simply by comparing the negotiating position of the West in the first Berlin crisis of 1948–9 and that in the second Berlin crisis of 1958–61. The element that has been irretrievably lost from the Western negotiating position is the consciousness on both sides of the relative physical invulnerability of America—the consciousness that it could not be knocked out since the bases of its strength were beyond the effective reach of Russia, and that there was therefore no prospect of Russian success in general war if either party chose to push the situation to that point. This condition no longer holds good, and it is by this measure that the general Western negotiating position is the worse, not the better, for the ten years' lapse of time.

Let us look first at the failure of the "posture of strength" side of the policy. The nature of this failure should not be minimized, since it was achieved in the teeth of the West's actual advantages —advantages, in the first or conventional-forces phase of population and militarily disposable population, of coal, steel, oil, and power production, and a failure in the second or missile phase despite the advantage of a higher general level of technological accomplishment.

The most optimistic summation of the cause of these failures would hold that it was a matter of deficient political leadership, especially in the period 1953–60. This would be an optimistic view, because political leadership is the one element in Western societies which may be changed relatively easily. More pessimistically, one might conclude that the difficulty was in the nature of Western political institutions (a pessimistic view since these are not easily changed) or the absence of any institution for joint political decision by the NATO powers.

The most depressing of the possible explanations would see the reason in the fact that the West is committed to a pluralistic decision-making process. The usual phrase is democracy, but this rather obscures the nature of the phenomenon. There may be pluralistic societies which are not democracies, and there are times when democracies, alarmed for a short time into a strong national consensus, cease to be pluralistic. But in general a viable definition of a free society would have to include the notion of the national scale of priorities being set pluralistically, by a multitude of tiny individual decisions, rather than centrally.

If this were the whole truth, it would imply that a pluralistically-deciding society could never compete with a centrally-deciding society except in periods when a crisis has in fact established a strong consensus. In the past this has tended to be after the outbreak of war or when war was already inevitable. In the days when one could go on losing a war for the first three years and still win in the end, this was not necessarily fatal. But things are different now, since *all* the decisions relevant to winning or losing a war must be made in time of peace. The staying power of the democracies under fire is no longer an important element of national strength. One should by no means discount the degree of disadvantage that this entails for the Western powers. It may well be mortal.

From the vantage point of hindsight, the months from early 1952 to mid-1953 look like the best negotiating time for the West, at least judged on the basis of relative strength. This period saw perhaps the most promising-looking "mix" of military strength actually attained *vis-à-vis* Russia. The Russians, it is true, must have had by then a fair stockpile of atomic bombs, but there is no indication that they had adequate means of delivery against America. Their first small show of long-range aircraft was not until about a year later. The invulnerability of the American home base, whose knocking-out was the basic condition of a successful war for Russia, was still assured. On the other hand, the sense of psychological nakedness, produced by the absence of conventional forces in Europe, which plagued the period of Western atomic monopoly, had been somewhat remedied by the growth of NATO conventional forces. There was no great military improvement for the West in terms of relative strength on the Central Front for some years after late 1952, since, though the quality of the Western divisions doubtless improved, there was a parallel improvement in Russian forces. Moreover, in 1952–3 NATO was just past the best period of its growth: its most ambitious forces goals had recently been proclaimed, and the limits of its potential were by no means as clear as they had become eighteen months later. Greece and Turkey had just acceded; the E.D.C. still looked a real possibility (the treaty was signed in May 1952). America's forces were still at their post-Korean peak. If NATO could have maintained the growth rate of 1951 for even a year longer, it might have become quite a formidable instrument. And Europe was psychologically on the upswing; the United Europe movement still had the immediate post-war impetus behind it.

August 1953 ought to represent the point at which actual success (as against survival) in war against America appeared as a possibility in Russian military calculations, since at that time success with the H-bomb was assured, and success with missiles at least visible over the horizon. Hence this date appears a logical terminal point for any concessionary negotiations by Russia. It may be objected that what appeared in August 1953 was not actual present strength but the prospect of it. But the whole moral of negotiation from strength, on the Western side, is that expectations about the future, rather than the realities of the present, determine attitudes to negotiation, and there is no reason to suppose that on this point Russian psychology would show much difference from Western. One is of course venturing on very speculative ground if one attempts to define with any precision the tract of time during which the exclusion of West Germany from the military strength of NATO appeared worth the loss of East Germany to the Russians. On military grounds, as has been said, August 1953 would appear the logical terminal date, but bearing in mind the June 1953 rising in East Germany and what that indicated about the prospects of the "political education" that the East Germans had received being of advantage to Russia in the future chances of a reunified Germany, one might move the date backward a month or two. On the other hand, Ulbricht in November 1961 interestingly accused both Beria and Malenkov of "advocating a policy of capitulation to imperialism" with regard to East Germany,[1] that is, presumably, favouring a diplomatic compromise with the West. If evidence from this source is to be regarded as of any value, it ought to mean that the period of compromise settlement might be extended forward until Malenkov's star began to wane, in the summer of 1954.

This line of reasoning would put the greater part of the optimum Western negotiating period into Stalin's lifetime. Is this an insuperable obstacle to acceptance of it? Is it clear that his successors have proved more promising as *vis-à-vis* for the West in diplomatic discussions? Looking at Stalin's policy against eight years' experience of Khrushchev's, one is struck chiefly by how limited, prudent, cautious, and willing to settle for partial gains Stalin appears, as against the sense of world (not just European) revolutionary destiny that informs Khrushchev's policy. There was no equivalent until October 1962 for Khrushchev of Stalin's 1946 retreat over Iran, or his 1949 acceptance of defeat on Berlin.[2] And though the "collective leadership" wound up the war in Korea, it was Stalin who initiated in June 1951 the policy of acceptance of stalemate and compromise there. In Marxist terms, one might say that Stalin's tendency was towards "opportunism" —i.e., to over-estimate the odds against success, as for instance in his estimate of the chances in respect of both the Chinese and the Yugoslav revolutions. Khrushchev's temperament ap-

---

[1] *Guardian*, November 29, 1961.

[2] This judgment was made during the Cuban crisis of October 1962. At the moment of writing, Khrushchev's withdrawal of missiles from Cuba appeared fully and directly parallel to Stalin's tacit concessions of a defeat on points in these earlier rounds of the Cold War.

pears far more sanguine and impulsive: to again use a Marxist term, he might be charged with "adventurism," i.e., a tendency to underestimate the odds against success. One can see this in the initial stages of the second Berlin crisis, and especially on Cuba, and it is obviously a quality that carries real danger of war through miscalculation. Again, it might be said that Stalin was more cynical and more inflexible than Khrushchev. But if he was the more cynical, he was therefore the more likely to sacrifice "the gains of the revolution" in East Germany for Russia's national advantage. And if he was the more inflexible he would be therefore the more apprehensive of German power and the more likely to pay a price for German neutralization. After all, throughout Stalin's life as an active political leader, Germany was the major problem of Russian foreign policy— from the ferocious treaty of Brest-Litovsk to the rise of Hitler and the just-warded-off near-defeat of 1942. With these memories to wince over, it seems unlikely that Stalin could have adapted himself as readily as Khrushchev to a situation in which Germany is a comparatively minor and manipulable issue in Russian foreign policy. It is perhaps hardly worth considering the popular supposition that the concept of "peaceful co-existence" only entered Russian policy with the death of Stalin. It was of course employed by Stalin whenever it seemed likely to prove useful, from the twenties on.

Much has been made of the change in the spirit of Russian government after Stalin's death, with the implication that the "liberalization" of the regime internally somehow made diplomatic accommodation with it more easily possible. But this does not necessarily follow: on the contrary, greater popularity on the part of a government *vis-à-vis* its own people may give it a more assured basis for buoyancy and adventurousness abroad. Except for the somewhat confused period between Stalin's death and the fall of Beria, a period during which Russian foreign policy certainly showed some uncertainty and effort to placate the outside world, the dominant difference between foreign policy under Stalin and policy since his time has been its greater degree of self-confidence and willingness to take risks. Nor is it at all self-evident that the substitution of some degree of competition for power, in Khrushchev's time, for the fairly secure monopoly of power that Stalin apparently enjoyed for the last few years of his life was necessarily likely to result in the putting forward of milder and more peaceful foreign-policy aspirations. To cite an obvious Western parallel, did the competition for power between Republicans and Democrats in 1952 encourage the putting forward of milder and more peaceful foreign-policy aspirations? On the contrary, it produced in "liberation" the most intransigent if also the least viable of American aspirations in the period under review. It is of course frequently argued that the competition for popular support in Russia results in more emphasis on consumer goods and thus an economy less geared to power. But the first exponent of this approach was Malenkov, and it cannot be said to have served him well. "Consumer sovereignty" in either a political or an economic sense is low in Russia, and the whole ethos of the society is directed towards future Utopias rather than present comforts. And of course the domestic competition for power is partly determined by the competition between Russia and China for leadership of the Communist *bloc.*

Surely the true reason for the usual assumption that negotiation was more possible with Stalin's successors than with Stalin himself is the unconscious importation into the argument of the "domestic change" rather than the "diplomatic adjustment" thesis? That is, that a more "liberal" Russia somehow acquired different diplomatic interests? And this in turn, as was noted before, is related to a theory of the causation of war that sees it as inherent in the nature of individual states (in this case the Stalinist tyranny) rather than in the nature of the relation between states—a morally comfortable view since it means that the only changes necessary for peace are those to be made by the other side.

Actually, there was a real and massive reason why negotiation was impossible in 1952 and 1953, but it related to the West, not

Russia: the American Presidential election. The inauspicious sign
of Yalta hung over the Democrats in 1952; the memory of their
own election campaign hung over the Republicans in 1953. Probably a "cube law" could be worked out in international politics
as in psephology to show that the number of political obstacles
to negotiation by an alliance is equal to the cube of the number
of major members of that alliance. It is always an inconvenient
time politically for one or the other.

One should not assume any abrupt change, of course, in
Russian policy. In 1954 Molotov was still prepared to work hard,
diplomatically, to block the E.D.C., and possibly even to make
actual concessions to that end. There may be an element of truth
in the interpretation of the success of the 1954 Geneva conference
in producing a truce in Indo-China as representing a Russian aim
of maintaining M. Mendès-France in office in the hope that he
would put the E.D.C. to the Assembly, and that it would be
defeated. One must contrast the assiduity with which the Russians appeared to seek the exclusion of Western Germany from
the Western military *bloc* in 1954 with their apparent unconcern
with any dangers from that source in 1955, as exemplified by
Bulganin's bland snub to Eden when the question of a guarantee
of Russia against Germany was brought up at Geneva. From
1955 to 1961, and especially since 1957, Soviet foreign policy may
be said to have shown a steady growth of the robust self-confidence already audible at the first summit meeting. Naturally
enough, since if any agreement was reached at Geneva in 1955
it was a tacit one to the effect that the Great Powers acknowl-
edged a common interest in avoiding the use of general nuclear
war to settle conflicts among themselves. The logical correlative
of this, however, was not that conflicts would necessarily be
settled by negotiation, but that they could safely be brought to
a higher degree of exacerbation by other means.

The balance of terror, if it is assumed to be stable, clearly
makes successful negotiation less likely, rather than more likely. If
the incentive to agreement in international politics is the fear of

the consequences of disagreement, then the down-grading of this fear must also down-grade the prospect of agreement. Of course there are other conceivable motives for agreement: for instance, a sense that the fabric of the society of state is legitimate and necessary to be preserved, and that therefore an obligation rests on individual states to avoid behaviour that will damage it. But this motive entails a belief that the state order and its members are legitimate and should be preserved—and Russia does not share the first of these views nor America (as regards Russia and China) the second. The understanding is simply that general war will not be contemplated for diplomatic interests of the order of importance which have produced it in the past. In Walter Lippmann's words: "Dulles said on Thursday that as a result of Geneva the diplomatists can now practice diplomacy without fear of war. Among the Geneva powers at least, this means that they are, as it were, disarmed: they do not have to make concessions and they cannot enforce their demands."[3] This remained valid as long as the operation of the "balance of terror" was symmetrical, but whether it continued so after that time is open to doubt.

We have now to consider the central puzzle of this entire historical episode: were there in fact any genuine "negotiable issues" between the West and the Communist powers during the ten years under review? In a sense it will never be possible to answer this question categorically, since it entails an estimate of intention, which cannot be finally known: certainly not for Russia and perhaps not even for the Western powers, since there were so many assorted and disparate intentions involved in the West.

It may be useful in this situation to endeavour to define the nature of negotiation more closely than has hitherto been attempted, and thus to isolate what might at least theoretically be expected to be the negotiable issues. The essential element that distinguishes negotiation from general diplomatic discussion is surely the putting forward by either side of propositions that may

---

[3] The *New York Herald Tribune*, July 1955.

seriously be expected to lead to an agreement on a specific issue. Each party to a bargain may be said to have an optimal and a minimal level of hopes with respect to the settlement: an "asking price" and an "accepting price." If we call the area within these two levels the "bargaining zone" of each of the parties, then we may say that true negotiation (as against preliminary discussion) only occurs when one side puts forward proposals which lie within or on the border of the bargaining zone of the other. The preliminary discussions are of course not necessarily purely for the record: they may be essential to discover where the "bargaining zone" of the other party is. One of the factors which unfortunately distinguishes diplomatic bargaining from industrial bargaining (or ordinary bargaining over the sale of a house or a car) is that there is no convention or ruling market rate which sets the limits of the bargaining zone of each party.

The aim of negotiation is a formalized accommodation of wills and/or interests on particular matters. The notion of formalization must be stressed since (though this is often lost sight of) diplomatic accommodations of various sorts do take place by other means than formal negotiation—by default, by tacit acquiescence, or by the mere lapse of time. One may say, for instance, that the Munich agreement was a formalized accommodation of wills, whereas in the episodes of the remilitarization of the Rhineland and the German invasion of Czechoslovakia in March 1939 there was an accommodation by default or by tacit acquiescence. Formal negotiation is indeed perhaps one of the rarer means of accommodation of wills in diplomacy, and it has one quality which made it more difficult than other modes of settlement for the West (or at least for America) in the decade under consideration. It requires an element of belief that a legitimate bargain may be struck. Now the forces which delimit the area of legitimacy in diplomatic bargaining at any particular moment for any particular people are complex, and probably slightly different for each of the fifteen members of NATO, but there can be no doubt that in this question the decisive limits were the American ones, which are still set by Wilsonian concepts of national self-determination. Therefore, most of the conceivable bargains in Central and Eastern Europe which would have been acceptable to Russia have not had and cannot for the foreseeable future acquire the element of legitimacy as far as America is concerned. This applies to all bargains formally accepting the *status quo* in the area.

Negotiations on disarmament obviously do not suffer from this disability: indeed disarmament is one of the few concepts in international politics which is agreed as legitimate by the whole spectrum of political opinion, from far Right to far Left. But disarmament was the least likely of subjects for agreement in the ten years under review. One of the main characteristics of the period, after all, was the asymmetry of the military establishments of the two contending powers, and the effort that each was making to reach equality with the other in the sphere in which it was at a disadvantage. The central problem of disarmament is the problem of equalizing advantage at each stage. It is difficult enough to convince the parties concerned that they are not being unfairly disadvantaged by any particular proposal even when their defence establishments are similar in structure. The problem becomes insuperable when the two defence establishments are unlike. This problem may seem to have become of less importance towards 1960, as the American and Russian defence establishments became similar, but it still existed in one respect which was enormously important from the point of view of the disarmament discussions—that of secrecy. Effective inspection must necessarily mean loss of secrecy, and while the differential advantage on this side is as great for Russia as it is at present, the probability of Russian agreement to systems of inspection and control is clearly very slight. On the other hand, the prospect of American agreement to any system *not* involving effective inspection and control is obviously nil, since any such system would be regarded in America as promoting insecurity, not security. If America could contrive to become as difficult a field for Russian military intelli-

gence as Russia is for American military intelligence, inspection might seem as advantageous to Russian generals as it does to the Pentagon. But America, as an open society, must continue to suffer from the inconveniences of its virtues. A difficulty even less likely to disappear, as far as disarmament is concerned, lies in the fact that more than ever before in history the chance of defeat or victory depends on arms-in-being at the beginning of a war.

The merit of the assorted disengagement proposals that emerged after 1955 was that they met, on the whole, the criterion of legitimacy, and showed signs of being adaptable to meeting the criterion of equalized advantage. They offered something to negotiate "away" as well as something to negotiate "from." And most of them were inextricably connected with the most obviously "negotiable" element in the Western position which was both legitimate and substantial enough to serve as a possible *quid pro quo* for Russian advantages in Eastern Germany: the West German military contribution to NATO. But as has been pointed out, official Western policy from September 1950 was based on the view that this must *not* be regarded as a negotiable asset, even in the period up to 1956 when the German armed forces existed only potentially, not actually. Thus the particular concept of strength-building officially adopted, even though it was not realized in actuality for most of the period under review, excluded the most genuinely negotiable issue. There is a strong tongue-in-cheek air about Western proposals for German reunification after September 1950, since the likelihood of Russian acquiescence in the basic Western precondition of agreement —Germany's ability to adhere to the West—was obviously discounted even as the proposals were put forward. And quite aside from the Russian attitude, which has been discussed, there is a second sense in which the lapse of time may be said to have perhaps foreclosed this possibility. The governing concept of what is a legitimate bargain in this field has more and more, since 1955, come to be the German one.

However, the immediate issues in dispute between America

and Russia—the points on which negotiation might have been undertaken—are related to the real cause of their quarrel as the one eighth of an iceberg that shows above the surface is related to the seven eighths below. Not that the visible one eighth is unimportant: it provides a market for the area of danger, and its configuration tells one something about the bulk of the issues attached to it. Issues like Berlin are obviously not only important in themselves but important as psychological rallying points. The *status quo* is physically expressed in a number of territorial arrangements, and a demand to change one of them is heavy with psychological significance. But the real tension is over the power relationship between the two states. This is not so pointless a contest as it may seem: each is in a real sense the author of the other's insecurity by the mere fact of its existence and power. The sovereign state, like other organisms, seeks to better its own environment so that it may flourish in security. When that environment offers only one substantial immediate possible cause for apprehension, as is the case for both America and Russia, the prescription for foreign policy is obvious. This would perhaps be true even if it were not for the ideological differences between them, but ideology adds to the reasons for the quarrel. As Niemeyer has said (in *Orbis*, summer 1957):

Each sees the other's aspirations as a threat to itself, and begrudges the other the power it now enjoys. . . . Each states its objectives in terms obviously unacceptable to the other. Each regards the other's power as a denial of its most basic values, a threat to its social order, and a death-warrant for its leaders.

The influence of this factor of competition about the over-all distribution of power on the chances of peace or war may best be understood by analysis of relationship of revisionist and *status quo* elements in the foreign policies of America and Russia. Each must be at present accounted both a revisionist and a *status quo* power. (The term revisionist is used in the simple meaning of "desiring change," not necessarily with any pejorative overtones.)

There is a stronger unconscious element of revisionism in American foreign policy attitudes than Americans themselves are usually prepared to perceive. This revisionism is nothing so crude as a demand for hegemony: it is best expressed in a phrase the author encountered in Washington, the idea of the "compatible world"—and that means compatible as much with American principles as with American interests. In the words of an influential policy-maker, Paul Nitze, American policy "has challenged Soviet policy not merely at a series of geographical points but over-all and in its essence" since "United States interests and United States security have become directly dependent on the creation and maintenance of some form of world order compatible with our combined development as the kind of nation we are and believe ourselves capable of becoming."[4]

Historically the American mood and the American intellectual tradition about the relationship between force and diplomacy or the military and the civil power have exhibited some sharp variations. On the whole, American tradition has been rather less pacific when any kind of genuine American interest was involved than it is sometimes represented as being. Or, rather, one may say that there are several American traditions of thought (as there are several English ones) and that Teddy Roosevelt is rather more in the mainstream than Cordell Hull. There is a notable contrast between the liberal-pacifist-isolationist mood of the twenties and thirties or of the prelude to World War I, which strove to ignore the relation of military strength to diplomacy, and the present situation, when the main intellectual effort of American political scientists seems to be going into an effort to work out a coherent theory of this relationship.

Negotiation from strength, if it is to be taken seriously and literally, can only mean an effort to improve the balance of military power, and to use your new position to seek a new *status quo*

---

[4] "Coalition Policy and the Concept of World Order," in Wolfers, ed.: *Alliance Policy in the Cold War* (Baltimore: Johns Hopkins Press; 1959), pp. 16 ff.

of a more satisfactory sort. It must therefore clearly be classed as a revisionist policy, even though the revision is to be through diplomatic leverage rather than the use of force. But there was an obvious incongruity between this basically revisionist aspiration and the military establishment planned to back it, which even at the most ambitious point of planning was not intended to be within leagues of the sort of strength required to back a serious revisionism in Europe—and actuality of course fell short of intention. This was even more clearly the case from 1953. A revisionist foreign policy is obviously incompatible with a defence establishment geared only to deterrence, since the essential quality of the deterrent strategy is that it supposes *reaction*, not initiative. A *priori*, it might have been said that one could take seriously the policy of deterrence or the policy of negotiation from strength, but not both. And when military policy is incompatible with diplomatic policy, one must recall that military policy is embodied in an actual military establishment, whereas diplomatic policies frequently have no more embodiment than the speeches in which they are set forth. In these circumstances, not surprisingly, it tends to be the military policy which makes itself good.

Even if, for the moment, one discards the notion of deterrence as a euphemism, or an unproven assumption, and regards the Western military establishment as being based on the policy of the nuclear strike, which theoretically might serve as the sanction of either a revisionist or a *status quo* diplomacy, the obstacles to taking American revisionism seriously are still very great. Faced with a clear prospect of encroachment on its sphere of power by a dangerous enemy, a nation may stake its survival on resistance to that encroachment, even if it is not a very great one, especially in a period in which the memory of Munich has been invoked unceasingly to prove that whenever anything is conceded, everything is lost. But a rich and happy country (like America) will not stake much for the hypothetical advantages of increasing its sphere of power. The prospect of loss is a stronger motive in international affairs, as in individual ones, than the hope of gain. This may not be logical, but it is reasonable enough. The powerful forces of anger and immediate fear reinforce calculation when loss is in question: where it is a matter of gain only a remoter fear can be enlisted to aid calculation, and a heavy inertia exists to dampen its schemes. A revisionist policy likely to incur any serious *costs*, even in the form of conventional warfare, would be difficult for a prosperous democracy to contemplate, still more difficult for one with America's constitutional arrangements. A revisionist policy backed solely by a power of nuclear strike would surely be possible only in a pathological state of political opinion among both the leaders and the led.

And, aside from these obstacles to taking seriously any revisionist intentions theoretically implicit in American policy, there is the fact that even if they had been wholehearted they could not have been put into operation without disintegrating NATO. Britain, France, and the minor powers would all have dissented from any true revisionism. Europeans as a whole had at best a more ambivalent attitude than Americans to the possibility of German reunification, and a firmer determination not to take risks or incur costs on its behalf. In the nature of things, the ability of an alliance to pursue a common policy is limited and conditional: limited and conditioned by the behaviour of the putative enemy, the lowest common denominator of individual cost, and the highest common factor of individual interest.

In view of these reasons for discounting, as far as action was concerned, the revisionism of American policy, it may seem unlikely that the rulers of Russia should interpret "negotiation from strength" *au pied de la lettre*. But whether or not they privately discounted the policy (at least after 1952-3), it was found on occasion a useful stick to beat the Western powers with, as in this passage from one of Khrushchev's speeches:[5]

---

[5] Published in *Soviet News*, December 23, 1957.

It is a fact that the essence of the imperialist "policy of strength" is to force the Soviet Union to accept the demands of the Western countries—demands having the character of ultimatums—and to "settle" certain political issues on terms which would be to the imperalists' advantage. . . . We say to the representatives of the Western countries and in the first place the United States: Throw your unreasonable and sufficiently compromised "positions of strength" policy on the rubbish heap of history, where it belongs.

Let us look now at the revisionist element in Russian policy, and determine whether it is affected in the same way as American revisionism by the present power balance. It should hardly be necessary to make the point that Russian policy is, in aspiration, revisionist *à l'outrance* in that it does contemplate, and has contemplated ever since the Bolshevik capture of power in 1917, not only an ultimate total remaking of the power map of the world, but a transformation of the nature of the whole society of states, and that it regards victory in this enterprise as inevitable and foreordained.

On the other hand, Russian leaders are not committed to pursue their revisionist aims by military force, to export revolution on the bayonets of the Red Army. Where they have done this, as in Eastern Europe, it has been incidental to military operations undertaken on a different basis, i.e., in the protection of Russian national interests, though they will clearly, as in Hungary, maintain by military force the enlarged sphere of power thus acquired.

One must class Russia therefore as essentially a revisionist power, with reservations as to the methods of her revisionism. Can one also detect *status quo* elements in her policy? There is one obvious sense in which she is a *status quo* power in Eastern Europe, the sense of being determined to preserve her *Machtgebiet* there against either a "forward policy" of the West or national uprisings of the peoples concerned. There is also, however, a sense in which she may be said to have acted as a *status quo* power in the wider meaning of one intent on resisting change in the over-all distribution of power, in the period of the rise of

Hitler, from 1933 to 1938. That is to say, when faced with a threat to the interests of the Russian national state the Russian leaders—Stalin in this instance—perceived the interests of Russia to be better served, for the time being, by a *status quo* than by a revisionist policy, and so one had the sight of the then Russian Foreign Minister, Litvinov, as a mainstay of that eminently *status quo* institution, the League of Nations.

And there is a sense in which Russia may be said at present to be insisting on her own classification as a *status quo* power, provided that her definition of the *status quo* is accepted. This emerges with particular clarity from the interviews given by Khrushchev to Walter Lippmann in 1958 and 1961, in which he proclaims in effect that "the revolution is the *status quo*." That is, he is presenting as one of the features of the world scene which Russia will use its diplomatic leverage to maintain and forward the process of revolutionary change in Africa, Asia, and Latin America which is already revising the power map of the world in a direction that may or may not ultimately prove beneficial to Russia but is certainly proving damaging to the Western powers. And he has indicated that he will meet Western efforts to counter this development with the threat of force.

An early instance was the Russian attitude in 1958, after Brigadier Kassem's *coup* in Iraq, when it appeared uncertain whether Western reaction would be confined to preventing similar developments in Lebanon and Jordan, or would aspire to the reversal of the situation in Iraq. Russian policy met this situation not only with the rather abortive summit conference mentioned in the last chapter, but with the statement that the U.S.S.R. disposed of means to turn the U.S. Sixth Fleet's ships into "coffins of molten steel." This remark, and the observation of the 1957 "kitchen conference" with Nixon that "we too can threaten," and the effort to use Russian strength to influence U.S. policy towards Cuba—all these are instances of the use of explicit military threat as a backing for diplomatic objectives, expressed with bluntness and violence not to be found in Western diplomacy. One of the many ill services that the Suez adventure did to the West was the Russian discovery that threats of this sort could be effective with opinion in the colonial world. So that there is a sense in which it can be said that the Russians have been able to use their air atomic power as psychological backing for revisionist political objectives—even to give some of the leaders of the colonial world a sense that some of this power has brushed off on to themselves so that one has the ironic spectacle of Egyptians and Iraqis, Cubans and Congolese trying to negotiate from the strength of Russian rockets.[6]

One may distinguish this kind of revisionism, whose advantages accrue to the U.S.S.R. as the carrier of a revolutionary political doctrine, from the direct military revisionism which might be pursued in Europe by Russia as a national power. May one claim at least that the American military establishment or the "balance of terror" acts as an effective sanction against this second kind of revisionism? Perhaps so, although revisionism backed by the ability to choose non-nuclear means in a situation where retaliation is only possible by raising the level of exchange to that of nuclear strike is quite a different proposition from revisionism without this option. And if the American power of nuclear strike operates against a "willed" or "deliberated" revisionism it does so only at the cost of placing a premium on what might be called a "pre-emptive" or "crisis" revisionism. *That is, the revolution in military technology has operated to displace status quo by revisionist intentions at a moment of crisis, since the military operations logically required merely to ensure national survival have become identical with those required by the most sweeping revisionism.* An example may help to make this clear. Let us assume, for instance, that East Germany were to experi-

---

[6] Dulles noted this phenomenon. Briefing Congressional leaders about Israel and Egypt in 1956, he remarked: "But now since the Russians have intervened they say that they want to bargain from positions of strength. They learned that expression from us." Sherman Adams: *First Hand Report* (New York: Harper & Brothers; 1961).

ence riots on the scale of 1953 or greater; that the Russian troops in East Germany were used to suppress them; that the rioters were receiving actual or alleged help from West Berlin; and that there was a Russian incursion of some sort into West Berlin, allegedly to end such assistance. This would be a situation of ambiguity in the sense that neither side could be certain whether the other side's intentions were revisionist or *status quo*. Let us take the most optimistic view, and assume *status quo* intentions on both sides. But each side must not only take into account its own intentions, and its estimate of the intentions of the other side, but must make an assessment of the degree to which the other side can tolerate defeat on so important a front, and must try to guess also at the other side's assessment of its own tolerance of defeat. For this is the point at which resort to nuclear strike must arise as a possibility *both* for the side which faces defeat in the contest of conventional forces (certainly the West in this instance) and for the side which is winning, and thus staking its survival on the other side's tolerance of defeat.

Once either side faces a situation in which *either* it believes that the other side has reason to actively contemplate a nuclear strike *or* it believes the other side to suspect that it is itself doing so, the case for the pre-emptive strike becomes overwhelming, *and is known by each side to be overwhelming for the other.* For even if it were true that neither side can "win" a war, in the sense of being in a more advantageous position afterwards than before, nevertheless *the side which strikes first* has a reasonable chance of holding damage to "an acceptable level"—even perhaps to a level below that of earlier wars—or possibly of being in a position to "bargain" itself out of any damage at all.

This possibility is not ruled out by the so-called "invulnerable deterrent." It may be enhanced by it. If, for instance, the Russians could, by a pre-emptive first strike at the S.A.C. bases and missile bases of the Western alliance, wipe out 50 or 70 per cent of American retaliatory power (which is not inconceivable), they would then be in a position to *bargain* with the Americans—in a very special sense to "negotiate from strength"—by trading a second strike at American cities against the President's "calling off" his slow reaction-time "invulnerable" retaliatory weapons, such as Polaris. That is to say, the balance of terror must be reckoned by Russian leaders in situations of ambiguity and friction, not as between the full weight of nuclear damage inflictable by the Americans versus no damage at all, but as between the damage that would be inflicted if the Americans strike first, versus the much lower level of damage that could be inflicted by what remained of the American strike force after a Russian first strike, *minus* what could be "bargained off" by the threat of a second wave of Russian strikes at American cities.[7]

And this might conceivably not include even that portion of the S.A.C. which was actually air-borne or on 15-minute alert, which would in any case not normally be more than one third of the total. For, with the present differential in time of delivery, while much of the American deterrent is still in bombers, the American "fail-safe" system may itself operate in the Russian favour. Assuming that the bombers take to the air at the alarm, there ensues a period of some hours by the end of which they must receive a message to proceed to their assigned targets. The American President, assuming the negotiating demand by Russia which we have envisaged, has this period to reckon whether to order them to continue a futile act of vengeance which will bring death in the second Russian strike-wave to about 55 million Americans, *and which will not be militarily decisive,* or to negotiate what bargain he can.

This weakness in the theory of deterrence is, of course, visible to American strategists, and has prompted a view that the re-action strike must be, and must be believed by the Russians to be, completely automatic. To quote one authority, "if the

---

[7] The American speeches of November 1961 insisting that American second-strike capacity was as great as Russian first-strike capacity were obviously inspired by American apprehension about Russian estimates on this point.

threat of unlimited war is to be effective as a deterrent, it must be
clear there can be no possibility of choice after the aggression."[8]
But to insist on an automatic reaction deterrent, with no possibility of human choice after the warning, is to maximize the
risk of accidental war (as against pre-emptive war), and so
merely to substitute one danger for another. In any case, the
direction of development seems to be towards the slow reaction-
time weapons, such as the Polaris submarines, and it is hardly possible to make such a concept credible in their case.

It is considerations of this sort that lead to the stretching of
the theory of deterrence to contemplate any enormity, even the
so-called "Doomsday machine" or "super-dirty" bomb loaded
with cobalt and other substances to maximize the residual radio-
active poisoning of the world. For, the reasoning runs, deterrence
is only effective so long as *he who strikes first* is faced with the
absolute certainty of devastating reprisal. Given the present advantages attending the first strike (which are tremendous), even
a small additional technological breakthrough, in a field like the
ability to confuse either side's warning systems, would offer
the prospect of holding damage to an acceptable level—and it
must be recalled that the benefit to be bought at the price of
this damage is the chance to eliminate a mortal threat and to re-
order the world according to one's own prescription. And it is
further calculated that Russian notions of an acceptable (or sur-
vivable) level of damage may be different from Western ones.
During the Second World War, the Soviet leaders lost control
and use for a time of 40 per cent of their people, many of their
greatest cities, much of their area and resources, a larger proportion of their population than any Western state.[9] Yet ten
years from the worst point of this ordeal saw Russia not only
restored, but raised astonishingly in magnitude as a power,

[8] George W. Rathgens, Jr.: "Nato Strategy: Total War," in NATO *and
American Security* (ed. Knorr), p. 72.
[9] Their temporary losses during the Napoleonic Wars and World War I
were on a similar scale.

from one that had to struggle desperately to ward off the German attack and then barely met it adequately, to one that is able to be intransigent with the entire Western world and make it abide Russian answers. From a Kremlin's-eye view it may look like a terrifyingly good illustration of the recuperative power of the system.

To sum up, it must be said that ten years of American endeavour to rally Western strength produced a military establishment which was not only inadequate to the half-hearted revisionism of its original diplomatic aspirations, and inappropriate as a sanction against the Soviet political-revolutionary revisionism endemic in the world outside Europe, but which reduced the probability of war-by-deliberated-revisionism only to enhance the possibility of war-by-mutual-panic.

Nevertheless, as was shown in the quotations which serve as epigraphs to this study, the idea of negotiation from strength has continued to be offered as an official aspiration for Western policy up to the Presidential election campaign of 1960 and even afterwards.[1] Why, one must ask, has the idea persisted into an epoch in which its relevance to the power balance of the present and the foreseeable future is so very dubious? The answer must surely be because of the difficulty of putting forward any alternative foreign-policy aspiration for the alliance. The reasons for this may be considered at several levels. At the level of the man-in-the-street there is a consciousness—associated in America with the name of Yalta and in Britain with that of Munich—that past negotiations from positions of weakness have had results that were unpalatable, and that therefore better future results may necessarily presuppose a better negotiating position. But beyond this the phrase has a sort of built-in and inescapable psychological and political appeal in that it consciously or unconsciously blends two theories of the nature of diplomacy: the liberal-optimist theory which sees it as a process of compromise and recon-

---

[1] See Dean Rusk's speech of October 1961 (*The New York Times*, October 1961).

ciliation, and the Machiavellian-pessimist theory which sees it as
a continuation of war by other means, a temporary shift of the
unceasing conflict to a less-than-lethal level. The adherents of
the first theory would of course put their emphasis on negotiations, and the adherents of the second on strength, but both
can feel reasonably happy with the phrase as a whole. And the
two theories of diplomacy represent not only intellectual traditions, but temperamental affinities among both leaders and led,
so that the phrase has the genuine and deep-seated appeal of the
best political myths.

But the widespread supposition that the man-in-the-street
always inclines to the liberal-optimist view, and that only the
disillusioned policy-maker is adequately pessimistic or realistic
about the prospects of peace, has not much basis in reality, as is
clear from such investigations as have been made of popular
opinion on international policy.[2] This is a point of some importance. The real basis of the case against negotiations, as seen for
instance by Dulles, was not so much simply that they were likely
to be unproductive, as that they would tend to induce a *détente*
(whether or not they produced results) and that in conditions of
détente it becomes impossible for the democracies to maintain
a posture of strength.

There is a great deal less in this argument than is usually supposed. If we consider the *détente* associated with the 1955 summit
meeting, which undoubtedly created some months of public
optimism about the international political prospects, it is notably
difficult to point to any specific way in which it impeded Western
efforts at military strength. The guided-missile budget was not
cut: indeed it started its precipitous upward trend in that year.
The American surveillance of Russia was not relaxed: in fact
both the U-2 flights and the radar watch from Turkey seem to

---

[2] The most interesting is perhaps a mass-observation study that reveals
much more of the background assumptions with which foreign affairs are
popularly discussed than the usual statistical approach (*Peace and the
Public* [London; 1947]).

have begun then. The decay on the side of conventional forces was not created by the 1955 *détente*; its origins were in 1952–3, and the die was irretrievably cast by 1954, which was a year of considerable tension, with an Indo-Chinese crisis in its early months and a Formosa crisis in its later months. Nor is it true to say that the Russo-Egyptian arms deal was made possible only by the summit *détente*: it was well under way in June, a month before the conference opened.

It is ironic to note that the approach to summit negotiations of Paris in 1960 and in Vienna in 1951 avoided this much apprehended danger in that they were wholly unproductive of any *détente*. But even if one judged that nevertheless it should be assumed that negotiations would normally be associated with a *détente*, and that a *détente* usually had effects on the public mind which made it more difficult for the Western powers to maintain their military strength, the case for tension would not become conclusive, for its dangers must be weighed against its advantages. The overriding consideration is the fact that war by mutual panic (i.e., pre-emptive war) is much the likeliest occasion of general nuclear war in the present period, probably the only really likely occasion, except for the possibility of a major swing in the power balance following a diplomatic reversal by a first-class power, or a notable technological breakthrough. Even these, assuming that war would be precipitated by the country adversely affected, would be special instances of war-by-panic. This danger must be set against whatever advantages may be held to flow from tension.

A concept that may be useful in arriving at a reasoned judgment is that of the "opportunity cost" of a policy. It is a notion normally used in assessing weapons, as for instance one might say that the opportunity cost of a particular missile system is the best alternative weapon that can be developed by the use of the same resources. Applying the concept to the diplomatic field, we may ask, what was the opportunity cost of "negotiation from strength"? Or, if that is too vague to be answerable, the oppor-

tunity cost of the decision that German troops must be an
element in Western armies? The answer must include, most im-
portantly, some realistic reckoning of the effect of the lapse of
time. There has been a suppressed premise in all arguments
against negotiation either that time is on the Western side or that
time is a neutral. But neither has proved to be true. It is obvious
enough that time has proved militarily to be against the West.
What is less often realized is that time has been against "negotiated settlement" of any sort, and on the side of "accommodation
by default or tacit acquiescence." In this sense time may be said
to have already made a settlement of sorts in Eastern Europe,
and perhaps in Eastern Germany also.

There is a still more important sense in which time may be
said to have modified the question of settlement. It has operated
within both the Eastern and the Western alliance to shift power
towards the revisionist element of each side. This is perhaps
clearer if one looks at the position of China in the Communist
side of the scales, but it is also visible if one looks at the position
of Germany on the Western side.

The contrast between the position of China *vis-à-vis* Russia in
1950 and its position in 1960 is particularly sharp and telling. In
1950 China was wholly dependent for protection on the treaty
with Russia and the supply of Russian arms. Without it, counter-
revolution by America in the name of Chinag Kai-shek would
have been a possible policy, though not necessarily an effective
or productive one. By the middle of the decade this situation had
already begun to change. China had become a force in its own
right, diplomatically independent of Russia at the 1954 Geneva
Conference and in Asia. By the last years of the decade she was
more independent still, demonstrating what may be classed as a
veto on Russian policy in the episode of the 1958 summit on the
Middle Eastern crisis, and competing with Russia in setting the
general objective and procedures in foreign policy of the Communist *bloc* at the conferences of 1960 and 1961. And it is more
than apparent that Chinese revisionism is far less tempered by

general satisfaction with the *status quo* than is the case with Russia.

In the case of Germany, the ultimate results of the change in position may be less formidable, but the change itself is hardly less striking, from a power in 1950 still under occupation, without full sovereignty, with very little influence over the diplomatic choices of the West, to the situation in 1960, when Germany supplied the largest single contingent of NATO's conventional forces. If it were not for the West's continuing reliance on nuclear weapons, Germany would be militarily the most powerful of the European members of NATO, and the trend back to conventional weapons which is now under way must enhance her diplomatic leverage. As has been pointed out, schemes of disengagement and neutralization have up to now had the advantage of meeting the criteria of "legitimacy" as seen by the dominant powers, but they are not likely to do so when the decisive criteria in this field are those of Germany.

There is, of course, a natural brake on the ability of the revisionist powers on either side of the balance to set the limits of settlement: the consciousness that if they press their respective friends too hard they may cause the latter to reflect, as it were, "*status quo* powers of the world, unite: you have nothing to lose but your more inconvenient allies." As Thucydides observed, mutuality of fear is the only sound basis of alliance, and there is bound to be, and has indeed proved to be, an asymmetry of fear in the attitudes of Russia and China to nuclear war. The much-speculated-upon possibility that the deteriorating fortunes of the West in the balance of power might be retrieved by a break on the Communist side of the balance, through the dissension between Russia and China,[3] cannot of course be discounted. Such an event would obviously create a new balance whose long-term implications for the West could hardly fail to be more promis-

---

[3] At the time of writing, this dissention appeared to be sharpening fast, as much because of the Russian retreat on Cuba as because of the Chinese aggression on the Indian border.

ing than those of the present balance. But short of dissension growing into rupture, and rupture into active hostility, the competition between Russia and China for leadership of the Communist *bloc*, like the domestic competition for power within Russia, is at least as likely to produce intransigence as mildness in attitudes towards the West.

If one had to put the meaning of this strand of history into a single sentence, one might say that the American aspiration to negotiate from strength came to nothing because the compounded pluralism of decision-making in an alliance of democracies vitiated the effort at strength, and the chosen concept of strength ruled out the one promising issue for negotiation. It is a melancholy fact that both what we believe about ourselves and what we believe about the Russians militated against our ever having been able to negotiate from strength, and militates in favour of their being able to do so. For the concept rests on a belief about willingness to use force or the threat of force as a sanction for the attainment of diplomatic objectives. But the rather flattering and unrealistic *persona* that Western opinion (particularly in America and Britain) constructs as the image of its own character in international dealings—an essentially law-oriented, reasonable, even idealistic self-image—is not really compatible with the degree of ruthlessness implied. Whereas the qualities we impute to the Russians, especially their alleged disregard for the human costs, even within Russia, of nuclear war is entirely so compatible. Thus the West tends to be hoist with its own psychological warrior's petard: the Cold War image of Russian society, constructed with some deliberation in the West, becomes in itself a means of diplomatic leverage to the Russians. Similarly, the whole basis of the theory of the deterrent was the belief that if one could force the other side to make their gambles big rather than small, they would decide not to gamble at all. A plausible theory, but it proved to be truer of the West than of the Communists.

If there is any consolation to be found for this failure, it may be in the reflection that the original assumption, that diplomatic settlements reflect only the negotiating strength of the parties to them, is not necessarily valid as a historical observation. The ethos of diplomatic settlement has changed so profoundly since the rise of the concept of national self-determination as the standard of justice in international politics that it would be dangerous to use analogies earlier than the interwar period. But looking at settlements since then, one may say that on the whole the pattern of settlement has owed less to the relative strength of the parties than to calculations at the time about the balance of power in the period after settlement. This was probably true of Munich, and is certainly true of such formal or *de facto* settlements as have been made after the Second World War. It accounts for the relative harshness of the early treaties, with Italy and the satellites, as compared to the extreme mildness of the treaty with Japan and what one might call the *de facto* settlement with Western Germany.

There are two possible reasons for not negotiating: because one is weak and cannot afford to, or because one is strong and does not need to. Unfortunately the psychological balance of policy-makers appears to be so delicate that it swings between these two extremes without ever resting at the point between them. This is perhaps inevitable so long as the attention of each is concentrated on strength *vis-à-vis* the other. When attention must be directed instead to the long-term prospects of the world power balance as a whole, each may find its own advantage in maintaining the fabric of the present society of states.

This is not necessarily to contend that settlement is now readily possible, or even that it was so earlier. But in a period when the dangers attending diplomatic negotiation have been constantly stressed, it may be useful to point out that delay is not enough, that the process of postponing settlement is a process of reduction of choices. To stand firm may be an admirable policy, but not if one happens to be standing in a patch of quicksand. Ten years under the sign of negotiation from strength saw the

Western powers work themselves into a situation where both
sides are terrifyingly conscious that victory and even survival
depend on the first strike; where the West cannot effectively back
a *status quo* diplomatic policy, much less sustain its original ambitions for a revisionist one; where the revisionist power in the
East—i.e., China—and the revisionist power in the West—i.e.,
Germany—both approach the power of veto; where the Russian
leadership both needs a victory and believes one possible; and
where discussion of a settlement in Central Europe has moved
from an issue—reunification—on which the West had something
to gain, to an issue—Berlin—on which it has only something to
lose. With all due consciousness of the dangers attending negotiated settlement, one must ask whether those attending settlement by default have not proved as great.

Bibliography

1. OFFICIAL DOCUMENTS—AMERICAN

Assignment of Ground Forces of the United States to Duty in the European Area: Hearings, Senate Foreign Relations and Armed Services Committees, 82nd Congress, 1st session. Washington, 1951.

In the Matter of J. Robert Oppenheimer: Transcript of Hearing before the Personnel Security Board. Washington, 1954.

Military Situation in the Far East: Hearings before the Senate Armed Services and Foreign Relations Committees, 82nd Congress, 1st session. Washington, 1951.

North Atlantic Treaty: Hearing before the Senate Committee on Foreign Relations, 81st Congress, 1st session. Washington, 1949.

Powers of the President to Send the Armed Forces Outside the United States: Committee Print, Senate Foreign Relations and Armed Services Committees. Washington, 1951.

Congressional Record (passim).

Department of State Bulletin.

2. GOVERNMENT DOCUMENTS—BRITISH

Cmd. 8501. Germany. Correspondence between Her Majesty's Government in the United Kingdom and the Soviet Government about the Future of Germany. March 10/25, 1952. (Germany No. 1, 1952.)

Cmd. 8551. Germany. Further Correspondence between Her Majesty's Government in the United Kingdom and the Soviet Government about the Future of Germany. April 9, May 13, 1952. (Germany No. 3, 1952.)

Cmd. 8610. Germany. Further Correspondence between Her Majesty's Government in the United Kingdom and the Soviet Government about the Future of Germany. May 24, July 10, 1952. (Germany No. 9, 1952.)

Cmd. 8663. Germany. Further Correspondence between Her Majesty's Government in the United Kingdom and the Soviet Government about the Future of Germany. August 23, September 23, 1952. (Germany No. 13, 1952.)

Cmd. 8903. Washington Talks. Documents relating to the Tripartite Conference. Washington. July 10/14, 1953. (Miscellaneous No. 9, 1953.)

Cmd. 8945. Germany. Further Correspondence between Her Majesty's Government in the United Kingdom and the Soviet Government regarding the Future of Germany. August 4, September 2, 1953. (Germany No. 4, 1953.)

Cmd. 8979. International Situation. Further Correspondence between Her Majesty's Government in the United Kingdom and the Soviet Government regarding the International Situation. Moscow. September 28, October 18, 1953. (Miscellaneous No. 16, 1953.)

Cmd. 9008. International Situation. Further Correspondence between Her Majesty's Government in the United Kingdom and the Soviet Government regarding the International Situation. Moscow. November 3/16, 1953. (Miscellaneous No. 21, 1953.)

Cmd. 9022. International Situation. Further Correspondence between Her Majesty's Government in the United Kingdom and the Soviet Government regarding the International Situation. Moscow. November 26, December 8, 1953. (Miscellaneous No. 22, 1953.)

Cmd. 9037. International Situation. Further Correspondence between Her Majesty's Government in the United Kingdom of Great Britain and Northern Ireland and the Soviet Government regarding a Four Power Meeting in Berlin. Moscow. December 26, 1953; January 1954. (Miscellaneous No. 1, 1954.)

Cmd. 9391. Statement on Defence, 1955.

Cmd. 9080. Berlin Conference. Documents relating to the Meeting of Foreign Ministers of France, the United Kingdom, the Soviet Union and the United States of America. Berlin, January 25, February 18, 1954. (Miscellaneous No. 5, 1954.)

Cmnd. 381. Correspondence between the Prime Minister and Mr. Bulganin, December 11, 1957, to February 8, 1958. (Soviet Union No. 2, 1958.)

Parliamentary Debates (passim).

3. OTHER WORKS CONSULTED

ACHESON, DEAN G.: *Power and Diplomacy*. Cambridge, Mass.: Harvard University Press; 1958.

——: "Prelude to Independence." *Yale Review*, Summer 1959.

ADAMS, SHERMAN: *First Hand Report*. New York: Harper & Brothers; 1961.

ALSOP, J. and S.: *The Reporter's Trade*. New York: Reynal & Hitchcock; 1958.

BALDWIN, HANSON: *The Great Arms Race*. London: Stevens & Sons; 1959.

BELL, CORAL: *Survey of International Affairs for 1954*. London, 1957.

BEAL, JOHN ROBINSON: *John Foster Dulles: 1888–1959*. New York: Harper & Brothers; 1959.

BEVAN, ANEURIN: *One Way Only*.

BLACKETT, P. M. S.: *The Military and Political Consequences of Atomic Energy*. London: Turnstile Press; 1948.

——: *Atomic Weapons and East-West Relations*. Cambridge: Cambridge University Press; 1956.

BRODIE, BERNARD: *Strategy in the Missile Age*. Princeton: Princeton University Press; 1959.

——: "Unlimited Weapons and Limited War." *The Reporter*, November 18, 1954.

BUCHAN, ALASTAIR: *Nato in the 1960's*. London: Institute of Strategic Studies; 1960.

BUNDY, W. McGEORGE: *The Pattern of Responsibility*. Boston: Houghton Mifflin Company; 1952.

BURNHAM, JAMES: *Containment or Liberation*. New York: John Day Co.; 1952.

BUTLER, D. E.: *The British General Election of 1951*. London: Macmillan & Co.; 1952.

BUTLER, D. E. & ROSE, R.: *The British General Election of 1959*. London: Macmillan & Co.; 1960.

CALVOCORESSI, P.: *Survey of International Affairs* for 1950 and for 1951. London, 1953 and 1954.

CHAMBERLIN, W. H.: *Beyond Containment*. Chicago: Henry Regnery Co.; 1953.

CHILDS, MARQUIS: *Eisenhower: Captive Hero*. London: C. S. Hammond, Hammond & Company; 1959.

COOKE, ALASTAIR: *A Generation on Trial*. London: Rupert Hart-Davies; 1950.

COLM, GERHARD, and MARILYN YOUNG: *Can We Afford Additional Programs for National Security?* Washington: National Planning Association; 1958.

COUNCIL ON FOREIGN RELATIONS: *The United States in World Affairs* (annual volume from 1949). New York, 1950/1960.

CRAIG, GORDON A.: "NATO and the New Germany." *Military Policy and National Security*, ed. W. W. Kaufmann. Princeton: Princeton University Press; 1956.

DINERSTEIN, HERBERT S.: "The Revolution in Soviet Strategic Thinking," *Foreign Affairs*. January 1958.

DONOVAN, ROBERT J.: *Eisenhower: The Inside Story*. New York: Harper & Brothers; 1956.

DRUMMOND, R., and G. COBLENZ: *Duel at the Brink*. New York: Doubleday & Company; 1960.

DULLES, JOHN FOSTER: *War, Peace and Change*. London: Macmillan & Co.; 1939.

——: *War or Peace*. New York: The Macmillan Company; 1950.

——: "A Policy of Boldness." *Life*, May 19, 1952.

——: "Security in the Pacific." *Foreign Affairs*, January 1952.

——: "Moral Force in World Affairs." *Presbyterian Life*, April 10, 1948.

EDEN, SIR ANTHONY: *Full Circle*. London: Cassell & Company; 1960.

EXLEY, R. A.: *The Campaign for Nuclear Disarmament*. Unpublished M.A. (Econ.) thesis of University of Manchester, 1959.

FEIS, HERBERT: *Churchill, Roosevelt, Stalin*. Princeton: Princeton University Press; 1957.

GARTHOFF, RAYMOND L.: *The Soviet Image of Future War*. Washington: Public Affairs Press; 1959.

GAITSKELL, HUGH: *The Challenge of Co-existence*. Harvard: Harvard University Press; 1958.

GARDNER, TREVOR: "Must Our Air Force Be Second Best?" and "Our Guided-Missile Crisis." *Look*, May 8, and 14, 1956.

GILBERT, MILTON, and ASSOCIATES: *Comparative National Products and Price Levels*. Paris: O.E.E.C.; 1958.

GOLDMAN, ERIC F.: *The Crucial Decade: America 1945–1955*. New York: Alfred A. Knopf; 1956.

HARSCH, JOSEPH: "John Foster Dulles: a very complicated man." *Harper's*, September 1956.

HILSMAN, ROGER S.: "NATO: the Developing Strategic Context." *NATO and American Security*, ed. Knorr. Princeton: Princeton University Press; 1959.

——: "On Nato Strategy," in *Alliance Policy in the Cold War*, ed. Wolfers. Baltimore: Johns Hopkins Press; 1959.

HOWARD, MICHAEL: *Disengagement in Europe*. London: Penguin Books; 1958.

INSTITUTE OF STRATEGIC STUDIES: *The Communist Bloc and the Free World: The Military Balance 1961*. London, 1961.

ISMAY, LORD: *NATO: the First Five Years*. Utrecht, 1955.

JACOBI, CLAUS: "German Paradoxes." *Foreign Affairs*, April 1957.

JONES, JOSEPH M.: *The Fifteen Weeks*. New York: Viking Press; 1955.

JOUBERT, Air Chief Marshal, SIR PHILLIP: "Long-Range Air Attack." *Soviet Air and Missile Forces*, ed. Lee and Stockwell. London: George Weidenfeld & Nicolson; 1959.

KAHN, HERMAN: *On Thermonuclear War*. Princeton: Princeton University Press; 1960.

KAUFMANN, W. W.: *Military Policy and National Security*. Princeton: Princeton University Press; 1956.

KENNAN, GEORGE: *American Diplomacy 1900–1950*. London: Martin Secker & Warburg; 1952.

——: *Russia, the Atom and the West*. London: O.U.P.; 1958.

——: "The Sources of Soviet Conduct." *Foreign Affairs*, July 1949.

KIRKPATRICK, SIR IVONE: *The Inner Circle*. London: Macmillan & Co.; 1959.

KISSINGER, HENRY A.: *Nuclear Weapons and Foreign Policy*. New York: Doubleday & Company; 1958.

KNORR, KLAUS: *NATO and American Security*. Princeton: Princeton University Press; 1958.

LEE, ASHER: *Air Power*. London: Gerald Duckworth & Co.; 1955.

LEE, ASHER, and RICHARD STOCKWELL: *The Soviet Air and Missile Forces*. London: George Weidenfeld and Nicolson; 1959.

LERNER, D., and R. ARON: *France Defeats E.D.C.* London: Thames & Hudson; 1957.

LIPPMANN, WALTER: *The Cold War*. London: Hamish Hamilton; 1947.

MASS OBSERVATION. Peace and the Public.

MIKSCHE, F. O.: *The Failure of Atomic Strategy*. London: Faber & Faber; 1959.

MILLIS, WALTER: *Arms and the State*. New York: Twentieth Century Press; 1954.

MILLIS, WALTER, ed.: *The Forrestal Diaries*. New York: Viking Press; 1951.

MILLS, C. WRIGHT: *The Causes of World War III*. London: Martin Secker & Warburg; 1959.

MURPHY, CHARLES J.: "The Eisenhower Shift." *Fortune*, January–March 1956.

NICHOLAS, H. G.: *The British General Election* of 1950. London: Macmillan & Co.; 1951.

NITZE, PAUL: "Coalition Policy and World Order." *Alliance Policy in the Cold War*, ed. Wolfers. Baltimore: Johns Hopkins Press; 1959.

PLATIG, E. RAYMOND: *John Foster Dulles: A Study of his Political and Moral Thought Prior to 1953*. Unpublished. Chicago Ph.D. thesis, 1957.

PUSEY, MERLO J.: *Eisenhower the President*. New York: The Macmillan Company; 1956.

RATHGENS, GEORGE W.: "NATO Strategy: Total War," in *NATO and American Security*, ed. Knorr. Princeton: Princeton University Press; 1959.

RIDGWAY, MATTHEW B.: *Soldier*. New York: Harper & Brothers; 1956.

RITCHIE, R. S.: *Nato: The Economics of an Alliance*. Toronto: Ryerson Press for Canadian Institute of International Affairs; 1956.

ROSTOW, W. W.: *The United States in the World Arena*. New York: Harper & Brothers; 1961.

ROVERE, RICHARD H.: *Senator Joe McCarthy*. New York: Harcourt, Brace & Company; 1959.

———: *The Eisenhower Years*. New York: Farrar, Straus & Cudahy; 1956.

SETHE, PAUL: *Zwischen Bonn und Moskau*. Frankfort: Scheffler; 1957.

SCHELLING, THOMAS C.: "Surprise Attack and Disarmament," in *NATO and American Security*, ed. Knorr. Princeton: Princeton University Press; 1959.

SHEPLEY, JAMES: "How Dulles Averted War." *Life*. January 16, 1956.

SLESSOR, Marshal of the R.A.F., SIR JOHN: *Strategy for the West*. London: Cassell & Company; 1954.

SNOW, C. P.: *Science and Government*. London: O.U.P.; 1961.

TAFT, ROBERT A.: *A Foreign Policy for Americans*. New York: Doubleday & Company; 1951.

TAYLOR, MAXWELL D.: *The Uncertain Trumpet*. London: Stevens & Sons; 1960.

TIMES, THE: *The Nuclear Dilemma*. London, 1957.

TRUMAN, HARRY S.: *Years of Trial and Hope*. New York: Doubleday & Company; 1956.

TUCKER, ROBERT W.: *The Just War. A Study in Contemporary American Doctrine*. Baltimore: Johns Hopkins Press; 1960.

VANDENBERG, ARTHUR H.: *The Private Papers of Senator Vandenberg*. New York: Houghton Mifflin Company; 1949.

WOLFERS, ARNOLD: *Alliance Policy in the Cold War*. Baltimore: Johns Hopkins Press; 1959.

Index

Acheson, Dean, 5–49, 72 ff., 142 ff.
Adenauer, Konrad, 46–8, 120–3, 187–9, 199, 204
Algeria, 124, 167, 203
Amery, Julian, 14
armed-forces levels: British, 58, 161; NATO, 48–51, 63–7, 161–7; U.S.A., 52, 55–6, 126–43, 146, 160; U.S.S.R., 49, 171–8, 214–15
arms control, 134–5, 222
atomic bomb, first Russian, 31 ff.
Atomic Energy Commission, 32–5
Attlee, Clement, 10, 59, 101, 107–9, 112, 140
Austria, 42, 114, 122, 127
Austrian Peace Treaty, 106, 120–5

Baldwin, Hanson, 41, 117, 145 *n.*
Belgium, 44, 49 *n.*, 52 *n.*
Benelux, 62
Beria, Lavrenty, 111–14, 215–17
Berlin, 22, 54, 112, 113, 146 *n.*, 149, 159, 161, 162, 166, 196–206, 209, 213, 216–17, 231
Berlin Foreign Ministers' Conference, 96, 105–6, 116, 118, 200
Bermuda Conference, 110 ff., 189 n.
Bevan, Aneurin, 59, 102–3, 112
Bevin, Ernest, 10, 13, 14, 21, 47
Bidault, Georges, 111
Bonin, Bogislaw von, 164, 184
Bradley, Omar, 32–5
Bricker, John William, 77–8, 85–7
Britain, 3, 5, 9–10, 12–13, 16, 21, 40–8, 54–62, 90–132, 160–96, 227, 234, 239; Conservative Party, 12, 26, 60, 100–1, 112, 117, 121, 183; Labour Party, 10,

12, 26, 58–60, 100–3, 112, 117–18, 182–5
Brussels Treaty, 12, 41
Bulganin, Nikolay, 127–32, 181, 189, 219

Camp David, 202–3
Campaign for Nuclear Disarmament, 181–3, 185–6
Canada, 44, 49, 57, 66–7, 202
Carney, Robert B., 27
"Carte Blanche," 164
CENTO, 93
Chiang Kai-shek, 94–5, 196, 237
China, 27, 45, 52, 61, 71, 79, 88, 90, 94–102, 113, 121–3, 127–9, 140, 168, 195–7, 203–6, 216, 218–20, 238–41
Churchill, Winston S., 5, 10–17, 59, 100–1, 106–23, 131, 143, 157, 179
Cockcroft, John, 159
Cole, Sterling, 117, 119
containment, 23 ff
Condon, Edward U., 171
Cuba, 209, 216 *n.*, 229, 230, 238 *n.*
Cyprus, 124
Czechoslovakia, 22, 63, 64, 125, 184, 194, 221

de Gaulle, Charles, 203–4
Denmark, 44, 49, 63, 65, 189, 191
deterrence, 143–6, 147–55, 226, 231–3
Dewey, Thomas E., 71
disarmament, 221
disengagement, 184, 222
Dulles, John Foster, 23 ff., 28, 61–2, 68–99, 110 ff., 114 ff., 121 ff., 129–30, 138, 146 ff., 162, 189 ff., 205, 220, 235

A Note about the Author

CORAL MARY BELL was born and educated in Australia. She received her B.A. from the University of Sydney and her M.Sc. and Ph.D. in Economics from the University of London. She served in the Australian Foreign Service from 1945 to 1951 and at Chatham House, as a writer and research worker, from 1951 to 1956. Thereafter, until 1961, she was Lecturer in Government at the University of Manchester, England. She has since come back to the Department of Government at the University of Sydney. In 1959 she was awarded a Rockefeller Fellowship and spent some time at Columbia University in New York, attached to the Institute of War and Peace Studies. She has published articles in British and Commonwealth journals, and was the author of the Chatham House *Survey of International Affairs for 1954* (Oxford University Press).

A Note on the Type

THIS BOOK is set in ELECTRA, a Linotype face designed by W. A. Dwiggins (1880–1956). This face cannot be classified as either modern or old-style. It is not based on any historical model, nor does it echo any particular period or style. It avoids the extreme contrasts between thick and thin elements that mark most modern faces, and attempts to give a feeling of fluidity, power, and speed.

Composed, printed, and bound by
The Haddon Craftsmen, Inc., Scranton, Pa.
Typography and binding design by
VINCENT TORRE